RIVER OF MISTS

CAITLIN PRESS INC.
3375 Ponderosa Way
Qualicum Beach, BC V9K 2J8
www.caitlin-press.com

TEXT DESIGN by Onça Publishing
COVER DESIGN by Sarah Corsie
COVER IMAGE by Tomas Handfield via iStock
EDITED by Meg Yamamoto
PRINTED in Canada

CAITLIN PRESS INC. acknowledges financial support from the Government of Canada and the
Canada Council for the Arts, and the Province of British Columbia through the British Columbia
Arts Council and the Book Publisher's Tax Credit.

Canada Council Conseil des Arts BRITISH COLUMBIA Funded by the Canada
for the Arts   du Canada   ARTS COUNCIL   Government
                                                of Canada

LIBRARY AND ARCHIVES CANADA CATALOGUING IN PUBLICATION

River of mists : people of the upper Skeena, 1821–1930 / Geoff Mynett.
Mynett, Geoff, 1946– author.
Includes bibliographical references.
Canadiana 20220217084 | ISBN 9781773860930 (softcover)
Subjects: LCSH: Hazelton (B.C.)—Biography. | LCSH: Hazelton (B.C.)—History. | LCGFT: Biographies.
LCC FC3845.H39 Z48 2022 | DDC 971.1/85—dc23

RIVER *of* MISTS

People of the Upper Skeena, 1821–1930

Geoff Mynett

CAITLIN PRESS
2022

To Peter Newbery
For his encouragement and enthusiastic support

Contents

Maps

Preface

The sketches in this book are of people who either lived in or visited Hazelton, a small town on the Skeena River in northern British Columbia, in the period from 1821 to 1930. By no means were all important. Some were merely visitors. But they all have a connection to Hazelton and have contributed in some way to the rich history of this beautifully situated town. My selection is admittedly and unapologetically whimsical.

The title of the book, *River of Mists*, comes from the Gitxsan name for the Skeena River. The Skeena was a famously difficult river to navigate—sometimes shallow, sometimes deep. The challenges included dangerous rapids, moving sandbars and swift, changeable currents. Steamers, it was said, had to be able to float on dew. Many people lost their lives in the Skeena. In 1907, for example, the river turned over and wrecked the sternwheeler *Mount Royal*, killing six of the crew. Ice closed the river every winter for four or five months. Even in summer, high or low waters could cause steamer captains not to risk the trip. The journey upriver could take from four days to three weeks, with six to seven days being typical. The journey down often took one day. It was, one passenger said, the journey of a lifetime.

Hazelton is situated at the confluence of the Skeena and Bulkley Rivers. Before 1871 this was known as the Forks of the Skeena or, locally, the Forks. Although Hazelton was always a small town, barely rising above the status of village, for the forty years commencing in 1871 it was the most important non-Indigenous settlement in the northern interior of British Columbia.

The names of the rivers are confusing. In the early days, the Bulkley was known as Simpson's River. Its Indigenous name was Watsonquah. Below the Forks and to the sea, the merged river was also known as Simpson's River. Fort Simpson was established at the mouth of the Nass River in the mistaken belief that it was the mouth of Simpson's River. The Babine River flowed from Babine Lake and joined the main river (the Skeena) below Kisgegas. From there to the Forks, it was called the Babine River and, occasionally, McDougall's River.

The Gitxsan Indigenous People have lived in the district for millennia. Their name for the confluence of the two rivers was Gwin Ts'ihl.[1] To avoid confusion, in this book I refer to it as the Forks. The Gitxsan village at the Forks, Gitanmaax, was the central village of the Gitxsan people. From three thousand to four thousand Gitxsan people—it is difficult to ascertain accurate numbers—lived in the district in villages such as Kispiox, Gitsegukla and Gitanyow. Across the Bulkley River in the huge area to the south lived the Wet'suwet'en Indigenous People.

The Forks of the Skeena has always been a place where Indigenous Peoples have met to trade. It provided a natural and convenient trading location for people from the coast, the Skeena, Nass, and Bulkley Valleys and beyond.

The non-Indigenous settlement at Hazelton was founded in 1871. For the next twenty years, goods were brought upriver by canoe and pack train. The first steamer managed the difficult journey upriver to Hazelton in 1891. Depending on conditions on the river, it was possible for steamers to reach the dozen miles beyond Hazelton to Kispiox. One need was to transport Gitxsan people who lived in Kispiox downriver in the spring to work in the fish canneries on the coast. Nevertheless, for all practical purposes, Hazelton was the highest point of navigation, and this made it an excellent location for trading posts and stores. Steamers brought goods from the coast to Hazelton, from where they were carried on by pack train into the hinterland. Miners on their way to prospect in the Omineca Mountains to the east bought their supplies, and often spent their winters, in Hazelton. Omineca is the Indigenous name for the whortleberry, a food staple for the inhabitants of the region.[2]

Gitxsan stories have been told by many others. Neil Sterritt has written about the Gitxsan people and their stories in his book *Mapping My Way Home*. I cannot add anything to what he has written, nor should I. I fear that I, with neither the knowledge nor deep understanding of Gitxsan culture, would not be able to relate them with integrity.

The Gitxsan people did not have a written language. This led non-Indigenous people to spell Gitxsan names any way they wanted, sometimes differently even in the same sentence. Spelling of Gitxsan names was, as a consequence, often wildly personal. Kispiox, for example, was variously spelled Kispiax, Kishpiax, Kishpyax, Kispioux, Kitsbyox and Kish-py-axe; today it is also called by its Gitxsan name of Anspayaxw.

The Gitxsan village at Hazelton, technically a separate place, is named Gitanmaax. Some of the settler names for Indigenous places are:

- Forks of the Skeena—Gwin Ts'ihl
- Fort (Port) Simpson—Lax Kw'alaams
- Kispiox—Anspayaxw
- Kitsegukla—Gitsegukla
- Kitwancool—Gitanyow
- Kitwanga—Gitwangak
- Moricetown—Witset
- Port Essington—Spaksuut/Spokeshute
- Rocher Déboulé—Stekyawden

On occasion I refer to the Hudson's Bay Company as merely the Company. With a strong prejudice against acronyms, I prefer to use the term "HBC" only in quotations.

During the years covered by this book, many non-Indigenous people used language about Indigenous people that today is considered deeply offensive and unacceptable. I have used the original language in this book only in the quoted passages from the time; not to set it down as written would be dishonest to the often uncomfortable facts of history. The damage done by colonial governance rightly requires the hard work of reconciliation and the changing of attitudes and practices of systemic racism. On the other hand, we should be cognizant that all historical fact is filtered in some way. Selection of facts, translation, transcription, the reliability of second- or third-hand information, wishful thinking, failing memories and deliberate distortion all shape our pictures of the past. As L.P. Hartley wrote in the prologue to *The Go-Between*, "the past is a foreign country: they do things differently there."[3]

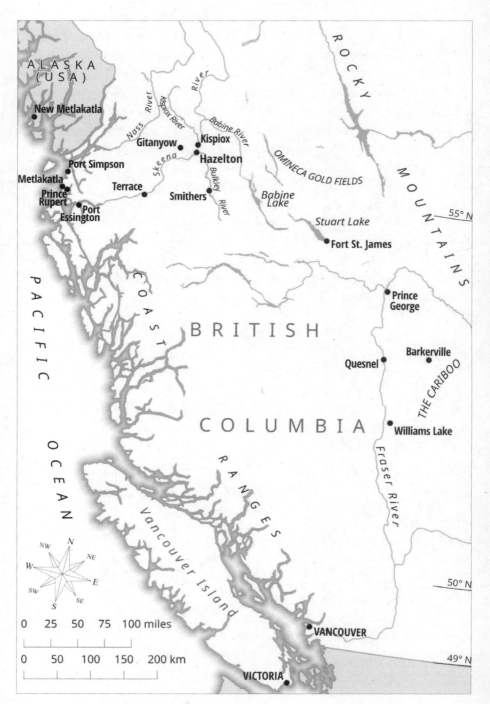

ALASKA
(USA)

New Metlakatla

Nass River

Kispiox River

River

Babine River

Gitanyow   Kispiox

Port Simpson   Hazelton

Skeena

Metlakatla   Terrace   Smithers

Prince
Rupert   Bulkley River

Port
Essington

OMINECA GOLD FIELDS

Babine
Lake

Stuart Lake   55° N

Fort St. James

ROCKY

MOUNTAINS

PACIFIC

COAST

BRITISH

Prince
George

Quesnel   Barkerville

COLUMBIA   Williams Lake

THE CARIBOO

OCEAN

RANGES

Fraser River

Vancouver Island

NW   N   NE
W   E
SW   S   SE

50° N

0   25   50   75   100 miles

0   50   100   150   200 km

VANCOUVER

49° N

VICTORIA

Map by Morgan Hite, Hesperus Arts, Smithers

1

William Brown, Simon McGillivray and Their Early Explorations

1821–1833

S imon McGillivray walked on the stones out to the point where the two rivers merged. He and his companions surveyed the scene before them in astonishment. The date was Thursday, June 20, 1833. They had just arrived at the Forks of the Skeena River. They were, as he reported to Hudson's Bay Company governor George Simpson, "the first Whites who have seen the Babine and Simpson's River so far down."[1]

This was the moment of his discovery. From his left flowed Simpson's River, now called the Bulkley. From his right flowed Babine River, now called the Skeena. "Une grande Rivière," his men kept saying quietly to one another as they looked at it. McGillivray wrote, "It is broader than Fraser's River and may be compared with Athabasca River in its greatest breadth. I cannot but call it a noble stream."[2] He would likely have been satisfied that he had accomplished the journey his colleague William Brown had tried, but failed, to make seven years before.

Across the fast-flowing river to his right were low cliffs covered with yellow-bark poplar trees. Over Simpson's River to his left, he could see the flat ground used for many years as a trading place by the Atnah (as the Gitxsan people were then called), the Wet'suwet'en, and the Tsimshian people, who came from the coast. The land then rose up to the majestic snow-tipped mountain known as Stekyawden or, later, as Rocher Déboulé. On the riverbank behind them grew a profusion of hazel bushes and flowering paintbrush. White fluff-like balls shed by the cottonwood trees floated in the air and fell to the ground like loose snow. Swarms of mosquitoes, emerging after the recent downpour, were buzzing around their ears. An eagle swept smoothly from a branch of a tree and, talons down and trailing behind, swooped across the water to snatch a fish. On the river, Atnah men were paddling their long cottonwood canoes toward the strangers.

Atnah people had lived in harmony with nature at the Forks for millennia. Across Simpson's River were the territories of the Wet'suwet'en First Nation. Already they were aware of the presence of people with pale skin, strange customs, bizarre clothing and beguiling merchandise, both to the east and in ships on the seas to the west. Within a few decades their hitherto largely undisturbed way of life would change forever.

The Forks of the Skeena River, with the Bulkley River coming in from the right to join the Skeena River on its journey to the coast. When Simon McGillivray stood there, the Bulkley River was known as Simpson's River and it continued under that name to the coast. The Skeena River was then known as Babine River or, on occasion, McDougall's River. Before the Simpson's River was renamed the Bulkley, it was also known as the Akwelgate (Hagwilget) River. Its Indigenous name was Watsonquah. Image courtesy of the author

For almost forty years after McGillivray first saw it, the Forks would remain quiet, and Indigenous possession of it would be undisturbed. Traders, prospectors and missionaries would not arrive in any discernible numbers until the 1870s. Many Gitxsan men and women would then find work bringing people and goods upriver by canoe. Nevertheless, the Gitxsan way of life would scarcely change until the turn of the twentieth century.

Traders and Indigenous people each had something the other wanted. The Gitxsan people trapped animals such as marten, ermine, silver fox and beaver for their furs, which they traded not only through Indigenous middlemen with the newcomers on the coast to the west but also with the trading companies to the east for metal, leather, axes and firearms. Until gold was discovered, fur, largely for the China market, governed the economy of the North.

For the first fifty years of the nineteenth century, a lively competition existed on the coast among the Russians, King George's men (the British) and the Boston men (the Americans) to acquire furs. These three rivals had been operating there since approximately 1790. (The United States would not buy Alaska from Russia until 1867.)

Before 1821, the trading company in the interior was the North West Company, the great rival to the Hudson's Bay Company whose monopoly technically applied only to the land drained by rivers flowing into Hudson's Bay. Since Alexander Mackenzie's epic journey to the coast farther south in 1793, the North West Company had been establishing trading posts, such as Fort McLeod in 1805 and Fort St. James, at the south end of Stuart Lake, in 1806. Simon Fraser had reached the sea near what is now Vancouver. But the northern land west of the Rocky Mountains, known as New Caledonia, was still almost entirely unexplored. The North West Company did not know what lay between Fort St. James and the sea.

The chief factor at Fort St. James between 1810 and 1817 was a God-fearing man from Vermont named Daniel Harmon. On Sunday, June 16, 1811, he wrote in his journal that six canoes of Indigenous people from the west had arrived at the south end of Stuart Lake and told him about six villages around the confluence of two great rivers. They told him that every autumn a number of white people came up the river to trade with the Indigenous people there, but they could not say what nation they had come from. "However, I imagine they are my Countrymen [Americans] who came round Cape Horn to make Coasting-trades—for I cannot learn that they attempt to make Establishments."[3] Here Harmon was suggesting that unnamed American traders could have been the first non-Indigenous people to visit the Forks. (These traders could, though, also have been Russians or King George's men.)

———

William Brown was born in Kilmaurs, Ayrshire, Scotland, in 1790. Like so many other Scots, he joined the Hudson's Bay Company as a young man and served at a number of posts, including Fort Wedderburn in Athabasca (now northern Alberta) and Fort St. James. Company records described him as a short, slender man of five feet eight, an excellent trader, fully qualified for the charge of a district, active, courageous and highly deserving of promotion. He was a good man for a difficult job. Governor George Simpson had a high opinion of him. "Permit me now to remark," Simpson wrote to Brown in 1820, "that the zeal you have uniformly manifested in the service merits the highest encomiums and it is extremely satisfying to me that the charge of Fort Wedderburn District is in such comfortable hands."[4]

In 1821, after some years of aggressive and at times violent competition, the North West Company merged with the Hudson's Bay Company. During the conflict between the two companies in the ten years preceding the merger, Simon McGillivray had a famous confrontation with Simpson and Brown. This took place in October 1820 at Fort Wedderburn, where Brown was chief factor. Simpson, who happened to be at the fort at the time, encouraged Mr. Grignon, a constable from Montreal, to arrest McGillivray. "Mr. Grignon seized Mr. Simon McGillivray," Brown wrote in the fort's post journal, "and at the same time called upon us in the King's name for assistance."[5] While waiting to be sent to Montreal for trial, McGillivray was imprisoned in the fort. During the following six weeks, Brown and McGillivray had time to become well acquainted. Then McGillivray escaped. One report said he was disguised in the clothes of his "country wife," as the Indigenous women who became the common-law wives of fur traders were known.[6]

A year later, in October 1821, the Company sent Brown to build and manage a new post on the long and narrow Babine Lake, west of Stuart Lake. Brown and his party managed the difficult twelve-mile portage from Stuart Lake to Babine Lake, found a suitable spot up the lake and started to build. By the end of the month, they had erected the first buildings of the new post. As the men raised a flag post and ran up the Company's flag, Brown christened the post Fort Kilmaurs. (Because the location was later moved, this post came to be known as Old Fort Babine.) They celebrated the event with a dram of liquor and a volley of shots. This frightened the local Indigenous people, who, thinking they were all about to be slaughtered, fled into the woods.

Brown was determined to discover what lay between his new home at Fort Kilmaurs and the Pacific Ocean—and it wasn't just explorer's curiosity. All was not well with the fur trade in this territory. In today's terms, he was losing market share. He had strong competition from the British, Russians and Americans on the coast who were trading axes, firearms and manufactured goods with the coastal Indigenous people, who then came upriver as far as the Forks to barter with Babine, Atnah and Sekani hunters for their furs. These they took to the coast and traded with the foreigners in their ships. Each year they were coming farther upriver. With their lower expenses and the resulting ability to outbid their rivals, together with their knowledge of local cultures, these middlemen had a worrying competitive advantage over Brown, which paid off with what Brown called "handsome profits."[7] They were already taking over half the furs from his territory. Brown knew it would not be long before they were encroaching on the Company territory around Babine and Stuart Lakes. This was serious competition. What could he do to stop it?

On April 3, 1823, Brown wrote to his superiors, recommending that the best way to fight the competition might be for the Company to open a post at the Forks and then take the furs downriver to the coast. A cautious Scot, he wrote that he thought at some time, sooner rather than later, he should explore the route to the Forks and assess the situation. On April 15, 1825, realizing that what he had feared had happened, he wrote that Indigenous middlemen from the coast had already

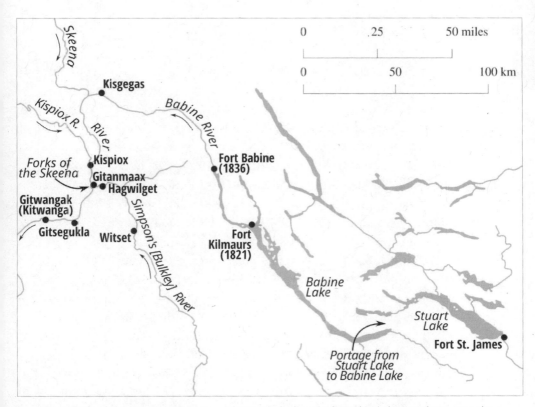

Map of the area between Fort St. James and Gitwangak, showing the Forks. In the period 1821–1833, the Bulkley River and the Skeena to the sea were called Simpson's River, and the Skeena was called the Babine as far as the Forks. (Occasionally the Skeena upriver from the Forks was also called McDougall's River.) Map by Morgan Hite, Hesperus Arts, Smithers

reached Kisgegas and were within a short distance of Babine Lake. Unless checked, they would reduce the supply of furs in the region even more.[8]

He decided it was time for him make the journey to the Forks. Governor Simpson approved and wrote to him, "I am rejoiced to find that you are preparing to undertake a Voyage of Discovery towards the Coast. It is an object of great moment that a friendly understanding should be established with the Indians as it is probable that the Committee will Direct that Posts be settled both in the Interior and on the Coasts as far to the northwards as the British territorial rights extend."[9] Brown had already visited the populous Wet'suwet'en village at Witset (Moricetown) at least once and had travelled some way up Simpson's River toward the Forks. Witset was located at the eastern end of the high, steep-walled canyon on Simpson's River. Brown noted that a rockfall in 1824 had led to the establishment of a Wet'suwet'en village named Hagwilget on a rise above a crescent-shaped, stony beach.

Brown's preferred route, though, was to go by water, down the Babine River, which he believed was navigable for most of the year. In 1825, he started his journey, first to visit the Forks and then to continue downriver to the coast. However, bad weather and sickness stopped him at Kisgegas, close to where the Babine River joined the main river, and he had to return to Fort Kilmaurs. He spent most of July and August in bed, immobilized. "Mr. Brown feels no bodily pain at present," the post journal said, "but he is weak—has in a great measure lost the use of his legs—and cannot leave his bed without the help of crutches."[10] In March of the following year, he set out again from Fort Kilmaurs to reach the Forks but once again fell ill at Kisgegas and had to return. He decided to return to the Company's headquarters at York Factory, Manitoba, and then go home to Scotland to convalesce.

On April 18, 1826, Brown left Fort Kilmaurs for the last time. "Here I have spent as anxious moments as ever I have had in my life," he wrote. "And now for the greatest part of the two last summers I was confined to bed with a sickness. Still, I leave the place with regrets as I never have had the means to carry the business to that degree of perfection which I often wished and could have done."[11] He joined a party coming up from Fort Vancouver and took over command of it for the arduous journey across the Rocky Mountains, across Athabasca to Norway House and then to York Factory.[12] Here he met again his adversary, now a colleague, Simon McGillivray. Conceivably Brown discussed with him the Forks, its opportunities and challenges. Eventually arriving home in Scotland, Brown found lodgings in Princes Street in Edinburgh. There, on March 19, 1827, ill with dropsy and other ailments, he died. He was thirty-seven.

By the end of the 1820s, the Hudson's Bay Company was determined to protect its territory in New Caledonia. It wanted to investigate the practicalities of establishing a trading post at the Forks. Could the Company establish a profitable link with Fort Simpson, the new company post on the coast, and squeeze out its competitors?[13] Should it indeed build a post at the Forks? Was there a practical route to get there? Thanks to Brown's reports, it already believed the Babine River was navigable. But if not, could horses be used on the land route? In 1833, the Company sent Simon McGillivray, the forty-two-year-old former North West Company trader, on an expedition to find out.

McGillivray was well connected with the former governors of the North West Company. His father, William, had been its last chief partner and, together with Simon's uncle, also named Simon McGillivray, had negotiated the merger with the Hudson's Bay Company. His godfather was the explorer Alexander Mackenzie. The North West Company had in some ways been a family affair. At one time or other, it had employed no fewer than eight members of the McGillivray family, not including relatives by marriage. After the merger, the Hudson's Bay Company kept the younger Simon McGillivray on. At its annual meeting on July 12, 1832, the governor and council of the Company appointed him chief trader at Fort St. James, working under Chief Factor Peter Dease.

What McGillivray thought of being assigned to this post is not known, but he soon submitted his formal notice of retirement for June 1, 1834. Meanwhile, he decided to attempt to complete what Brown had started. In April 1833, he was writing to Governor Simpson, "Should means permit, it is our intention at present to explore the Babine and Simpson's Rivers this summer and I certainly will consider it a very good achievement if we can reach the Sea Coast."[14]

Means did permit. His objective was to reach the Forks of the Skeena and to confirm that the sea could be reached from there without difficulty. In making his plans, he still believed the Company post at Fort Simpson was at the mouth of Simpson's (Skeena) River, when in reality it was at the mouth of the Nass River. His plan was to follow Brown's route up Stuart Lake, portage to Babine Lake, past Fort Kilmaurs (Fort Babine), and then go down the Babine River to the Forks.

McGillivray intended to leave Fort St. James on Friday, June 7, but because his men were superstitious about starting a journey on a Friday, he postponed his departure until the following day. He set out with six men, including two gentlemen, Jacques Telehoult and Louis Vandale, and others described just as "men": Maurice Dupré, Alexandre Gendron, Jean Baptiste Regnier and a troublesome fellow named John Simpson.

Those first few days on Stuart Lake were tough. At one point the rain and particularly the wind drove them to seek shelter on the shore for an hour, "the men much exhausted by pulling against a head wind."[15] They reached Babine Portage by eight o'clock on the Sunday evening. This was the twelve-mile stretch of land between Stuart Lake and Babine Lake over which they would have to carry their canoes and supplies. "We might have gone farther on," McGillivray wrote, "but I do not like to exhaust the strength of the men."[16] The back-breaking work of portaging their canoe was too much for them to reach their destination of Babine Lake that first night. Despite the incessant rain, they did manage to complete the portage by mid-morning of the following day.

At Babine Lake, McGillivray looked for a guide. Someone had recommended a man named Chilcowan, who had experience of the route to the Forks and down to the sea. Chilcowan agreed to go with them. He told McGillivray, to the latter's great surprise, that Simpson's River did not reach the sea at Fort Simpson. Although near, Fort Simpson was at the mouth of the Nass, an entirely different river. He did say, though, that the journey from the Forks to the sea by canoe could take as little as a day and a half.

McGillivray had heard stories that the Babine River was navigable down to the Forks. After all, William Brown had declared it to be so. Chilcowan, though, warned him that it was not, that there were too many rapids and high precipices. The advantages of going down by canoe were large, however, and these persuaded McGillivray to take the risk. He should have listened to Chilcowan.

They carried on up Babine Lake to Fort Kilmaurs, occasionally now being called Babine Fort. A man called Waccan—Jean-Baptiste Boucher—joined them. A useful man, he had the reputation of being an enforcer of Company rules. Here they heard more stories about the dangers of the Babine River. These contradictory reports confused and upset the men. McGillivray wrote that "secret murmurings were the order of the day."[17] McGillivray, though, knew that the Atnah people traded with Fort Kilmaurs, so he believed the men's fears were unjustified. He hired an Atnah youth to work as an interpreter and introduce them to the people at the Forks. The party left Fort Kilmaurs and paddled up the lake and into the Babine River. McGillivray soon found the going too difficult. "There is water enough to float our canoe with six men, but not with all hands on board. ... The farther we go down, the rapids will be worse."[18]

By Sunday, June 16, he had had enough and decided they could proceed no farther. The risk of injury or even death was too high. He wrote, "The moment we entered the river, it became a succession of rapids without intermission and, although the water was high, there was not a sufficiency to float our canoe, with all hands into it, and to avoid breaking, five of us walked about four miles. The rapidity at which the canoe went down this part of the river baffles all description and I became alarmed for the safety of those who were in it."[19] He turned back.

Time for Plan B. This was to take the overland route. "I therefore retraced my steps to Babine Lake and resolved to go by land to Simpson's River to ascertain whether it was navigable and at the same time to find a practical road for horses."[20] Since they had no horses, they would have to walk. They lightened their loads, cached their canoes and surplus supplies and set out on foot at nine o'clock on the morning of Monday, June 17. "We have a good beaten path before us, which led us to the foot of the mountain. There we had to ascend and, with the loads on the men's backs, it was a job of some difficulty. ... Fortunately the mountain was bare of trees. Some snow impeded our progress."[21] That first day they travelled about sixteen miles.

The next day they carried on and entered a gorge. "The river is bounded on each side by perpendicular precipices, which form frequent strong rapids and in some parts make it impossible for a canoe to jump it or even let down with a line."[22] This suggests that they had reached the Hagwilget Canyon below Witset.

In his letter to Governor Simpson, McGillivray described the fallen rocks at this place:

Roche Débouléz or fallen rocks in Simpson's River is a remarkable place. 2 immense large rocks have fallen from a high precipice on the south side of the River which has almost blocked up the passage, leaving a small channel open. When the water is low, the salmon cannot go beyond this spot, which accounts for the number of houses and inhabitants resorting here in summer and winter. It was in 1824 these rocks fell into the river. When the late Mr. Brown on Derouines [going to trade with Indigenous people in their own villages] to visit the Babine Indians of Simpson's River he found them about 20 miles [at Witset] above this spot, these rocks had not then fallen. From what I saw of Simpson's River above the Fallen Rocks, I should pronounce it rather hazardous to navigate with boats or canoes owing to strong rapids and eddies.[23]

Journeying that Wednesday was hard for them all. McGillivray wrote, "Started early. We are all much tired by yesterday's exertions."[24] At five that evening, June 19, they came to a wooden bridge across the river. This was likely the famous one at the Wet'suwet'en village of Hagwilget. Here McGillivray had some trouble with one of his men:

About 5 p.m. we reached a wooden bridge, which crossed the river. It is not wider than 60 yards. Some of my men had already crossed, whilst myself, Regnier, Waccan and Vandale dare not attempt it without imminent peril to our lives. I therefore ordered my men to come back. All obeyed except Simpson, who took his bundle and Gun and was proceeding alone, dividing himself from our party when we were not far from the Indian camp. I threatened to shoot him if he disobeyed my orders.

He at length obeyed and on remonstrating with him for his imprudent conduct in attempting to go in among a camp of strange Indians who did not expect us, he began to swear and said that if I fired he would have done the same. Upon which a scuffle ensued. He threw me on my knees and Waccan coming to my assistance the affair ended here, but not without Simpson having received a few heavy blows in the face with the butt end of a pistol. He moreover cut his left hand, for he had impudently torn the scabbard off in the scuffle. His conduct is infamous, particularly in the presence of my guides. This lad ought to be sent out of the Country. He is an unruly character and would resort to any foul means to get the better of his master.[25]

Not long after this, they arrived at Rocher Déboulé (the village at Hagwilget). The Indigenous inhabitants, threatening to destroy them, "came rushing out like wild beasts, armed with long muskets." The guides managed to calm the situation and explained who McGillivray was. McGillivray said he then shook hands with them all individually and gave them each a piece of tobacco. "At our first interview, they did not like our visit, stating that we were on a voyage to our people at the Great Fort (Russians) to inform them to sell the goods dearer, adding at the same time that both forts had entered into an agreement to sell their goods higher. ... When reassured, they became much friendlier. On informing them of the particulars of my voyage, the object of it and the benefits they would derive from it, they became pleased at this explanation and before I left them, the younger ones had formed plans of carrying our property across this portage should we ever come with it from the sea."[26]

With friendly relations established, some of the Indigenous people cut firewood for them and gave them salmon to cook. They also gave them a house to stay in, particularly welcome no doubt because it was raining heavily. McGillivray noted the carvings on the houses and the totem poles. He also described the carving of a three-masted vessel, very well depicted, under sail, with two rows of cannon. Could this have been a clue that non-Indigenous people had been there before them? In the village, he counted fifteen houses on one side of the river and three on the other.

The following morning, Thursday, June 20, he learned, probably to his considerable surprise, that there was a letter waiting for him at Gitanmaax, the Atnah village at the Forks. He "immediately furnished the Atnah man with a piece of gold to go and get it."[27]

McGillivray and his men then set off to find where the two rivers merged. They took the direct route over land, following the Babine Trail, roughly along the present road from the Hagwilget Bridge to Old Hazelton. They would have passed through the trees where the present hospital now lies and then reached the brow of the hill, near the present pioneer and Gitxsan cemetery. There they would have looked out onto the Babine (Skeena) River flowing from the right and joining Simpson's (Bulkley) River flowing from the left. In the middle distance two or three miles away, at last, was their destination—the merging of the waters of two mighty rivers. In the trees near the confluence, they could see the Atnah village of Gitanmaax. Towering above Simpson's River was Rocher Déboulé Mountain. If the weather had been clear enough after all the rain, they would also have been able to see the Seven Sisters mountains in the distance to the west.

McGillivray and his companions walked down from the bluff and made their way down to the point where the rivers merged. It was here that the astonished men proclaimed it "une grande Rivière." McGillivray walked along the stony beach until he reached the channel. This was probably the Hazelton Slough, since dried up. Some Gitxsan men from the nearby village of Gitanmaax fetched a small canoe. He then crossed the slough to the small island that he named Smith's Island after a friend. With some vermilion, he marked the date and his name on a tree. He then went up the Babine River for a short way, noting it was as wide as Simpson's River and more powerful.

Having reached his destination and knowing that from here it was only two days' journey by canoe to the sea, McGillivray had no need to stay longer. Time to return to Fort St. James. The party made its way back to Hagwilget, where a woman gave McGillivray a handful of ripe strawberries. Back at the village, he found approximately twenty villagers from a more distant Atnah village, who had arrived on a trading expedition. Some had not seen white people before. They had some fine muskets, he said, but were otherwise destitute of materials of European manufacture. One man in this party spoke a little English. He had been captured as a child by Indigenous people from the coast and kept as a slave. When he had seen his fellow countrymen, he grabbed the opportunity and escaped. McGillivray gave him some tobacco and a few brass rings. The man counted them in English and said they were "very small."[28]

The man McGillivray had sent to fetch the mysterious note had returned. It was from Peter Ogden, the chief factor at Fort Simpson. Dated February 23, 1833, it read, "Reports are in circulation here that a party of whites are in quest of this place. If so, I shall be happy to see them. Peter Skene Ogden."[29] This note raises the questions of how Ogden knew they were coming, when MacGillivray's plan was formulated and what the communication system in the district was at the time. It tantalizes the historian with questions of how much might have happened that was not written down.

The party set out on their return journey. The way back to Fort St. James was uneventful. It seems to have rained most of the way. McGillivray described the trails, the mountains, the trees, the rain and the availability of grass for horses. When they reached Babine Lake, they retrieved their canoe and the supplies they had cached, all happily undisturbed. They carried on and arrived back at Fort St. James on July 3.

McGillivray reported to Governor Simpson that, yes, there was pasture for horses on the route to the Forks. With a better road, it could be a practical trading route. The distance, he said, was not more than seventy-one miles. He regretted not being able to go down the Babine River all the way but hoped it might be possible with better conditions on the river. He was prepared to try that route again.

He was generous in his praise for his Indigenous helpers. "Should any expedition be made in that quarter in summer, I would recommend the same guides which I had, to be employed. Chilcowan knows the country well, and is respected

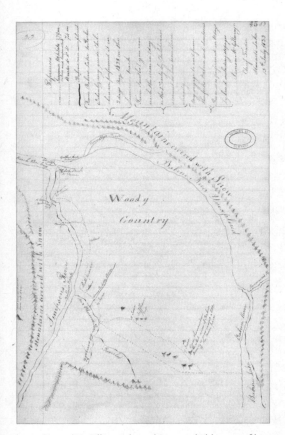

Simon McGillivray drew this remarkable map of his journey from Fort St. James in 1833. The significance of this map, which is in the Hudson's Bay Company Archives, was only recognized a few years ago. Simpson's River, Babine River, Hagwilget and the Forks are clearly identifiable. Map drawn by Simon McGillivray, D.4/126, HBCA, pp. 33/63–36/65

among the Indians. The Atnah lad is a good interpreter, active and obedient withal. They promise to be in readiness if required. During the whole voyage, I never saw these Indians out of temper; and their information I always found accurate."[30]

With his report, McGillivray included a map he had drawn of his journey. This map is remarkable for its accurate depiction of the Bulkley River. On the map he marked two bridges across the Hagwilget Canyon, one at the east end at Witset and another near the western end at Hagwilget.

McGillivray had achieved his objectives. He had reached the Forks of the Simpson and Babine Rivers. He was satisfied the journey from there to the sea by canoe was possible in two days. In his report of July 15 to Governor Simpson, McGillivray repeated Brown's recommendation that the Company set up a trading post at the Forks. He wrote:

This intercourse and traffic [Indigenous trade with traders on the coast] will never be stopped till we have our supplies via Simpson's River, and it would be necessary to form a post at the Forks of the Babine and Simpson's River; we will then be able to forestall all other traders by underselling them. The sooner this plan is effected the better. The advantages will be great to all persons concerned and the voyage hardly worth speaking about.[31]

His own view was that the route from the interior to the coast by way of the Forks could become practical if, first, the trading post at the mouth of the Nass

River—Fort Simpson—were moved to the mouth of Simpson's (Skeena) River and, second, a trading post were established at the Forks. He floated the idea of meeting with the men from Fort Simpson to discuss this, but nothing came of it. Company politics may have played a part. Fort Simpson was part of the Columbia River Department, whereas Fort St. James and Fort Kilmaurs were part of the New Caledonia Department.

In 1836, the location of the fort on Babine Lake was moved. The new fort was named Fort Babine, and Fort Kilmaurs became known as Old Fort Babine.

The Company did not, however, accept McGillivray's recommendation. Being possible for one intrepid explorer was one thing; being practical as a route for the regular transport of goods was another. Even if Babine River was navigable for much of the year, it was not practical as a reliable trade route. What about the land route that McGillivray had taken? Probably considering the practicalities of setting up a pack train system for a mere seventy-one miles too troublesome, the Company did nothing. Consequently, it would be more than thirty years and require the enticement of gold before the Company would think it worthwhile to establish a post at the Forks.

McGillivray did retire, but his retirement did not last long. For whatever reason—financial hardship, loneliness, nostalgia—he wrote to Governor Simpson in 1836 asking for a job. Simpson laid the proposal before the council at its meeting on June 1, and it agreed to rehire him as a clerk for £150 a year, with the chance of promotion to chief trader when a vacancy came. This was a sad comedown for a chief trader, but he accepted.

The Company sent McGillivray to its North West River post on the coast of Labrador. A more distant and remote place could not have been found, and he was not happy there. In March 1840, the governors in London wrote to the Company officers in Winnipeg. One of their directions was to move McGillivray from Labrador to take over the Fort Liard post on the Mackenzie River. McGillivray, consequently, set out on the long journey. But he never arrived. On October 15, the chief factor of Fort Liard wrote, "Snowing this morning. I was very surprised at 12 a.m. to see Mr. Bribou arrive to relieve me of my charge but very sorry to hear from him that McGillivray was no more, having departed this life at Bas de la Rivière."[32]

Thursday, June 20, 1833, was therefore a significant day in the history of the Skeena River. What William Brown had strived to accomplish, Simon McGillivray had achieved. When McGillivray walked out onto the stony point and was astonished at the confluence of the rivers, he was the first non-Indigenous person recorded as having visited the Forks. The non-Indigenous history of Hazelton had begun.

2

George Chismore and the Western Union Russian-American Telegraph

1866–1871

Finally they had arrived. After a week paddling upriver from the coast, George Chismore and his companions came at last to Kispiox, about a dozen miles upriver from the Forks of the Skeena. As soon as their cottonwood canoe rounded the point, they saw the large Gitxsan village with its houses and totem poles stretched out along the left bank. Indigenous children were playing among the canoes, which had been pulled up the bank away from the water for safety. Chismore's gaze naturally swung round to the Kispiox River tumbling in from the left, almost taking him by surprise because the confluence had been hidden by the point. And there was Fort Stager, the supply base for the Western Union Russian-American Telegraph Company. Workers from the base had already seen them and were coming down to give the arrivals a welcome and help unload the canoes. It was September 1866.

Twenty-six-year-old George Chismore clambered out of his canoe and looked around with interest and anticipation. He was starting his first day on site as staff doctor for the Western Union Telegraph. He was almost certainly the first non-Indigenous doctor to visit both Kispiox and the Forks of the Skeena.

The telecommunications challenge of the 1860s was to link North America to Europe by telegraph. The entrepreneur Cyrus Field was making valiant efforts to lay a cable under the Atlantic Ocean. Numerous failures, however, had proved to almost everyone that this was impossible. The cable always broke. While Field persevered, Perry McDonough Collins thought he had found another route. Why not go in the other direction, he argued, through British Columbia, Alaska and Russia? He acquired the requisite rights and commenced the project. Although Western Union soon took over the project, it is still often referred to as the Collins Overland Telegraph. When Chismore arrived, this telegraph had already been constructed up through the colony of British Columbia as far as Kispiox. Now it was pushing farther north. Chismore was looking forward to his new adventure.

George Chismore had been born in 1840 in Ilion, New York, where his father reportedly had worked in the Remington rifle factory. According to one account, his father sent young George to sea in a New England whaling ship when he was eight years old. Another account, arguably more plausible, records that, after a row with his father when he was fourteen, he went to New York and signed on as a ship's cabin boy.

Chismore arrived in California in 1854, having come round Cape Horn. He then went to Nevada and worked at prospecting sites for a time. Interested in medicine, he reportedly picked up the rudiments of dental and medical knowledge. Always adventurous, he then went back to sea. He worked between 1857 and 1860 on the whaler *America* with the rank of green hand and between 1862 and 1866 on the whaler *Corinthian*, both ships on North Pacific stations and in the Arctic. While whaling, he became familiar with the northern coasts. He also may have become acquainted with coasts south of the equator. At one point he compares the mosquitoes on the Skeena to those he had met at "Yaquila" (possibly Guayaquil) on the Ecuadorean coast.

He seems to have spent time both whaling and mining. The 1860 United States census records him as being at Mud Springs Township, California. In addition to being a famous mining community, Mud Springs was a staging post for the Pony Express, which operated from April 1860 to October 1861. Chismore became president of the Cosumnes Grove Copper Mining Company and later had stories to tell about the mining desperadoes there. This mining experience proved useful when he went prospecting in the Omineca Mountains in the summer of 1871.

Without formal training, Chismore acquired enough practical medical and dental knowledge and had read enough medical books to consider a career as a doctor. Accordingly, he took some preliminary courses in medicine at Cooper Medical College in California. This secured him a job as a medical officer with the Western Union Telegraph in 1866. Conceivably the American Civil War had drawn many fully qualified medical men into service in the East, and those who returned to California wanted a quieter life.

After a twenty-two-day journey from San Francisco, Chismore arrived in Victoria on July 14, 1866, on the bark *Onward*. This was a Western Union ship, loaded with material for the telegraph line. After a passage up the coast from New Westminster on the *Mumford*, he waited at Port Essington for Edward Conway, the young engineer-in-chief for the telegraph project and his new boss, to arrive. Chismore stayed on board the *Mumford* for a short jaunt in the Lower Skeena River. He recounted that, despite the captain's repeated warnings, two Indigenous men hitched their canoes to the back of the steamer for a tow. One of the canoes came to serious grief when it came too close to a moving part of the stern wheel. The canoe was badly damaged, but no one drowned.

When Conway arrived with William Manson and Thomas Hankin, two Hudson's Bay Company men, they all transferred to canoes. Chismore was in canoe number three, the five-man crew of which included four Indigenous men. They all started their journey up the Skeena River on September 13, 1866.

They toiled upriver. "The stalwart boatmen," Chismore wrote, "by pulling and jumping over in the cold water, managed to drive the canoe over some very strong rapids. They are wonders of strength and endurance at this kind of labour, working from daylight till dark, soaking wet all the time."[1] They camped for the night on gravel bars. Chismore admitted that, although many in the United States ridiculed the English idea of travelling with so much baggage, he found it "mighty nice" to have a tent, a good meal of meat on a table equipped with a tablecloth and his "regular cocktail and plates, knives and forks."[2]

Chismore's medical skills came in useful on the way upriver. One old Indigenous man was brought to him for treatment for a "colossal ophthalmia."[3] Chismore treated him and was annoyed when the man left without expressing a word of thanks. He revised his opinion the following day, however, when the man, with much improved eyesight, returned with a beautiful girl—"a winsome dame," Chismore called her—for his temporary possession.[4] With some regret, he turned this offer down, though not without much raillery from his companions at his lack of gallantry. In her stead, he did accept a pair of moccasins.

Near the Kitselas Canyon, they stopped to visit the Gitxsan village there. It was raining so hard here that Chismore wrote himself a memo "to bring a d—n good gum-coat" the next time he came to that locality.[5] He was not at all impressed by the totem poles in Gitwangak and the other villages they stopped at, which had "all kinds of grotesque figures in all kinds of queer positions."[6]

Since Simon McGillivray's visit in 1833, gold had been discovered in the Skeena and farther to the east in the mountains. Reports of the presence of gold had enticed many prospectors to the river and to streams that fed into it. Chismore noted many canoes with prospectors on their way to or from their explorations on the river and in the mountains. Among them was the notable Joseph Shaft, whom Chismore described as "the best model of endurance I ever saw: middle-aged, tall and strongly-made, bronzed and strongly-marked features, whereon hardship seemed to have done its utmost and failed to leave more than a few deeply marked furrows. ... I shall not soon forget the searching glance of his eager, restless eye, the self-reliant poise of his head, and the manly bearded face so full of character and expression."[7]

The party reached the Forks on September 20, 1866. Here Chismore noted the big river coming in from the right. This would have been the Bulkley River, which had just emerged from the high and narrow Hagwilget Canyon four miles upstream. He likely stopped at the Western Union supply camp on the flat land at the confluence of the rivers (later known as Mission Point, now Anderson Flats

Provincial Park) and met Charles Morison, the young man in charge there. At the Forks, ever the hunter, Chismore proudly noted he shot the head off a wild goose seventy-five yards away with his Remington pistol. He then continued with the others up to Fort Stager.

During the couple of days Chismore stayed at Kispiox, he went to observe a fellow medical practitioner—a Gitxsan *halayt* (shaman)—treat a sick Chief:

> A circle of twenty or thirty Indians sat around the patient, beating kettle drums and gourds and thin strips of board, while the chief doctor stood stamping the ground, with his head bowed nearly to his feet gesticulating wildly, perspiring at every pore, with a fantastically-carved gourd containing rattles in his hand, which he shook in a peculiar manner incessantly. Over the patient sat two assistant doctors and an old squaw, the whole group chanting a monotonous wail, while every few moments a boy poured buckets of cold water over the doctor's head. Altogether it was a wild scene and continued for hours.[8]

Thomas Hankin and William Manson, his canoe mates on his journey upriver, both had names that would echo down through the history of the Skeena. At this time, Manson was the chief trader at the Hudson's Bay Company post at Fort Simpson. Both he and Hankin were looking for a better route to transport supplies to, and furs from, the Company's posts in the interior. Manson was to travel to Babine and Stuart Lakes and then on to Fort Fraser. Hankin was to explore the Bulkley Valley. Both men arrived back at Fort Simpson in early November. Later that year, Hankin was sent to open a trading post at the flat land at the Forks, becoming one of the first settlers there.

After saying goodbye to Hankin and Manson, Chismore left Fort Stager and rode on horseback to the Western Union work camp twenty-seven miles up the Kispiox Valley. There he found telegraph workers busy clearing the path for the telegraph and connecting wire to posts. As the telegraph line moved approximately four miles a day up the valley, the camp and Chismore moved with it. He started work, providing medical help for hurt and injured telegraph workers. "The camp looks quite lively," he wrote, "with the cheerful log-fires and the 200 men scattered about the tents this fine night. The snow comes nearer every night and the temperature is rapidly falling."[9] By September 25, the hills were covered with snow.

Mile by mile the telegraph line moved up the valley. First the surveyor, rough sketch map in hand, went ahead with a few axemen, who blazed trees to mark the way, keeping as straight a course as the landscape permitted. After him came a team of about eighty choppers who cut down all trees within a swath of about twelve feet. A man then paced out the ground and drove in a stake every seventy yards. A group of Chinese labourers following him then dug a hole at the marked spot. Another party of axemen cut down the trees that would become the telegraph poles on which the wires would be strung. The pole setters then nailed a bracket on the pole, fixed the insulator on and set the pole firmly upright in the hole, packing the earth down firmly. The wiring party came next and strung the wire to the poles. Finally, John McCutcheon, the telegraph operator, attached his key and connected to the outside world.[10]

One message that arrived at the end of September was that, despite the doubters, a cable had been successfully laid under the Atlantic Ocean. (Why it took so long for the news to reach them is a puzzle. The news of the achievement had arrived in Victoria on July 30.[11]) This immediately made the Western Union telegraph to Europe through Russia redundant. Already winding down for the winter, work did not resume the following year when it became clear that, unlike previous cables, this new cable to Europe was not going to break.

Along with most of the other workers, Chismore then returned to the coast. Some of the telegraph workers, though, did stay in the district to prospect for gold. The Gitxsan villagers at Kispiox soon burned Fort Stager to the ground. The post journal of the Hudson's Bay Company at Fort Simpson recorded that Chismore arrived back at nearby Metlakatla on October 18. "He reports," it said, referring to Chismore, "that the whole party have finished for their season on the Skeena. And that there will be about one hundred here in boats and canoes tomorrow to await the arrival of the Otter to take a passage in her to Victoria."[12] Chismore did not go with them but stayed in the North.

Charles Morison was the young man employed by the Western Union to guard its supply depot on the flat land across the Bulkley River. Although he lived there for only a few months, he claimed the bragging rights of being the first non-Indigenous person to live at the Forks. He and Chismore became colleagues and friends. Morison later recounted that, when he and Chismore were together at Wrangell, Alaska, that winter, they had to deal with the results of a conflict between Indigenous people raging there at the time.[13] Chismore taught Morison how to treat wounds. Both warring Indigenous clans soon recognized that the two men were neutral players and brought their wounded warriors to be stitched up and made ready for battle again. Morison stayed in the North and later settled in Hazelton.

Chismore returned to California. In August 1867, he became an assistant surgeon on a contract with the United States Army, for an annual compensation of $115. He served in various frontier postings on the Gila River in Arizona and in Orange County, California, at a time when it was still desert. In October 1867, the United States bought Alaska from Russia, and early the following year it sent five officers and approximately fifty soldiers of the Second United States Artillery to Fort Tongass, Alaska, to establish its authority. This fort was only fifteen miles across the British Columbia border from Fort Simpson. In April 1868, the army posted Chismore there as its medical officer.

In May 1868, the traveller Emil Teichmann visited Fort Tongass and described the fort as being in a state of building confusion. The soldiers were cutting down trees and the whole place was obstructed by stumps, tree trunks and lumber being used to build a blockhouse. There was no room for the soldiers to form a straight line to parade. He decided that Chismore was the most interesting person at the fort and with his knowledge of the North was eminently qualified for his position. "The relations of the military officials with the Indians," he wrote, "were very good, thanks to the mediation of the doctor, who enjoyed in the settlement a respect which was not common amongst the Indians in consequence of some successful operations and cures which he had performed, and his reputation had already spread beyond the boundaries of Tongass. ... Medicine was also supplied without charge to the natives he had befriended."[14]

In May 1870, the much-travelled Lady Franklin and her niece Sophia Cracroft also visited Fort Tongass. Lady Franklin was the widow of the famous Arctic explorer Sir John Franklin and had earned a reputation as a redoubtable searcher for what had happened to him. They had first visited the Colony of Vancouver Island in 1861. Now they were back on the Pacific coast. Sophia Cracroft wrote about their travels. She described how "Mr. Cheesemore" showed them round the fort and the First Nations village, where the inhabitants welcomed "Cheesemore" warmly and without ceremony.[15]

Chismore served at Fort Tongass for two and a half years and came to love the area and the people, even to the point of thinking he might stay.

In 1870, the army gave Chismore a leave of absence, and he used it to return to the Nass and Skeena Rivers. He first went up the Nass. His guide for this trip was Arthur Wellington Clah, who helped him navigate the difficulties of journeying through Indigenous territories. Clah was a Tsimshian Chief and prospector and one of the colourful people on the Skeena in the mid-nineteenth century. He was one of the few Indigenous people from that time who left a written record.

Chismore wrote about his travels in the November 1885 edition of the *Overland Monthly*. He described visiting "Kil-a-tam-acks" (Gitlaxt'aamiks, on the Nass) and "Kis-py-aux" (Kispiox, on the Skeena):

> Near night we arrived at the village of Kil-ack-tam or Kil-a-tam-acks, beauti-
> fully located on a bold bluff on the right bank of the river, one of the finest
> Indian towns I ever saw. It contained thirty houses, and had a population of

about six hundred. The principal Chief Mus-ke-boo (Wolf) welcomed me at his home during my two days' stay. So far as I could learn, four whites had previously visited this village—Hudson's Bay Company officers and explorers in the employ of the Collins Russian-American Telegraph. No one has published any account of the vicinity of which I am aware.

My host's house, an unusually good one, was built on the plan prevailing generally among the aborigines of British Columbia and Alaska, which it may be well to describe.

At the four corners of a square space of level ground, timbers, deeply grooved on the sides facing each other, are firmly planted, rising some ten feet above the surface of the soil. At intervals along the lines, similar timbers, of proper height, grooved on the edges, are erected. Thick planks, split with wooden wedges from spruce or cedar logs, and cut to right dimensions, are slipped into the grooves, one on top of the other, till the walls are formed.

Just within the walls at each end of the building equidistant from the sides to the central line, two large uprights are solidly fixed, saddled at the tops to receive the main supports of the roof. These supports consist of two immense spars, hewn perfectly sound and true, and extending the whole length of the structure. When raised and placed in position, their great weight causes them to remain *in situ*. Round poles are used for rafters. Their butts rest upon the walls, and project to form the eaves; their centers are upon the spars, and the tops are notched together to form the ridge.

Other poles are laid across the rafters, and the whole covered with sheets of bark, lapped to shed rain, and kept in place by heavy stones. The ends are then finished to the gable. The pitch of the roof is very low. In the center of the ridge a large square hole is made to serve in lieu of chimney and is covered by a raised movable shelter that can be shifted, as the wind changes, to make it draw well. The floor is planked, leaving a large opening in the center over which to build the fires. No partitions are used; each dweller has a portion of the space allotted him, in accordance with his importance in the tribe. The best and warmest part, that opposite the door, is reserved for the Chief. Each house affords plenty of room for from twenty to fifty persons, sometimes for many more. Some of the planks are very large. One in Mus ke-boo's dwelling measured fifty-four in length, four feet one inch in width, and five inches in thickness.

In front of most of these houses a pole is raised, sometimes sixty feet high, carved from base to tip with grotesque designs, and surmounted with the owner's crest. More rarely, several houses have but one pole, centrally located. In either case, those of a crest own the houses in common, and form independent tribes, having power to make peace or war without involving their neighbours. Usually each village elects from the heads of the various houses someone who is called the "Chief of Chiefs," and who has a nominal authority outside of his proper crest.

The principal crests are the eagle, bear, wolf, crow, stork and killer [whale]. Even among tribes speaking widely different tongues, they are substantially the same both in British Columbia and Alaska. Indians travelling to strange villages go to their own crest, and are received as brothers, though never known before. No man and woman of the same crest can marry. All children take the crest of their mother.

The houses, though somewhat dark, are exceedingly comfortable. The door, a small one, is in the center of the front end, and is often circular. In some cases, the crest pole is pierced near its base, and entrance to the house is made through the opening.

The country about Kil-ack-tam was very attractive at that season. Within a mile both up and down the river, the Indians had little gardens planted with potatoes, which do well there.[15]

On July 5, 1870, Chismore and Clah started up the grease trail, a trail used by the Indigenous peoples of the coast to bring oolichan grease into the interior to trade. Chismore and Clah followed the trail over the mountains and down into Kispiox. They came across the place where the Western Union telegraph line had ended and then recognized where they were. Chismore noted that the Gitxsan people of Kispiox had taken down all the telegraph poles and taken the wire for their own use. He arrived in Kispiox two days after a bear had killed a Gitxsan woman who had been gathering berries. The inhabitants had killed the bear and scattered its body over the place where the woman had been killed. As he entered the village, the residents were holding a ritual dance of celebration.

Chismore's description of the famous Indigenous bridges is probably the first detailed written description of them. In 1872, he gave a newspaper in California a sketch of a bridge over what the paper called the "Hun Kun River"—probably the same as the "Har-Keen River" Chismore describes—on the grease trail he took from the Nass over to the Skeena.[17]

Although there were many such bridges in the district, the most famous of them was the one crossing the Bulkley River at Hagwilget. Chismore described how these bridges were built:

Bridges span the wider streams; one, a suspension bridge crossing the Har-Keen, built long ago, replacing a still older one, has a clear span of ninety-two

AN INDIAN BRIDGE.

George Chismore's article in the *Pacific Rural Press* was accompanied by this illustration of the bridge across what the newspaper called the "Hun Kun River." It was an important bridge on the grease trail, one of the trading routes the Indigenous people used to carry transport goods including eulachon oil.

Pacific Rural Press, volume 4, Number 8, August 24, 1872, p. 121

feet. It is located at a point where opposing cliffs form natural abutments and is thus constructed. From each bank two tapering logs, parallel to each other—some ten feet apart and with points elevated to an angle of ten degrees—are pushed out over the stream towards each other as far as their butts will serve as a counterpoise. Then two more are shoved out between the first, but nearer together and almost horizontal. The ends on shore are then secured by piling logs and stones upon them.

Then a man crawls out to the end of one of the timbers, and throws a line to another in the same position opposite. A light pole is hauled into place, lashed securely, and that arch completed. The three remaining sets of timbers are treated in the same manner. The upper and lower arches are then fastened together by poles, cross pieces put in, foot-plank laid, and handrail bound in proper position to steady the traveler in crossing the vibrating, swaying structure. No bolt, nail, or pin is used from first to last. Strips of bark and tough, flexible roots form all the fastenings.[18]

Chismore went on to the Forks and there met Morris Moss. One of the Jewish pioneer in the colony, Moss had a colourful past and would have a mysterious future. He had been a packer and fur trader. He had witnessed the murder of a policeman, been shipwrecked on an uninhabited island for three months and been held prisoner by Indigenous people for another month before escaping. He had also been a government agent, magistrate and adviser to the government on Indigenous matters. Years later he was to disappear mysteriously from Victoria and be found dead in Denver, Colorado, reportedly the victim of a murder. But now he was at the Forks, with a party of approximately twenty prospectors, having come from the Peace River country to the east. Moss told Chismore he was astonished how much easier the Skeena route was than the one up from the Cariboo. He pronounced it would become the most favoured way for prospectors to travel to and from the Omineca Mountains.[19]

Chismore then took a canoe down to the coast and described the rapids and canyons of his journey. He loitered at the mouth of the Skeena until it was time for him to return to Fort Tongass, where he arrived the day before his leave expired on October 7, 1870. There he had a surprise. The United States was closing the fort and bringing the soldiers home. Chismore and his friend Lieutenant Franklin Ring made a pact to meet in the Omineca Mountains the following summer to try their luck looking for gold. Meanwhile, Chismore agreed to stay on at the fort for a while as the custodian.

Keeping faith with his friend, the following year Chismore set out for the Omineca. He started up the Skeena in a canoe at 6:20 a.m. on June 14, 1871. He was in a fleet of four canoes that the travellers christened the *Merrimac*, the *Alabama*, the *Guard Boat* and the *Great Eastern*, indicating the American origins of his fellow travellers. Chismore was in the *Merrimac*, which carried eleven people, only two of whom were Indigenous canoemen. He said he was the only one of the white men who knew anything about paddling. Sore backs and arms and blistered hands, he noted, were the order of the day. Nevertheless, on average they managed ten to fifteen miles a day.[20]

After an arduous journey upstream, much of it in the rain, the canoes reached the Forks on June 26. On the way they passed a canoe carrying "Thomas Hunkin" (Hankin), whom Chismore would have remembered from his 1866 journey up the river. If they had stopped to chat, which would have been likely, Hankin would have told Chismore he was going downriver to be married. On June 20, Hankin married Margaret MacAulay at Fort Rupert, at the northern end of Vancouver Island.

When Chismore arrived at the Forks, he may have had a surprise. The previous October, when he was there last, the settlement, such as it was, had been south of the Bulkley River, on the flat land there. Now it had moved. He "found the old station abandoned and the new town of Hazelton located on the left bank of the river, about a mile above the Forks."[21] He described it as "a little camp of miners to and from the Peace River mines, consisting of several tents and three stores."[22] He stayed there a couple of days and then, on June 29, with one companion and three porters (two men and one woman, each carrying one hundred pounds of goods) continued on his journey to the goldfields. He stopped to see his friend Moss, who was then at the trading post at Babine Lake, and took the opportunity to have a good meal and a bath. He stayed with Moss in his tent for three days and was grateful for his generosity.

By mid-July, he had reached the mining community of Omineca City, which he described as being a "struggling log and tent city on the left bank of the creek. There were saloons everywhere and gambling in all. Two Virginians, old Fraser [River] miners and merchants, Peter Dunlevy and Jim Sellers, had quite a large assortment of goods, mining tools, picks, shovels and pans, hammers, files, saws, whip-saws; everything having been packed in by canoe boats, porter Indians, mules, donkeys and horses, from Victoria. ... Besides, they had an assortment of food and liquors, ammunition, guns, matches, fish-hooks, combs, brushes, writing-paper etc., all of which they sold at prices that would make your head spin. There was the most curious currency. The standard was one dollar. Lots of queer coin silver— English silver, shillings at a premium. Spanish pistorines, old and worn, pesos split and mutilated."[23]

Omineca City, he wrote, was a small mining town with a mass of prospectors, traders, Indigenous workers, Chinese and many other nationalities, saloons and all the inevitable camp followers. Others had more critical assessments of the mining camps in the Omineca. One correspondent of the *Washington Standard* wrote in August 1871, "I have been to a great many mining excitements in California, Oregon, Idaho etc., but I never yet have seen the want and misery I witnessed on Germansen Creek [another one of the Omineca mining communities]. There were hundreds of men without provisions of any kind, except a few beans and what they could pick up in the shape of mushrooms and a few fish; trying to drag out an existence in hopes that something might turn up."[24]

Chismore came across an acquaintance from his time with the Western Union. This was Judge Thomas Elwyn, who was now gold commissioner in the Omineca. Chismore described him as a perfect English gentleman. From him Chismore learned that Franklin Ring, his friend from Fort Tongass, had a claim on Black Jack Gulch, a stream twenty miles away that fed into the gold-rich Manson Creek. Together Chismore and Ring prospected there for a while. How seriously is a matter for conjecture. He certainly did find some gold. "I got $5 now and again," he wrote, but manifestly he did not make his fortune.[25]

Chismore's medical and dental knowledge, though, did stand him in good stead. But he made friends rather than a fortune by it because, although he was not averse to receiving gifts, he did not charge for his medical services. "I had my old six-shooter Colt from the Telegraph Company and there was a cone wrench and a screw-driver with it. This was good luck! When a miner had a tooth he

Manson Creek, heart of the Omineca mining district. Image A-04070 courtesy of the Royal BC Museum and Archives

wanted pulled, I was the only dentist in the outfit, and the screw-driver was the tool that did it. That grateful patient would usually pay in a 'pinch of gold' out of his sack—sometimes an ounce nugget."[26]

By early September, Chismore had decided to leave—perhaps he had never intended to stay for the winter anyway—and he left to travel to the coast, not thinking he would return. Or did he? The record does show that on August 27, 1872, he and a few friends, including Morris Moss and Franklin Ring, were granted a prospecting licence on a piece of land in the Omineca, and they later filed notice of their intention to apply for a Crown grant.

Passing through Hazelton on his way out, Chismore found that his friend Thomas Hankin, now married, was back in the village. He spent several days with him before going down to the coast. Then he headed home and, after spending "the jolliest week" in Victoria with his friend Ring, he arrived back in San Francisco on November 13, 1871, on board the *Prince Alfred*.[27] Among the ship's passengers were Ring, a man named William Downey and the noted prospector and bar owner Peter Cargotitch. Downey had journeyed up the Skeena in 1859 and reported on its gold-bearing potential. He and Chismore doubtless had much in common to talk about.

George Chismore. *California State Journal of Medicine* 4, no. 2 (February 1906), p. 65

Chismore was still attached to the United States Army. Possibly his arrangement with it enabled him to take breaks between contracts. In 1872, he was in charge of the smallpox hospital at the Presidio military base in San Francisco. The army then sent him as a replacement medical officer to Fort Halleck in Wyoming. Located on the famous Overland Trail, this fort had the reputation of being one of the most primitive military bases in the country. This experience may have encouraged Chismore to end his connections with the army, which he did in October 1872.

He was not yet ready to give up his adventuring, however. He signed up as a medical officer with the expedition that Octave Pavy was organizing to find a passage to the North Pole.[28] With his knowledge of Alaska and northern waters from his whaling days, Chismore would have been of great use to such an expedition. It was said he had his whole heart in the expedition. However, Pavy never left San Francisco for reasons that remain mysterious but seem to have been related to problems that included the suicide—or murder—of his financial associate hours before the expedition was to leave.

Chismore seems to have then decided to finish his medical studies, settle down and establish a career. On November 5, 1873, he qualified as a doctor of medicine at Pacific Medical College.[29] His graduation ceremony was held in Calvary Church at Powell and Geary Streets on Union Square in San Francisco. Starting a medical practice at that time was not easy. At first he was doing so badly that, reportedly, he once had to live on nothing but milk for a few days. While building a practice, he shared with a friend a three-room apartment that also served as their medical office. His friend slept in the bedroom, and he slept in the waiting room. The third room was their medical office and laboratory. But he persevered and prospered, becoming a specialist in genitourinary problems, writing many articles for learned medical journals.

In March 1877, he married Harriet Innis, with whom he had a daughter, Emma. His wife later divorced him and married her divorce lawyer, who then physically abused her.

For the rest of his life, Chismore practised medicine in San Francisco. In time he became one of the city's leading surgeons. Famous for his stubborn mispronunciation of words ("back-silly" for bacilli, "tremdous" for tremendous), he may never had been inside a regular schoolroom. He was a founder and patron of the California Women's Hospital. He retained his outdoor enthusiasms and became a celebrated wilderness hunter. He was a bon vivant. He founded and became the enthusiastic leading light of the San Francisco Bohemian Club. He also wrote what his friends called "acceptable" verse. "He had the gift of radiating kindness," a friend wrote of him, "a wonderful gift in a physician, especially when united with a knack of helping those in difficulties."[30]

As he aged he became a notable eccentric. Early in his practice, a bailiff had seized his horse and buggy, and thereafter he would not own a vehicle and walked everywhere. He slept with a pile of books and revolvers by his bed. A friend wrote that his bed was his library and shooting gallery. He was also observant in a Sherlock Holmes sort of way. A friend once brought an odd piece of lead he had picked up in China for him to identify. Chismore peered carefully at it and declared it was two rifle bullets from the Chinese-Japanese war, one Chinese, one Japanese, fused at having collided in flight—see, here were the different identifying marks on the bullets, and, moreover, it had entered the body of a Chinese soldier; see, here was the blue thread from the unfortunate man's uniform.[31]

When, much beloved, Chismore died in 1906, a newspaper described him in a headline as "one of California's great men." He was, the newspaper said, "bravely an adventurer, splendidly a scientist and quietly a gentleman."[32]

3

Thomas Hankin and the
Founding of Hazelton

1866–1871

Well, it wasn't his fault, whatever people said. The Hudson's Bay Company post at the Forks of the Skeena River had failed, and that was that. Business had not, admittedly, been good. But the Company shouldn't be blaming him, Thomas Hankin, for the fact that many Indigenous trappers brought in furs of inferior quality. And when they had good furs, they held out for the higher prices obtainable on the coast. The truth was that the post at the Forks did not pay. And now ... well, he didn't know what was going to happen to him. He was twenty-five years old and his future looked bleak.

Hankin had arrived at the Forks eighteen months before, in November 1866. Since then he had been managing the Company's Hagwilget post on the flat ground south of the confluence of the rivers.[1] Apart from the time his assistant James Otley had been with him, he had been the only white man living in the area. He had not, though, been totally isolated. In addition to the Gitxsan and Wet'suwet'en trappers and hunters coming into the post to trade skins and fur, a steady stream of prospectors was always passing by, going up and down the river on their way to search for gold. He would have noticed their need for supplies.

He looked across the Bulkley River to the stony point where Simon McGillivray had stood a little over thirty years before. Around the forested point lay the Gitxsan village of Gitanmaax, where more than three hundred Gitxsan people lived. Although it is hard to be precise about numbers, between three and four thousand Gitxsan people lived up and down the river in villages such as Kispiox, Kisgegas and Kitwanga (Gitwangak).

As Hankin stood there, waiting to leave, Michel Lacroix, who was taking over the post from him, was looking round and wanting him to be away, as successors do. Hankin was ready. The canoes were ready. He had thrown his sack of belongings into the canoe to return to Fort Simpson on the coast, 180 miles away.[2] The time had come for him to leave the first non-Indigenous settlement at the Forks of the Skeena River.

Hankin himself might not have felt he was at fault. However, the mighty Hudson's Bay Company, founded in 1670, one of the oldest and most powerful companies in the world, with quasi-governmental powers over approximately 1.5 million square miles, an area larger than India, with trading posts all over what would soon be the Dominion of Canada, with fleets of ships and wood-panelled rooms in London where dignitaries sipped port with the noble and great, begged to disagree. It saw matters very differently from young Mr. Thomas Hankin.

––––––––––

Thomas Hankin had been born into the minor gentry in Stanstead Abbotts, in Hertfordshire, England, in May 1843. His father, Daniel, was the local squire and farmer. On his farm he produced most of the food for his large family.

When Thomas arrived in British Columbia is not known. His daughter Constance said he came to Vancouver Island from India in 1857 to rid himself of yellow fever. Indeed, his family did have strong connections to India. In his book *Mapping My Way Home*, Neil Sterritt wrote that Constance once said Thomas spent 1856–1858 in India when Daniel was serving with the British Army medical corps. However, this sounds unlikely. Daniel was an irascible English squire, set in his ways in rural Hertfordshire. He was a farmer, and farmers seldom wandered the globe. In his memoirs, Philip Hankin, Thomas's brother, makes no mention of a medical or Indian background for their father.[3] Daniel, though, could well have sent Thomas to India in the same way he ordered his thirteen-year-old son Philip into the Royal Navy. Two of Thomas's brothers became colonels in the Indian Army, one becoming the military secretary to the government of Madras. His sister married a major general in the Madras Army.

In these years, 1857–1860, British Columbia was very much on the minds of four of the Hankin brothers. Philip was the eldest, followed by Thomas, Charles and then Graham. Philip was a naval officer. He had first come to Vancouver Island in 1857 as the mate on the government surveying vessel HMS *Plumper*. He later became an important figure in the colony as police chief, a member of the executive council and, after the sudden death of Governor Frederick Seymour, the administrator of the colony. Helpfully for Thomas's plans, in April 1869 Philip was sworn in as colonial secretary.

Philip may have told his brothers about the attractions of British Columbia, one of which was gold. Charles probably arrived in the colony in late 1858, bringing with him another brother, thirteen-year-old Graham. Though there is no confirming evidence, it is possible that Thomas came with them. Thomas does appear to have been in the colony in 1859. Speculation suggests that all three brothers went prospecting on the Fraser River. In 1859 Charles was trying to buy a thousand acres of land near Fort Langley, but he and his brothers soon moved north to the Cariboo. Here Charles found work as a clerk with a man called Thomas Elwyn (George Chismore's friend), who was a magistrate in charge of government business. In 1862, Charles and Graham became original partners of the gold miner

Thomas Hankin. This, the only known photograph of him, illustrates an article in *Native Voice* written in 1958 by his daughter Constance. We may consequently assume it is authentic. *Native Voice*, 1958

Billy Barker of Barkerville fame. Indeed, Charles was still the secretary of Barker's company as late as 1864.[4]

Thomas joined the police in Cayoosh, a settlement that, in 1861, changed its named to Lillooet. Elwyn wrote that in June 1861 Thomas moved from there to join the police at Williams Lake. That July the Gold Escort was formed, and Thomas joined it as second-in-command. The Gold Escort was created to guard gold being sent out to Victoria. Because the government would not guarantee the shipments, prospectors and banks did not use it much. In New Westminster it was highly unpopular because the main beneficiaries seemed to be in the other colony on Vancouver Island. In August 1861 Thomas was in New Westminster making arrangements for barracks and provisions.

An article in the *British Columbian* severely criticized Thomas Hankin for his management of the Gold Escort. "This institution," it said, "we very much fear, bids fair to end in a miserable fizzle, unless steps be taken forthwith to place it under the control of officers of a different stamp from those, or some of them at least who now have command of it. ... It seems that Mr. Hankin, the gentleman to whom we allude ... has become so puffed up with self-importance since being raised ... to the dignity of an officer in the Gold Escort."[5] However, people sprang to his defence. A letter in reply said, "With the present efficient officer (Mr. Hankin) who Capt. Elwyn has as second-in-command, I may say the officers are worthy of the confidence of the public. One word in relation to Mr. Hankin. In justice to that gentleman, I would state that after travelling in company with him for two weeks, I was surprised to see an article in your paper reflecting severely on that gentleman's character as a public officer. I come forward voluntarily now to contradict that statement, which was no doubt made by some party with a view to injure him."[6]

Well run or not, the Gold Escort did not pay, and later that year the operation was terminated.

In April 1863 Thomas and a friend applied for a pre-emption for 320 acres on the east bank of the Fraser River approximately nine miles from Fort Alexandria in the Cariboo. There he likely would have become acquainted with William Manson, who was the manager of the Hudson's Bay Company post at Fort Alexandria. It is not clear what Thomas did then, but it seems he may have gone to Victoria and joined the police there. In mid-1864 he resigned from the Victoria police. Then we lose sight of him again.

Sometime early in 1866, the Hudson's Bay Company engaged Thomas Hankin as a clerk and sent him north to Fort Simpson, on the Nass River, where William Manson was now the chief trader. The post journal recorded that at 3:00 p.m. on March 25, the Company's ship *Otter* arrived, bringing with it "a young man the name of Hankin for the Fort."[7]

Within days of his arrival, Manson sent Hankin to work as a clerk at an outpost on the Nass, and he stayed there until early July, when he returned to Fort Simpson to await further orders. He was set down in the fort's records as Mr. Hankin, as opposed to merely Hankin; that is, as a clerk, he was of the officer class. With his education, he spent most of his time in the store, trading and keeping the records. He worked at the Nass with a fellow employee named Donald MacAulay and became acquainted with his eleven-year-old daughter, Margaret, whom some years later he would marry.

At this time, the Hudson's Bay Company had a problem. The cost of taking goods and supplies into its posts in the interior by way of the Fraser River was increasing. The Company was looking for ways to reduce this cost and was therefore investigating the possibility of shipping the goods by sea from Victoria to Fort Simpson. Then it would send them up the Skeena and on overland to its posts such as Fort Babine and Fort St. James. To this end, on August 23, it directed William Manson, first, to send men to explore trails from the Forks of the Skeena into the interior and, second, to open a small post it called Hagwilget (variously spelled Hacwillgate or Ackwelgate) on the flat ground at the Forks. This place was approximately four miles downstream from the Indigenous village of that name.

Chief Factor Roderick Finlayson wrote to Manson on August 23, 1866:

The establishment of small trading Posts up the Skeena and Nass from Fort Simpson is very desirable, to prevent the furs getting to the Coast. And we trust to your making some arrangement without going to much expense in keeping Mr. Cunningham trading up the Naas River for the Winter and Mr. Hankin up the Skeena, and to be supplied with the necessary Outfits for this purpose. ... As the cost of sending supplies by the Fraser route to New Caledonia is very high, and bears heavily on the trade, we are of the opinion,

that we can get supplies in cheaper to that district by the Skeena route. You
will therefore please as early as possible, after receipt of this, organize a party
at Fort Simpson and proceed up that river, and examine it well, to the head
of Navigation for a small stern wheeler, drawing from two to 3 feet of water,
and from that point explore the Country to Lac de Francois. ... Examine also
the river as far as Roche de Bouillet [Rocher Déboulé], where the telegraph
line intersects it, and see, which is the best way to get our supplies in, either
to Babine Lake or Lac de Francois. ... Now that the telegraph line is cut
through to Skeena and will be finished this Autumn to the Stekine [Stikine]
River, we must make arrangements shortly for opening trading stations,
where it intersects those rivers.[8]

In compliance with the first directive, Manson and Hankin left the post
at Fort Simpson on September 12 to go up the Skeena. This was the journey
where they travelled upriver with George Chismore, the doctor for the Western
Union Telegraph Company. Hankin and Manson separated at Kispiox, with
Manson going farther into the interior. Hankin made his own explorations around
the Forks and of the route to François Lake and returned to Fort Simpson on
November 6, with Manson arriving back a few days later. Hankin reported that the
Indigenous people at the Forks had an abundance of furs to trade.

With winter and freeze-up of the Skeena River approaching, Manson had no
time to lose in implementing the second directive. Almost immediately, he ordered
Hankin to go back up the Skeena to set up the post. Hankin left Fort Simpson
on November 17, taking with him James Otley, who had signed on as his assistant
for one year, and Kiona, a man who was to help them build some small houses
to winter in and then return to Fort Simpson. Since this was land where Charles
Morison had spent a few weeks in charge of the Western Union Telegraph stores
only a month or so before, it is possible that there was already a building or two
on site or at least some cut lumber they could have used.

The results from that first winter were not good. William Tolmie, one of
the senior factors of the Hudson's Bay Company in Victoria, was clearly not
satisfied with Hankin's efforts. On August 12, 1867, he wrote to Manson, "We are
disappointed at the unsuccess of Mr. Hankin, as well in the explorations undertaken by him last winter, as in his trading operations at Ackwelgate [Hagwilget].
You will please strictly and impartially to investigate his conduct in these regards
generally; and if not considered by you a faithful, efficient and zealous clerk let
him be sent to Victoria in the *Otter*."[9] What Manson did about this is not clear, but
Hankin was allowed to stay another winter to prove himself.

That winter, alas, was no better than the first. By the spring of 1868, Tolmie and his colleagues had had enough. In April the Company changed the management at Fort Simpson, replacing Manson with Robert Cunningham and at the same time giving Cunningham express instructions to relieve Hankin. Cunningham went upstream to the Forks with a man named Michel Lacroix and sent Hankin back to the coast.

On April 17, Finlayson wrote to Hankin:

Immediately on receipt of this you will take stock of all the property belonging to the Company at Hackwillgate [Hagwilget], close the accounts of the place as of that date and come down with them to this place with as little delay as possible, leaving the goods in charge of Michael Lacroix, who is now ... with you, with the necessary directions to carry on the trade until further notice. On your arrival, Mr. Cunningham has received directions as to your occupation afterwards, and I have to request your attending to his directions as coming from me, as I have explained to him fully the arrangements we have in mind respecting the trade here this summer.[10]

On May 10, Tolmie instructed Captain Lewis of the *Otter* to bring Hankin back to Victoria with him on his next trip. Given the Company's views about Hankin's abilities and lack of success, it is more than likely that Tolmie then informed him that the Company had no further need of his services. As far as can be ascertained, Hankin no longer featured in lists of Company employees.

Lacroix, left in charge of the post at Hagwilget, was also unsatisfactory. The Company later accused him of desertion and closed the Hagwilget post. As for so many others, the lure of gold in the Omineca may have been too hard to resist, and he may have gone to prospect in the mountains.

In October 1870, James Bissett, a chief trader, set out the Company's thoughts about the Hagwilget post for James Grahame, the chief factor in Victoria. At this time the Company was still wondering whether it should re-establish a post there. It all depended on the existence of good trails from the Forks to the Omineca Mountains, which the government seemed to have no interest in building, and on how long the streams there would continue to yield gold to prospectors, which seemed uncertain. Bissett wrote:

It would appear necessary again to have an outpost on the upper Skeena, in order to secure the furs which find their way to the sea coast via that river. Acwellgate [Hagwilget] is the point where the coast Indians meet those from the Interior for the purpose of trade. The furs from whence at one time formed part of the returns of Fort Simpson. A small post was established there with that object in 1867 [1866], but unfortunately the charge was assigned first to an inexperienced person—a perfect stranger to the Company's service—and was afterwards left with a labourer unfitted to deal with the Indians, and who subsequently deserted from his post, which circumstances combined, appears to have led to its abandonment by the Company.

The trader already alluded to (Mr. T. Hankin) now established near to Ackwellgate, is the gentleman who was first in charge there for the Company, and who it would seem failed then to give satisfaction as their trader. On his own account, he now appears to succeed better, and I may be permitted to remark for this obvious reason, he first acquires an experience at the expense of the Company, and is afterwards allowed, without an effort on our part to prevent it, to occupy the same field for his own benefit.[11]

So, in the summer of 1868, Thomas Hankin was out of a job. What should he do now? He was no fool. He had likely already recognized the growing business opportunity on the Skeena. While working in the store at Hagwilget, he would have seen the often-irrational enthusiasm and determination of the prospectors passing by and their need for supplies. No one really knew how rich the gold streams in the Omineca were. How soon would they be exhausted? A major discovery of gold in Vital Creek in the Omineca Mountains in June 1869 touched off gold fever in prospecting communities. The stream of prospectors on the river grew.

It appears likely that during the rest of 1868 and 1869, Hankin mulled over a plan to exploit this opportunity. Why should he not set up a couple of stores along the Skeena, one at Hagwilget and another somewhere farther downriver? This plan was sufficiently formulated by 1870 for a map of the Cariboo and Omineca goldfields to be published in Victoria. This marked Hankin's store on the south bank of the river at the Forks: that is to say, where he had managed the Company's post and not at what was to become the new location of Hazelton. It also marked a second Hankin store at Gitwangak. Since this map cited Hankin as a source, it likely reflected the reality on the ground. Who would publish a map with a store marked on it that didn't exist? Travellers would rely on being able to buy supplies there and would be more than angry to arrive and find it did not yet exist. The fact that the Hudson's Bay Company had noted on October 12, 1870, that Hankin's store at Hagwilget was proving to be quite successful suggests that the store had been open long enough to prove how well it was doing.

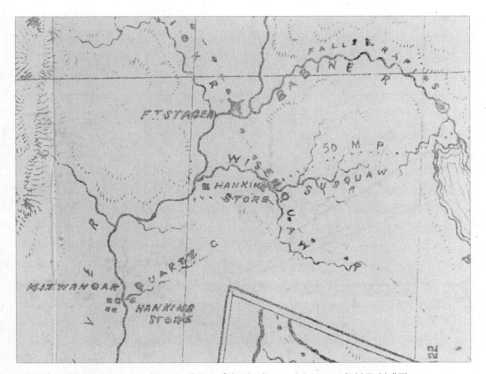

Detail from the March 1870 publication "Map of the Cariboo and Omineca Gold Fields." The map was compiled from reputable authorities (one of whom was Thomas Hankin) by William D. Patterson, Victoria, BC. Hankin's store at the Forks was on the south side of the Bulkley River on the flat land known as Hagwilget (although the Indigenous settlement of that name is a few miles away, at the canyon) or, later, Mission Point. His other store was at Kitwanga (Gitwangak). In this map the Bulkley River is named the Wisenquah. Fort Stager is located at Kispiox. Detail from image GR-1372.68.708 courtesy of the Royal BC Museum and Archives

While he was at Fort Simpson, Hankin likely shared his ideas with Robert Cunningham, the Company's manager there. This was the man who had come upriver to relieve him of his job at Hagwilget. Cunningham was an Irishman about six years older than Hankin. Described as a man with a jolly white face and strikingly white skin, he had come to British Columbia in 1862 to work with the notoriously difficult missionary William Duncan at Metlakatla but, probably after a row with Duncan, had left mission work. In 1866, he had gone to work for the Hudson's Bay Company at Fort Simpson.

What the two men were planning was to open a store at the Forks that would compete with the Hudson's Bay Company. Since Cunningham was in charge of the Company's post at Fort Simpson, this plan clearly had to be kept quiet.

Their idea appears to have been that they would become partners and then acquire land at the mouth of the Skeena, then known as Skeenamouth, and also at Hagwilget, where Hankin had already spent eighteen months. They would bring goods up from Victoria, warehouse them at Skeenamouth and then send them upriver to their new store at the Forks. From there they would sell to passing prospectors and also pack goods on mule trains into the Omineca. For good measure, they could also make the Skeena route easier by starting a freighting business. They would offer a service of canoes that would take the prospectors and their goods upriver. An easier passage meant more prospectors would use this route and lead to an increased demand for goods from their store. They would need some capital, of course, to buy their inventory, but happily, as his daughter Constance related many years later, Hankin had a substantial legacy from his godmother that enabled him to establish the business.[12] His father died in 1870, and Hankin perhaps also inherited a legacy from him. Cunningham invested money into the venture as well. In effect, Cunningham was subsidizing a store that would be in competition with his employer, the Hudson's Bay Company.

In April 1870, Cunningham applied for land on the north bank at Skeenamouth near land occupied by a man named William Woodcock. Was this application for land on his own account or was it part of the partners' plan? Was Cunningham already working with Hankin as early as April? The record does not provide an answer.

Sometime in October 1870, the Company got wind of what Cunningham was doing. It would have seen this as a direct threat to its monopoly, and the Company did not take kindly to such threats. It tackled Cunningham. It looked as if he was in a partnership with a competitor. Was that true? What the heck was he playing at? Cunningham had some fast talking to do. With his Irish charm, he was able to talk his way out of trouble. He had only loaned money to a friend. He really had no idea that a small store run by Hankin at the Forks might be a problem. It really hadn't occurred to him.

That October chief trader James Bissett wrote about this to Chief Factor James Grahame in Victoria:

This leads me to bring to your notice an irregularity on the part of Mr. Cunningham, our officer in charge of Fort Simpson. I was given to understand that Mr. Hankin had received aid from the private means of Mr. Cunningham, for carrying on his trade on the Skeena river, and under an arrangement akin to a partnership. In explanation, Mr. Cunningham states that he lent Mr. Hankin the money from a friendly desire to assist him in

starting a small business for himself; that the Company having no post on
the Skeena, he did not think it would be considered wrong to do so, and that
the interest or return for the use of the money would be contingent upon
the success of Mr. Hankin's operations. I explained to him the Company's
view of the matter: he now sees it in a different light, and expresses regret (I
believe sincerely) and further assures me that he will withdraw his money
at once. I may add that no mischief has resulted beyond a support and
countenance to Mr. Hankin's actions, which might have ended in a strong
opposition beyond the Skeena.

However, unless constant vigilance is maintained and every tendency
to tampering with the Company's trade in furs be nipped in the bud the
evil would soon attain a power beyond our control. The Skeena (along with
the Nass) river may be regarded as the key to the valuable district of New
Caledonia from the coast. The officer entrusted with the charge of this
outpost should be a man of some judgement, who, while endeavouring to
prevent the furs from falling into other hands, would not encourage the
interior Indians to come out to the coast.[13]

Somehow, Cunningham had managed to persuade the Company not to take
the matter any further. Then, showing considerable gall, he asked for a pay raise.
This request the Company turned down. Grahame wrote to Cunningham on
November 11, 1870:

Your letter of [September 19] is creditable to you and the matter you refer to
will not be discussed any further. The establishing of a store on the Skeena
River will depend on the future: our last effort by you in that quarter was,
you are aware, a failure while our late agent there [Thomas Hankin] seems
to thrive better on his own account.

... There are many clerks in the service no better paid than yourself
who have been far longer in the employ and are satisfied throughout the
whole country at very large stations who would be only too glad to get your
place. We will of course be sorry to part with you should you determine to
leave us. For I have every reason to feel pleased with what I hear of you and
would be quite satisfied did I see the expenses of the establishment at Fort
Simpson retrenched. With the present expenses there, the place cannot bear
the burden of advanced wages.[14]

Soon, though, Cunningham could not hide his involvement any longer.
Probably in the last two weeks of November, he resigned from the Company. One

account says that when his request for a pay raise was turned down, he angrily resigned on the spot.[15]

Hankin's plan depended on the supply of gold in the creeks in the Omineca continuing. Reports from there were at times encouraging and at other times discouraging. "The diggings are rich and extensive," the *Daily British Colonist* said on January 7.[16] A few days later it quoted a prospector as saying, "There's a second California there—aye, and an Australia on top of it."[17] Alarmingly, though, Vital Creek, the creek that sparked interest in the Omineca in 1869, soon started to show signs of giving out. Disillusion set in. "It is a grand farce, so far," one prospector said, "and nearly all the men have left."[18] Nevertheless, many men were coming up from the Cariboo, where the *Cariboo Sentinel* was noting how dangerous the route up the Skeena was.[19] Although this was in part to persuade the hopeful to come through the Cariboo and buy their supplies in places like Ashcroft and Soda Creek, it was not entirely untrue. At least half a dozen men drowned in the Skeena that year.

In July 1870, James Germansen, Jim May and two others discovered gold on a creek thereafter named Germansen Creek. This promised to be rich. In November it was reported in Victoria that May was taking out twenty-five to fifty ounces daily. (Germansen Creek became one of the richest creeks in the Omineca and over time produced approximately half a million dollars.) The promising discoveries continued, and this probably fortified Cunningham and Hankin's resolution to proceed. Without this discovery on Germansen Creek, the stream of prospectors going up the Skeena would have dwindled, making a store there unprofitable. Hankin and Cunningham's enthusiasm might then have flagged. In one way, therefore, in discovering gold on Germansen Creek, Jim May and James Germansen contributed to the birth of the community at the Forks that came to be called Hazelton.

Of significance for the governance of the North, that August the Hudson's Bay Company transferred all its rights on the land basically west of Ontario. This included all the land in northern British Columbia.

In December 1870, the *Colonist* reported that the quality of gold dust from the Omineca that the Victoria jeweller Julius Ludwig Jungerman was displaying in his store was attracting great interest. As was the nugget weighing 24½ ounces, half of which was gold, that M. Guichon had taken out of Germansen Creek and brought to Victoria. A great stampede north was forecast for the coming spring. "Omineca has at length emerged," the editorial in the *Colonist* said on December 28, "from the cloud of doubt and contradiction which hung over it last year. Its auriferous creeks are numerous, and they are rich—rich beyond precedent. In the very nature of things, Omineca will attract a considerable population next season."[20]

No longer a Company employee, Cunningham was now free to proceed with Hankin. The two men travelled to Victoria, arriving on December 10, 1870, and spent over two months there.[21] It is likely that they went to obtain whatever licences they needed and to buy goods to stock their stores. They would then ship these north to the warehouse Cunningham was planning to build at Skeenamouth. But first they had to acquire more land.

On December 12, Cunningham applied for 160 acres of land at Hagwilget. A few days later, Hankin applied for 160 acres of land on the south bank of the Skeena at Skeenamouth, next to Woodcock's Landing.[22] It may have helped that on June 11, 1869, Thomas Hankin's brother Philip, who was colonial secretary, had been the administrator of the colony for the two

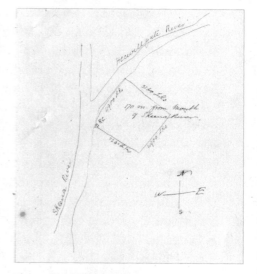

Thomas Hankin's original 1870 pre-emption on land at the Forks. This is also the location of the Hudson's Bay Company post where he had spent 1866–1868. Detail from image GR-1372.68.708 courtesy of the Royal BC Museum and Archives

months between the sudden death of Governor Frederick Seymour and the arrival of the new governor, Anthony Musgrave. Relatives in high places can always be useful. (British Columbia had not yet joined the Dominion of Canada.) On December 20, 1870, Philip was appointed to the executive council of the colony.

On December 24, a deputation of traders and prospectors, including Cunningham, went to see the governor. (Had Hankin used his connection to arrange this?) Eager prospectors knew all about the difficulties of the trail from the Forks to the Omineca, and they wanted a better one. Presenting him with a petition containing two hundred signatures, together with maps and cost estimates, they asked the governor to authorize construction of a trail from the Forks to Babine Lake. Unsurprisingly, the names of Cunningham and Hankin headed the list of signatures. The governor listened and pleaded a lack of money but said he would think about it.

The government did more than think. It acted surprisingly fast. Shortly after, it requested tenders for the construction of the requested trail. It also directed a well-connected surveyor named Edgar Dewdney to go up to the Skeena and survey for it.

Cunningham and Hankin were not alone in seeing the trading opportunity of a store at the Forks. Among the petitioners to the governor were other traders who also wanted to set up stores there. These included William Farron, John Mitchell, Thomas Currie and Lumley Franklin, the prominent Victoria real estate agent and auctioneer who had until recently been the mayor of Victoria. Franklin, who seemed to have capital to invest, was also a mining investor and chairman of the Eureka Copper Company. These were competitors. Hankin and Cunningham had no time to lose.

The most dangerous threat to the venture was not from these small traders, though, but from the behemoth of the Hudson's Bay Company itself. What if it reopened the store at Hagwilget? With its resources and supply connections, it could blow any and all competitors out of the water. The Company, though, was not prepared to take the risk of loss that failure of the Omineca gold streams and the lack of trails would lead to. It was happy, nevertheless, to let private enterprise or the government construct the trails, and then, if it saw fit, it would use them. It was watching Hankin quite carefully. Nor was it wrong about the gold. The Omineca Gold Rush did peter out in 1871, but by then the route up the Skeena was well established. The gold was still there in smaller quantities, but it was enough to entice men to prospect there for many more decades.

Hankin and Cunningham now changed their plans. They would swap positions. Hankin would go to the land at Hagwilget, and Cunningham would take possession of the land at Skeenamouth. It is indeed possible they had agreed to this earlier. It was, after all, Hankin's stores that were marked on the 1870 map. When they applied for approval to exchange their land, which they did on January 28, 1871, they may have been merely catching up with the paperwork.[23]

Cunningham called his site at the mouth of the river Port Essington, and it quickly grew. (Many years before, Captain George Vancouver had named the estuary Port Essington. The Indigenous name was Spaksuut/Spokeshute.)

On January 20, 1871, the *Daily British Colonist* and the *Victoria Daily Standard* both carried the partners' first advertisements. Both read, "Omineca Gold Mines, Skeena River Route. We have means at our command that will enable us to freight Goods from the mouth of Skeena river to the Forks for two and a half cents per lb. We will also convey Passengers from the Mouth to the Forks for fifteen dollars each. Each passenger will be allowed to carry 100 lbs of freight without extra charge. We are also prepared to supply miners with outfits and General Merchandise at reasonable rates and shall transact a forwarding and commission business. Cunningham & Hankin."[24]

On February 20, 1871, when he was still in Victoria, Hankin applied for the job of postmaster at the Forks, without pay. This was clever. He knew that every prospector would come into his store to ask if there was any mail from family or friends back home. Being postmaster would give him an edge on his competitors. Having been the Hudson's Bay Company postmaster while at the Hagwilget post, he had the necessary experience. The partners were also appointed the agents on the Skeena for the *Daily British Colonist.* This too was clever. Who wouldn't want to keep up with the latest news from the outside world when travelling in and out of the isolated world of prospecting in the wilderness?

Cunningham and Hankin travelled back to Port Essington on the *Otter*, which was the first vessel to go up the coast that year. It left Victoria at 7:00 a.m. on February 21 with 115 tons of goods on board, only 20 of which were for the Hudson's Bay Company posts. The rest was for traders, including Cunningham and Hankin.[25] They arrived on February 29.

Now that the partners were back on the Skeena, they had to move as fast as the state of the river, still closed by ice and bad waters, would allow them. They started to build their store at Skeenamouth. Until he moved to his new site at the Forks, Hankin was still living at Port Essington. He made a quick trip to the Forks by way of the Nass in early March. Indeed, his trip there and back in eighteen days set a record.

In late 1870 or early 1871, Hankin realized that his site at the Forks on the flat land south of the Bulkley River was the wrong place for a store. The trail to the Omineca started close to Gitanmaax and went north of the Bulkley River. Any prospector who wanted to come to his store at Hagwilget would have to cross the river either by the rickety Indigenous bridge or by canoe, paying the canoeman's fee. Any merchant with a store close to Gitanmaax on the Skeena itself would consequently have a significant trading advantage. Sometime in this period, therefore, Hankin moved his place of business across the Bulkley River and almost a mile up the Skeena.[26] He set up shop on land adjacent to Gitanmaax, probably building a log cabin and stocking it with goods.

Hankin knew that when prospectors came upriver, they would come in a rush. He knew he had to be ready for this wave as soon as the river became navigable. Prospectors, about twenty of whom had spent the winter at Port Essington, were already waiting impatiently for the river to open. Soon many more arrived from Victoria. More were arriving all the time. Excitement and urgency would have been in the air. They all knew those who got to the Omineca first could select the most promising unclaimed streams. At least one man had already drowned in an early attempt. By mid-April, approximately one hundred miners, ignoring warnings that it was too early, had started up the Skeena even though the ice was not out of it. A month later, over four hundred men had gone upriver.

Hankin had to work fast. Other traders were already arriving. On March 17, William Farron, who had also acquired 160 acres of land a little farther upriver from Hankin, applied for and was granted a liquor licence.[27] Farron and John Mitchell went into partnership and started advertising in Victoria, proclaiming they had the only storehouse on the river.[28] In Victoria, William Moore was building a large boat with which he intended to take goods up from Port Essington to the Forks. Very suddenly, it appears, the Forks of the Skeena was the place to be. This is where the buzz of mercantile action was at that moment.

This new community now needed a name. Hankin had noticed the hazel bushes all around and so he named it the town of hazel bushes—Hazelton. In his book *The Skeena: River of Destiny*, R. Geddes Large gives an alternative explanation of who settled there first and who named it. He suggests that workers from the Western Union Telegraph stayed in the area after the project was cancelled, and, settling on that spot on the Skeena, they named it Hazelton.[29] History is seldom neat and tidy. It is possible that some men did set up shacks at this point. Whatever the facts of who was the first non-Indigenous settler, Hazelton was now a small community, with stores, tents, settlers and at least one bar.

In April 1871, Cunningham and Hankin sent four canoes upriver from Port Essington with a total of eight tons of supplies for their new store. Arthur Wellington Clah brought another four canoes upriver with goods for them in May. This load included ten traps, forty-seven pounds of salt pork and one hundred pounds of axes. Clah had with him two white men and four Indigenous men. They had an exceptionally difficult journey upriver, having to hire additional bearers to portage the goods around the Kitselas Canyon. This journey took them a total of twenty-two days. Clah made two more journeys for the partnership that year.

Hankin then made another quick trip from Hazelton to Port Essington, arriving there on May 19. This would have been a quicker trip by canoe now that the river was open. However, the river was in an uncertain state, having risen six feet almost overnight and still rising. There had been more fatalities on it. The following month Hankin had a happier but still hurried trip. In June he went downriver and on to Fort Vancouver at the northern tip of Vancouver Island. There, on June 20, he married Margaret MacAulay.[30] It was on this trip that he met George Chismore coming upriver.

By mid-May, Hazelton was buzzing. Prospectors were arriving in ever-increasing numbers. Although one of his canoes had been wrecked on its journey upriver—split to pieces below Gitwangak—Hankin had his store ready with supplies. He would also have been negotiating with the Gitxsan packers to take supplies by pack train into the Omineca, where stores were springing up in the various mining communities. The firm of Sterling & Smith was building a warehouse at

Germansen Creek and had commissioned Jim May to build a storehouse for it. They would be needing supplies to fill it.

There was also the problem of the trail. The better the trail from Hazelton to the Omineca, the easier it would be for miners to reach the gold streams there, and more prospectors would consequently use the Skeena route. Without the mining in the Omineca, there would have been little need for any stores in Hazelton. The merchants needed better trails as much as the prospectors. Soon the government surveyor Edgar Dewdney arrived to survey for a better trail.

On July 20, 1871, in the middle of this frenzy of eager prospectors coming in and out of Hazelton, the building of houses, shacks and warehouses, the hustle and bustle of a new town, the Colony of British Columbia joined the Dominion of Canada as a province. Perhaps not many people in Hazelton paid much attention. In any event, the news would take several weeks to get there.

Robert Cunningham remained a pillar of the Port Essington community all his life. Tragically, three of his children with his first wife died in infancy. His wife and another son, aged seventeen, drowned. He died, aged sixty-eight, in 1905.

Thomas Hankin remained in Hazelton as one of its leading citizens. His store was the leading business in town for many years. He bought some land up the Skeena across the river from what is now Glen Vowell, where he grew hay and pastured horses and mules used in the pack train business. He also acquired an interest in the Inverness Cannery at Port Essington. He died in Port Edward in March 1885. His widow, Margaret, later married Richard Loring, the Indian agent who arrived in 1889 and who lived in Hazelton until 1920.

Hankin lived long enough to see the Hudson's Bay Company re-establish a post in Hazelton. In 1880, it appointed Alfred Sampare as its first manager at the Forks since Hankin in 1866. Clearly, he had succeeded in the business they had given up, and from that he likely took some wry satisfaction.

4

Edgar Dewdney, Charles Horetzky and Other Passersby

1871–1872

One day in late spring 1871, Edgar Dewdney picked up a mallet and the wooden stake. He looked around at the Skeena River flowing swiftly past him and then at the jumble of tents and shacks that was Hazelton. Thomas Hankin, William Farron, Thomas Currie and a few others stopped what they were doing to watch. Some Gitxsan inhabitants from the village of Gitanmaax, near the confluence of the rivers, stood and stared.[1] Dewdney then hammered the post into the ground. To it he nailed the notice he had carefully written. It read:

Notice

Notice is hereby given that a tract of land extending from the mouth of the Agelgate [Hagwilget, or Bulkley] River to a stake about 4 chains above this Notice is Reserved by the Government of British Columbia. And further that a portion of this summary claim thereon 30 chains from this point and ½ mile back from the River Skeena is reserved as a town-site.

The formal line of a few lots are staked in order that parties wishing to build may do so with some regularity. No one will be allowed to build closer to the River than the line staked.

The size of the lots are 66 feet by 132 feet. The usual rent of $2.50 per month must be paid by occupiers to the Government.

Any further information can be obtained from

Edgar Dewdney, J.P.
Government Agent[2]

Edgar Dewdney was a long way from Bideford in Devon, where he had been born in 1835.[3] Usually it was the younger sons who struck out for the colonies to make their fortune, leaving eldest brothers at home to manage the estate, business or shop. Dewdney, however, appears to have been the eldest son. Trained as a civil engineer in Cardiff, he had come to British Columbia in 1859, perhaps hoping to make his own fortune in the Fraser River Gold Rush.[4] He set himself up in Victoria as an auctioneer, surveyor, architect and land agent. With his training, his knowledge of surveying and his connections, he soon found work laying out new roads. The most important of these was the Dewdney Trail. For twenty-five years, this was a vital route joining the interior of the colony to the coast. Dewdney was active in colonial politics for a time but stepped down from his position on the Legislative Council of British Columbia to work as a surveyor. In early 1871, the government sent him north to survey a better route to the Omineca goldfields.

The notice Dewdney hammered into the ground was the official laying out of Hazelton. He wrote to Benjamin W. Pearse, the government's chief surveyor, on May 20, 1871, reporting on the town-site he had laid out and on the trail he was planning (the full report is set out in Appendix 1):

Edgar Dewdney in 1865. Image A-04735 courtesy of the Royal BC Museum and Archives

Since my arrival here I have selected a starting point for the trail and reserved for the Government all the land situated between the Agwilgate [Hagwilget, or Bulkley] River and the lower line of a pre-emption taken up by Messrs. Mitchell and Farron. A portion of it I have reserved as a town site, the remainder as an Indian reserve for a tribe called the Ket-en-macks [Gitanmaax].

On the proposed town site I posted a notice (a copy of which I enclose). By it you will see that I have staked off a few lots, and should you think it advisable to lay out a small town site here before I return, I should be obliged if you would forward me the necessary instructions. The work would not take more than a week, as the ground is open and free from any underbrush. Three lots have been taken, one by Messrs. Cunningham and Hankin, one by a Mr. Reed and one by Wm. Moore. And buildings will be put up at once.

I trust that you will agree with me that it is fortunate I have been enabled to reserve a small tract for a town site as is invariably the case all the land that was thought to be open for pre-emption was taken up in the vicinity of the supposed starting point, and this would not have remained unoccupied had not the parties who had settled above the Reserve been of the opinion that an Indian Reservation existed from the mouth of the Agwilgate River two miles upstream.[5]

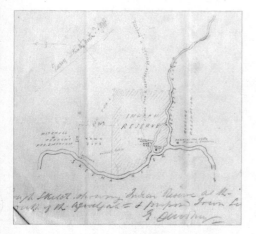

Edgar Dewdney drew this map when he
was in Hazelton in early 1871. Note that
it marks the location of "Kit-en-Maax"
(Gitanmaax) as being close to the island. In
approximately 1875, the village was later
moved to the bench above Hazelton. Note
also that Thomas Hankin's old store on his
pre-emption is identified as having been
"burnt by Indians." The channel between the
island and Gitanmaax over time became
the Hazelton Slough and then dried up.
*Topographical Sketch Map of Omineca and Finlay
River Basins* (detail), 1917, Northern BC Archives
& Special Collections, University of Northern
British Columbia

This letter seemed to take the authorities in Victoria by surprise. It is almost as though one senior official asked a colleague, "Did you authorize this?" whereupon the other replied, "No, did you?" Pearse wrote:

Submitted for his Excellency's information with regards to the town site. I am quite ignorant of what instructions may have been given to Mr. O'Reilly on this point. I instructed Mr. Dewdney a long time before to secure any location that appeared to him suitable for a town site, as well as to reserve all lands occupied by the Indians and to post up notices that such lands were reserved to them. It would be advisable, I think, to lay out a few lots, which might be leased for the present and sold by auction at a future time.[6]

This led to the following comments:

I concur in Mr. Pearse's opinion. If I remember rightly there were no directions given to Mr. O'Reilly respecting a town site.

and

Forwarded for the information of Mr. Pearse. No special instructions were given to Mr. O'Reilly respecting a reservation of a townsite at Hazelton.[7]

In any event, they endorsed Dewdney's actions and the townsite of Hazelton was approved. The O'Reilly referred to was Peter O'Reilly, the gold commissioner in the Omineca and the closest government authority.

On May 5 Dewdney left Hazelton to explore the terrain to determine which of the bad trails to the Omineca should be improved. Not that his activity stopped

At Christmas 1872, Charles Horetzky took this photograph of Hazelton and the Skeena River from the bluff above Hazelton. It shows the growth of the village. Image PA-022559 courtesy of Library and Archives Canada

the prospectors from complaining about the slowness in making a trail for them. "We all think here," they wrote in a letter to the *Daily British Colonist*, "that we have been shamefully treated."[8]

Many prospectors may have been impatient at what they considered the unconscionable delay in constructing the trail, but that did not stop them setting out. By mid-May 1871, four hundred of them had already travelled up the Skeena and on to the Omineca.[9] By July, a correspondent to the *Colonist* was writing that Dewdney had blazed the trail all the way from the Forks to Takla, and that William Woodcock had commenced to cut and grade it. He also noted that seven hundred prospectors had arrived at Germansen Creek. This correspondent wrote, "The Forks of the Skeena will, I think, soon become quite a place. There [are] now three business houses here, Messrs. Cunningham & Hankin, Mr. Woodcock and Messrs. Farron and Mitchell. There is no doubt but the Skeena will be the route of supplies to the Omineca country. The miners to a man are of that opinion."[10] Certainly the flow of prospectors upriver was increasing. By mid-1871, O'Reilly reported to the colonial secretary that there were at that time twelve hundred prospectors on the streams and creeks of the Omineca.[11]

Although Dewdney surveyed and blazed the trails, he didn't do the work of building and improving them himself. Cunningham & Hankin had one of the

A photograph Charles Horetzky took in 1872 of Hazelton from across the icebound Skeena River looking toward Rocher Déboulé. Image PA-117929 courtesy of Library and Archives Canada

contracts to do that, with Woodcock in charge of the actual building and William Moore in charge of the transportation.

When George Chismore visited Hazelton on June 26, 1871, he described it as having three stores and many tents. By the autumn, the settlement had grown and had six buildings and a tent. Hankin was said to be about to build a warehouse. Judge O'Reilly, the gold commissioner, visited the town and held a court. Although he did approve three spirit licences, one of which was to William Farron, he denied a man named Peter Cargotitch a licence to build a saloon. Since he had already given Farron one licence, he may have thought one bar for such a small hamlet was enough.

Toward the end of 1872, Chismore, who had spent the summer prospecting in the Omineca without much success, was back in Hazelton. He was returning to San Francisco to resume his medical work with the United States Army and then to continue his medical training. Knocking on Hankin's door, he was happy to find his friend and his new wife thriving. He stayed at Hazelton for almost a week and then went on his way.[12]

Christmas of 1872 was lively. Thomas Hankin and his wife threw a party for the Gitxsan children, setting up a Christmas tree and distributing presents to one and all.

Charles Horetzky, another passerby in Hazelton, knocked on Hankin's door that Christmas. He had emigrated from Scotland to the Australian goldfields when he was fifteen but had found his way to Quebec, where, in 1858, he joined the Hudson's Bay Company. He spent some years at the Company's Moose Factory post, where he became an expert photographer. He seems to have been disputatious, because he was fired from that job. His family's friend, Charles Tupper, a minister in the Dominion government, was able to persuade Sir Sandford Fleming—at that time the chief engineer for the Canadian Pacific Railway and surveying for possible routes through the Rocky Mountains—to hire Horetzky as the official photographer on the northern survey from Winnipeg.

Fleming asked Horetzky to journey to the coast and see what else he could find. In the winter of 1872, he was walking from Fort Edmonton in Alberta to Fort Simpson on the coast. He took the first photographs of Hazelton, the Hagwilget Bridge and the British Columbia North.

Horetzky related how he arrived in Hazelton just before Christmas:

Midnight had just gone, when, through the now thickly falling snow, the Indian pointed to the scattered collection of log huts one hundred and fifty feet below, which was dignified by the name of Hazelton. In front of this silent village, the Skeena could be distinguished by the black line of its unfrozen waters, down which coursed—tumbling, tossing, and grinding against each other, as if eager for precedence—huge, white floes of ice. With the exception of this narrow streak of rapid water, the entire landscape was white and desolate to a degree. ... A steep sideling trail had been cut down the bank, and we were just preparing to descend, when I, incautiously approaching too near the brink, slipped upon the icy ground, and reached the lower level before my companions, who, immensely amused at the exploit, followed in a more leisurely manner.

We at once sought out Tom Hankin's store, where, after a little delay, Tom Hankin himself appeared, and gave me a hearty welcome. "Just in time for Christmas," said Tom; and instantly called up "Charlie," the cook—a fat, good natured Indian of the Hyder [Haida] tribe—who poked up the fire, and with the celerity of a city waiter, soon placed before me hot tea and eatables. "Just in time for Christmas week. We're going to have a time of it, and you may make up your mind to remain here for three weeks, until there is good going. It's no use," said he, as I deprecated such a long delay. "Not an Indian will budge from here to New Year, anyhow, so you may keep cool."

To confess the truth I did not feel averse to spending a few days with such a hospitable entertainer, and, convinced of the soundness of his argument, I resigned myself to the delay consequent upon a fortnight's sojourn at "The Forks." After partaking of a homeopathic dose of hot scotch, we separated for the night, Charlie, the cook, having provided me with a "shake-down" on the floor, where I speedily forgot all my troubles, and slept very soundly till seven a.m. when I was awakened by the preparations for breakfast. As we sat down to that meal, Tom introduced me to his wife, a very nice, agreeable person, who seconded her husband's endeavors towards my comfort. ...

My first visit after breakfasting with Tom was to his partner Mr. McK. [likely Charles McKinnon], who lived in an adjoining house. These two gentlemen were engaged in the fur trade, and carried on, besides, a miscellaneous traffic with passing miners, of whom there were some score or more then wintering at the "Forks." As might have been expected, there was, besides the dwelling houses and stores, a saloon, which formed the favourite resort of the residents during those hours of leisure when "poker," "euchre" and "forty-five" absorbed the attention of the jovial and reckless population.

Owing to the want of accommodation at Hankin's house, I shifted my quarters to the saloon, and was located in a log house, containing but one room and a closet, where the bar-tender kindly provided me with a bedstead, on which I hoped to pass, after a civilized fashion, a few really comfortable nights: but, unfortunately for me, I reckoned without my host, and did not calculate upon the disorganization consequent upon the rioting and festivities of Christmas week, then close at hand.

The weather had again become settled and on the morning of Christmas Eve the thermometer stood at twenty-two degrees below zero. This was, however, a much higher temperature than is usually experienced at this place. I was informed that the previous winter forty, and even fifty, degrees below zero had been, by no means, exceptional readings at the corresponding period.

From early morning until far into the evening the miners and everyone else at the place were busily occupied in getting up shooting matches and other games with which to usher in the time-honoured holiday; and at midnight of the 24th, the bursting of a bomb consisting of 25 pounds of gunpowder securely tied up in many thicknesses of strong canvas announced the day which Englishmen so much delight to respect. Simultaneously a dropping fire of muskets and revolvers, accompanied by shouts and yells from the excited crowd, resounded through the air, and forthwith the major part of the population of Hazelton crowded into the saloon, where ample justice was done to the occasion in many a flowing bumper, the exciting effects of which were soon manifested by eager demands for music and dancing.

An old accordeon and tambourine, the only instruments at the place, were called into requisition, while the crack dancers took to the floor, among whom, and chief of them all, figured Dancing Bill, of British Columbian renown.[13]

The fun grew fast and furious; the legitimate instruments already in use, and soon rendered almost unserviceable, were not found sufficient to satisfy the terpsichorean tastes of the miners; frying pans, pokers, shovels, anything in fact, capable of producing sound, were therefore added to the list, and helped swell the din become now almost demoniacal.

To sleep through such an uproar was, of course, out of the question; so, seizing the first opportunity, I made myself scarce and sought refuge in a neighboring shanty, where I managed to elude the vigilance of the noisy crowd, and snatch several hours of quiet rest.

These demonstrations of mirth and loyalty continued for several days, and to avoid them I was glad of the occasion to make a short tour of exploration around the base of the Rocher Déboulé and up the Wotsonquah [Bulkley River], in which I was joined by Tom, who had now become sick and tired of the several days of consecutive festivity.

After a short journey up the Skeena in the direction of Kyspyox, with Mr. McK—for my companion, when we photographed several places of interest, amongst others Hazelton and the mountains in its vicinity—Tom Hankin and I, accompanied by Charlie and another Indian, started on a little trip up the Wotsonquah, taking with us my camera.[14]

After spending Christmas at Hazelton, Horetzky went on his way and ended his epic trek to the coast on January 23, 1873. After writing about his travels, he rejoined the Hudson's Bay Company, becoming a persistent and annoying advocate for the northern route for the Canadian Pacific Railway. Fleming, who believed the southern route was unquestionably the best, eventually grew exasperated and fired him. Horetzky spent most of the rest of his career with the Ontario government, supervising public works.

Edgar Dewdney returned to Victoria and reported to his superiors. He then returned to politics. In the 1872 election, he won a seat in the Dominion Parliament for the riding of Yale. He spent the rest of his life in senior political and governing positions. Prime Minister John Macdonald appointed him a member of the federal cabinet in 1879 and, in 1881, lieutenant-governor of the North-West Territories, where he served until 1888 and was also the Indian commissioner. In that capacity, he earned a highly controversial reputation for his policies toward Indigenous Peoples. He was lieutenant-governor of British Columbia for the years 1892 to 1897. Current re-evaluation of his record has resulted in increasing criticism of his contribution to Canadian history.

The community of Hazelton was now well and truly established. Although a steady stream of people passed through and many prospectors spent the winters there, the number of non-Indigenous residents grew slowly. Even by 1880, there were under a dozen settlers. The numbers started to increase after the first steamer reached Hazelton from the coast in 1891. By 1900 there were approximately 40 inhabitants. (The adjacent Gitxsan village of Gitanmaax had approximately 300 to 400 residents.) After the turn of the century, the numbers started to increase. In 1909, James Maitland-Dougall, the new police chief, counted 154 residents. This being a higher number than previously estimated, he felt able to increase the licence fees on the local hotels.

Few of the lots Dewdney laid out were taken up. When Richard Loring arrived in 1889 as Indian agent, he appears to have laid out thirteen acres for the town. Because the site was surrounded by Gitxsan land on three sides and the Skeena River on the fourth, Hazelton was never able to grow in land area. Its future was set.

5

Jim May and the Miners of the Omineca Gold Rush

"We had a couple of cows and a spare mule walkin' behind the wagon," Jim May, the old-time prospector, told Rev. Dan MacLean in Hazelton one day in about 1912. "And I was the one who had to herd them along, so I walked most of the way out there. When we heard of the gold strike in Barkerville, I walked to San Francisco and got a boat to Victoria, and from there to Yale. Then I walked from there to Barkerville, and ten years later I walked to Manson Creek, so you could say I walked most of the way."[1]

Of all the prospectors and old-time miners in British Columbia, few had such deep and broad experience as Jim May. And few prospectors, if any, were more respected for their honesty and judgment.

James Jasper May was born in Bedford County, Tennessee, in 1833. His father, William, who came originally from North Carolina, had a restless streak. When Jim was about seventeen years old, William took his family west and settled in Prairie, in Davis County, Iowa. On the way, Jim did his part scouting for their wagon train, foraging for game and watching out for hostile inhabitants. He helped his parents set down roots in Prairie, putting up buildings and harvesting their first crop. Then, leaving his parents and his younger siblings, Louisa, Susan, Nancy and eleven-year-old John, Jim May followed the lure of gold and went west. It is unlikely he ever saw any of his family again. He arrived in California in 1850, a few months too late to be a forty-niner. He then spent several years there on the gold streams, learning his trade as a placer miner. One day in 1858 or possibly early 1859, Jim was wandering along the waterfront in San Francisco. The captain of a ship there, needing more passengers to make his voyage pay, told him about new discoveries of gold somewhere up north of the United States border at a place called the Fraser River. Fired by the news, Jim went on board and came north.

In 1858, the discovery of gold in enticing quantities had sparked the Fraser River Gold Rush. Hopeful prospectors, mainly American or European immigrants, found their way to the streams and bars on the river. Their rowdy presence raised the real prospect they might pull the land into the United States as a state or territory. Though not assuredly one of the rowdy ones—he was too much of a gentleman—Jim May was one of these prospectors. The invasion of the often scofflaw American miners led to an urgent need for the authorities in Victoria to establish, and then maintain, law and order. This resulted in the creation of the Colony of British Columbia in 1858 and later to the merger of the Colonies

James Jasper May, the prospector who walked from Tennessee. Image G-04489 courtesy of the Royal BC Museum and Archives

of British Columbia and Vancouver Island in 1866. This united Colony of British Columbia joined the Dominion of Canada in 1871.

The search for gold built British Columbia. The pattern of discovery repeated itself time and time again. Photographs show us these prospectors of the Old West—the man with shaggy beard, trousers held up by suspenders, a floppy hat and the gleam, part hope, part despair, in his eyes. Such a prospector would find gold in a gravel bar on a lonely stream but be unable to keep his discovery secret. Inevitably, a rush of eager miners would soon descend on the stream and its neighbours. Before long the area would be a mess of diggings, channels of water, sluice boxes, piles of dirt, shacks and saloons. When the streams were all staked or the gold deposits exhausted, the prospectors moved on to explore another river some-where farther north.

It all happened quickly. In 1856, Indigenous people showed some gold to the chief trader at the Hudson's Bay Company post at Kamloops. This led to the search for and discovery of gold in the Fraser River and, in turn, to the frantic rush in 1858.[2] By 1859, prospectors were spreading out and trying their luck in the Cariboo. This led to discoveries in one river after another. The Fraser, the Cariboo, the Stikine, the Omineca, the Cassiar, the Atlin—it was a familiar pattern. Quesnel, Williams Lake, Cayoosh (Lillooet), Alexandria and Barkerville, among other places, became celebrated mining towns.

At much the same time, prospectors were exploring the Skeena River. People already knew gold was there for the finding. In a letter of August 26, 1852, the factor at the Hudson's Bay Company post at Fort Simpson, William Henry McNeill, wrote that "gold was reported 'by Indians' to have been discovered up the Skenar River on the 8th April last."[3] Although this discovery was not confirmed at the time, in view of the fact that gold was later found to be abundant in the river, it could well have been true. McNeill did report on the promising amounts of gold on the Queen Charlotte Islands (now Haida Gwaii). This led the government to send Major William Downie in July 1859 to investigate. After failing to find anything of value on the Queen Charlotte Islands, Downie went up the Skeena River to see if he could find gold there. Indeed he did. He reported that the "whole country was auriferous" with gold-yielding potential. "We could go no further," he wrote, "than Kittamarks [Gitanmaax], the Forks of the Skeena, in a canoe."[4] The publicity given to Downie's journey in newspapers and official documents stimulated prospectors—who never seemed to need much encouragement anyway—to explore the creeks and gravel bars of the Skeena River.

Throughout the 1860s, prospectors followed up on Downie's discoveries. They went farther afield and also explored the Stikine River country, which led to the gold rush of 1861–1862. Rumours of gold in the Peace River country on the eastern side of the Omineca Mountains led them to explore the upper reaches of the Skeena and the Omineca. What followed was the gold rush in the Omineca Mountains in 1870–1871.

Sebastopol was one of the first prospectors for gold on the Skeena River. His real name was Nathan Simpson, but almost everywhere—the Fraser, the Cariboo, the Skeena—he was known as Sebastopol. A successful prospector on the Fraser, he had left Victoria in early October 1860 on the schooner *Langley* to look for gold on the coast.[5] Perhaps that wasn't too successful, because he then spent a year or so in the Cariboo, developing a claim on a hillside known as Sebastopol's claim. He went north to the Nass in 1863. He and his party spent the winter of 1863–1864 at Fort Simpson. They built a boat there and came back up the Skeena in it.[6] In 1865 he went over a grease trail from the Nass to the Skeena. He wrote that he and his party "struck the Skeena about 200 miles above its mouth at an Indian village called Kit-wan-car [Gitwangak] and got a prospect with a rocker of about $6.00 per day. Prospected over 100 miles above this place as far as the village of Kis-pew-yort [possibly Kispiox] and found gold on all the low bars."[7] The *Daily British Colonist* reported in August 1864 that Sebastopol was having "fair success at the Skeenah river mines, taking out from $5 to $7 a day."[8]

Believing gold was to be found in the Omineca was one thing. Getting there, however, presented problems. The area was remote. Would-be gold magnates worked their way there by two principal routes. Neither was easy.

A growing number came up the Skeena River to the Forks and then went on to the Omineca. In Hazelton, after 1870, Thomas Hankin and his store were waiting for them.

Parties of prospectors had ventured north from Quesnel in the Cariboo in the early 1860s. In 1861, William Cust and Edward Carey found gold in the Peace River district on the eastern flank of the Omineca Mountains. In 1862, they returned with a party that included Ezra Evans and Peter Toy. They found more gold. Because of the difficulties of getting there and back and the high cost of supplies, a period of apparent inactivity followed. On May 3, 1869, a party known famously as the Peace River Prospecting Party set out from Quesnel. One of the committee of three organizing this expedition was Edgar Dewdney.[9] At this time he was farming near Soda Creek. He and his friends invested $1,200 in this project. Another investor, Dewdney said, was Governor Anthony Musgrave, who put in $1,000. Dewdney also said that one of the workers on his farm was named James Germansen.

Among the prospectors was a French Canadian from La Prairie, Quebec, named Vital LeFort (occasionally spelled LaFort, LaForce or LeForce). Before coming to the goldfields, he had worked with the surveying parties that had delineated the United States–British Columbia border at the forty-ninth parallel. He had also been a scout and trailblazer for the Western Union Telegraph. (Conceivably, he was one of the men who had stayed behind to prospect after the telegraph project was cancelled. Could he have been one of those who set up a shack on the site that is now Hazelton after that project was cancelled?) That summer of 1869, Vital LeFort made a rich strike on the creek in the Omineca that became known as Vital Creek. The richness of this strike fired the interest of eager prospectors. Although the party tried to keep the richness of the find quiet, when LeFort spent $2,500 in the store at Fort St. James people drew the obvious conclusions, and the rush started. The discovery on Germansen Creek in 1870 maintained the interest. The buildup for the Omineca Gold Rush of 1871 now began.

Ezra Evans, a Welshman from Caernarfon, joined the party. He came out to California reportedly after failing his second-year medical exams in Wales. He signed on to bring camels to Barkerville, which went well until a contretemps with a horse pack train at Clinton ended the venture. The experience of trying to round up the panicked and stampeded camels was not one, it was said, he liked to be reminded of.[10] He reached Barkerville and started his career of prospecting in the North. Evans was a partner of Henry Fuller "Twelve-Foot" Davis, so-called because he had spotted a twelve-foot section on Williams Creek in the Cariboo River after an improper survey. He took $12,000 out of that twelve-foot lot. Dancing Bill Latham, a Rhode Island man, was another pioneer. Among his jobs was running a dance hall. He was one of those who spent the winter of 1881 in Hazelton. And then there was Nellie Cashman, famous throughout the North. She was young and pretty with blonde hair, tough as nails but generous and energetic. By 1875, she was keeping a saloon in Laketon, a small mining community farther north.

As news of discoveries of gold in the Omineca spread, so did the excitement and the eagerness to get there. Although prospectors from the Cariboo still went to the Omineca from there, those coming from Victoria and the United States usually found the Skeena route easier. They came in ever-increasing numbers. Many prospectors spent the winter of 1870–1871 in Port Essington, waiting for the Skeena to become navigable after the winter in order to make an early start. Then they flooded up to the new settlement at the Forks, now called Hazelton, and then over the bad tracks to the Omineca. Many returned to spend their winters in Hazelton. In the spring, they set out again for the Omineca.

The Omineca Gold Rush of 1871 did not last long. Prospectors soon learned that the gold streams there were not as rich as they had hoped. It was the old problem: too many prospectors, too little gold. Within a year, many of them left for the more promising gold-bearing streams in the Cassiar.

Hopes of finding gold in the Omineca, however, did not die. Prospectors stayed and sifted through the gravel and bars on the streams for decades. A small number of prospectors roamed the known creeks—Manson, Vital, Omineca, Tom, Germansen—panning, digging and always hopeful. Prospecting continued over the years with varying degrees of intensity, enthusiasm and success. Toward the end of the century, mining became more industrial, requiring larger machines and larger amounts of capital. The arrival of the railway in Hazelton in 1913 spurred the surge of exploration and mining of silver and coal, as well as other metals and minerals in the short-lived Hazelton mining boom. The First World War and the high freight rates charged by the railway ended this.

––––––––

Jim May's story is typical of many. After frustrating delays on the sandbars and mud flats at the mouth of the Fraser, he reached Hope Bar. Sadly for him, he was too late. The claims were mostly worked out. After he heard of discoveries in the North, he moved farther up the river. At Cayoosh (Lytton) he met a group of prospectors that included Billy Barker, the most famous of all the British Columbia prospectors. May carried on north to the Cariboo. By June 1859, he was at Fort Alexandria, where gold had recently been found. He wrote to a friend in Victoria:

> I embrace this opportunity of writing you a few lines to let you know that we are well. ... The water is very high now, and we cannot work; but I think it will not be hard to find ten or fifteen dollar diggings when the water falls. We are located on Canal River, about twenty-five miles above Fort Alexander. ... If you and the boys come you had better buy ... enough grub to last you until cold weather sets in. Don't fail to see the boys and tell them I think there is a good show. ... MacDaniels thinks that he can make one hundred Dollars per day when the water falls. He has made as much as fifty dollars per day.[11]

This letter places May at the very beginning of the Cariboo Gold Rush. He remained in the Cariboo to prospect and achieved some success when, reportedly, he was one of the discoverers of the Antler Creek claim. Eager prospectors heard of this and rushed to the creek. May then heard of the discovery of gold in the Omineca Mountains and thought it was time to move on.

May arrived at the gold-bearing creeks in the Omineca in 1863. Sperry Cline, who wrote about the North, said Jim May was one of the discoverers of the Black Jack Gulch claim.[12] At that time there were approximately 150 men working the creeks. Like many prospectors, May had disappointments, but he nourished the hope that the next pan, the next shovel, the next creek, would bring his fortune. He did have successes, those moments of excitement and joy that kept prospectors such as him going. In 1866, the *British Columbia Tribune* described him as an old and well-known Cariboo miner who had struck a very rich claim on French Creek. "Jim May," it said, "is one of the pioneer prospectors of Cariboo, and he has traversed as much of that mountain region in pursuit of gold as any man who has ever ventured into the upper country."[13]

After the discovery of gold in Vital Creek, May moved his attention there. The Omineca mines record book showed that on November 15, 1869, James McMillan, Duncan McMartin and James May registered the following claim: "We, the undersigned, claim three claims of one hundred feet each on Vital's Creek about one and a half miles from its mouth."[14]

At first, he had little success. On June 8, 1870, May wrote to his friend John McLean in Barkerville:

> Friend John, I received your letter. Times are rough here yet. Nothing struck. We bottomed our shaft at 44 feet and found nothing to pay. Black and Sylvester bottomed last night at 30 feet. No prospect. We are now working in the creek claims, and I think it will be deep there. Shallow diggings on this creek are played out. If you are doing anything, you had better stop until you hear from me again. There is a chance for big diggings on this creek, and it may be a square bilk [hoax or deception]. The new chums are selling out and leaving. The Chinamen have all left. If we find nothing in the creek, I will let Vital creek slide. I am in hopes that the next time I write I will be able to give you good news. J.J. May.[15]

His luck did change. Jim May and James Germansen were two who gave up on Vital Creek and, following a hunch of Germansen, explored another creek. That July they made one of the richest finds. After the discovery, they paced out their claim and then named it Germansen Creek. Two of the party went back to Vital

Creek to tell the others about the find. "An intense excitement sprang up at once," Germansen told the *Daily British Colonist*, "some men leaving that same night with lighted candles in broken bottles to pick their way over the ground. The next morning there were only four men in camp. At Omineca some of the party built rafts and floated down 60 miles to Germansen Creek and took up claims. ... Nearly every man who went to work made money immediately."[16] This revived the flagging enthusiasm for the Omineca. By the autumn, prospectors had taken out $55,000 worth of gold. For a time, May was taking $25 to $50 a day out of the creek. But the old story repeated itself. Prospectors flocked to the creeks and mined much of the most easily found gold.

Jim May persevered. Having spent the winter of 1872 prospecting without much success, he spent the following summer building a store for Sterling & Smith. He took a party to prospect at Bear Lake but found nothing there either. So he returned to Vital Creek. The years passed. In August 1875, a letter in the *Colonist* from Joyce Heath (who were they? one wonders) said that "Jim May had found some good diggings in Omineca. Can't vouch for the truth. I am very much like the Virginny preacher. 'Blessed am dey dat expect nuffin. Dey ain't guinn to be disippinted.'"[17] May, however, never did make his fortune.

Romantic myths have made these old-time miners into honest men who had a fierce code of honesty, rough but fair. Not everyone, however, played by such chivalric rules. Theft was one problem prospectors had to contend with. A man called Joe Shuck was once working at one of May's sluice boxes and, when he thought no one was looking, scooped almost eight ounces of gold dust—worth about $125—into his handkerchief. At the next assizes, the judge sent him to prison for two years.[18]

Over the fifty years from 1860, Jim May became a respected and familiar figure in the mining camps of the Omineca Mountains and in Hazelton, where he wintered and bought his supplies. He became known for his honesty and fair-mindedness—a fountainhead of wisdom, someone once called him. He was often called upon to arbitrate disputes among miners about claims. So respected was he that when Premier Joseph Martin's government passed the Alien Act to restrict the rights of American miners in British Columbia, May was reportedly told by "the responsible authorities high in Government office"[19]—Cline's words—that the law would not apply to him. Cline also related that once May was offered an honorary colonelcy in an organization called the Legion of Frontiersmen. May turned it down, saying he wasn't a colonel and did not like pretending.

One of May's best friends was Joe Lyon, another Hazelton old-timer. Their friendship went back to the days of the Fraser River Gold Rush. The camp they were in was run by a group of men who had already been run out of California and who formed the local vigilante committee. They gave Lyon the job of constructing a chimney for a new building for twenty-five dollars. The committee told him that if the chimney smoked, they would hang him. May took Lyon's side in case of trouble, but fortunately the chimney did not smoke and Lyon did not hang.[20] The friendship endured.

They were as different as chalk and cheese. May was a soft-spoken, mild-mannered Southern gentleman, whereas Joe Lyon was a hard-headed Yankee. Mining partners throughout the American Civil War, they were said never to have mentioned the conflict in each other's presence.

Year in, year out, May and his friends and partners, men like Ezra Evans, Joe Lyon, William Keynton, Jimmy Wells and Charles McKinnon, prospected in the Omineca Mountains in the summer and usually spent the winters in Hazelton. The 1881 census shows that all except Wells were in Hazelton in the winter of 1880–1881. On January 1, 1895, many notable prospectors were among the winter residents of Hazelton, including Jim May, Ezra Evans, Jimmy Wells and Joe Lyon.[21] When Evans went to spend the winter of 1903 in the South, the *Skeena District News* said it was the first time he had gone out of the North to what it called civilization for twenty-seven years.[22] Charles McKinnon had been one of the original settlers of Hazelton with Thomas Hankin in 1871. In 1897, McKinnon took out of one creek a nugget of gold with a value of sixty-nine dollars. Such finds kept these men going. In 1911 McKinnon was sharing a cabin in Hazelton with his friend Ezra Evans.

May's last mining venture was at Tom Creek. He persevered with this claim over the years. In February 1907, he obtained a ten-year renewal of his mining lease there. In March 1909, May returned to Tom Creek, and that summer, with two partners, he took out $12,000 worth of gold. Here he and his partners had worked through the deep ground on the bench until they reached the gold they knew was there. That October, the *Omineca Herald* reported that May, Evans and seventeen others had arrived back in town and would winter there. It described Jim May and Ezra Evans as the two patriarchs of the Omineca mining district. The only concession they made to their age was to ride a horse instead of going on foot. May, the newspaper noted, had spent a full half century in the Omineca district. "In spite of his seventy-seven years, the old pioneer still looks fit and none the worse for his long hike."[23] The citizenry gave a "smoker" (party) for May and the other miners to welcome them back for the winter. The evening, the *Herald* reported, was filled with songs, recitations and reminiscences of the old days—the days of Barkerville and Billy Barker, Nellie Cashman, Dancing Bill and Twelve-Foot Davis and, for those with even longer memories, those days on the gold creeks in California.

The prospectors lived. They mined. They aged. They died. Few made fortunes. Working until he was about eighty, May sold his claim and retired in Hazelton.

Ezra Evans, in a white shirt and a vest, standing with Jim May outside the door of Evans's house in Hazelton, with St. Peter's Church behind. Image B-01334 courtesy of the Royal BC Museum and Archives

He was one of the pioneer miners who ended his days there, along with such other old-timers as Ezra Evans, Charles McKinnon and Joe Lyon.

Not all had peaceful last years. In January 1912, Vital LeFort, the famous prospector from the first days of the Omineca Gold Rush, shot himself in his cabin in Saanich, near Victoria. He was eighty. He was a man, his obituary said, of indomitable energy and many expedients. It was reported—how reliably is not clear—that he had once made the journey from Fort St. James to Hazelton in three days by rigging up a sail on his sled and using his shovel as a rudder. At one time of hardship, he had lived for days on grass, ferns and roots, like a moose.[24]

Ezra Evans spent his winters in Hazelton and his summers prospecting on Manson Creek, where he also had a store for a while. He kept going as long as he could. In August 1904, the government granted him a twenty-year lease on the south side of Manson Creek for hydraulic mining purposes on fifty-five acres at an annual rental of fifty dollars. He was appointed the mining recorder for Omineca at a commission of 20 percent on all moneys collected by him. For the last two years of his life, though, he hadn't been able to get up there. Suffering dizzy spells,

Vital LeFort, one of the pioneer prospectors of the Omineca Gold Rush, in 1912. Image G-09469 courtesy of the Royal BC Museum and Archives

he finally had a collapse at the end of December 1911 and died in the Hazelton Hospital soon after.

Constance Cox, Thomas Hankin's daughter, related that for many years Ezra Evans had cherished an old oak box. He would never let her look inside, which she had often tried to do, seeking candy or gold nuggets. After his death she opened the box and found neither candy nor gold, but a pair of lady's white gloves, a lace handkerchief and a withered, faded bunch of forget-me-nots.[25] Could Ezra Evans have left Wales not because he failed his medical exams but because of a disappointing love affair?

Between 1891 and 1896, Joe Lyon was the manager of the Hudson's Bay Company store in Hazelton. His life, too, had a sad end. While prospecting at Tom Creek in the summer of 1902, he was stricken with paralysis and became physically and mentally helpless. The following January, Richard Sargent, Edward Stephenson—both justices of the peace—and the Anglican missionary John Field wrote to the government asking it to provide care for Joe Lyon in a hospital or asylum. He deserved it, they said, for being one of the pioneers of the North.[26] When Joe died the following year, he owed several hundred dollars to the merchants of Hazelton. Although he was in no way responsible for them, Jim May insisted on paying his old friend's debts.

In March 1917, May performed one last service for his old friends. When the daughter of his now dead friend and mining partner, William Keynton, was married by Rev. John Field in St. Peter's Church in Hazelton, he led her down the aisle and gave her away.

Jim May enjoyed his daily tot of rum at the Hudson's Bay Company store in Hazelton. Wiggs O'Neill wrote:

Every day Jim would pull on his gum-boots, pick up his stick and hobble down the road and slowly wend his way to the Hudson's Bay Company store. There was an armchair just inside the door, which was known as Jim's chair, and he would sit in the big chair and everyone entering the store would always greet the old man and shake hands. ... It was an unwritten law that as soon as Jim arrived one of the clerks or perhaps the manager himself went out to the famous store cellar in the enclosure and brought in a glass of Hudson's Bay rum and placed it beside Jim's chair. The old boy would sit and sip and greet his many friends—and he would usually stay about an hour and then hobble off home.[27]

James May's gravestone in the Hazelton cemetery. As upright in death as he was upright in life. Image courtesy of the author

O'Neill was himself a pioneer, but of a later age. May was a pioneer of the gold rush days. O'Neill was a pioneer of machines, sternwheelers, motor launches on the Skeena and automobiles. He wrote that he took May for a ride in his new Russell-Knight automobile, which must have been an interesting experience for someone who had walked to Hazelton from Tennessee.

When May was ill and needed help at the hospital, he refused to go, fearing that Dr. Horace Wrinch, the hospital superintendent and a well-known temperance advocate, would deny him alcoholic remedies. Dr. Wrinch, though, promised him he would still get his daily medicinal tot of rum there, and so May went.

May spent much of his last year at the Hazelton Hospital. When he was approaching death, Dr. Wrinch asked him if there was anything he could do for him and if he was prepared to meet his end. "Doctor," Jim said, "I have never been mean to anyone in my life and Gabriel can toot his horn any time he wants to."[28] His only request was that he be buried next to his friend Joe Lyon in the cemetery on the top of the bluff. He died in December 1917. As requested, he was buried near his friend.

His funeral was a requiem on the disappearing age of the pioneer miners. Rev. Field conducted the service in the church, and Dr. Wrinch, a Methodist minister in addition to being the town doctor and the hospital superintendent, conducted the burial ceremony. Along with a sprinkling of old-time miners—there weren't many left—the pallbearers were the luminaries of the town: Richard Sargent, a leading merchant and a local legend in his own right; Richard Loring, Indian agent since 1889; and May's friend Constable Sperry Cline.

When Jim May died, the *Omineca Miner* called him the "pioneer of pioneers."[29] In March of the following year, it reported there was no marker over his grave. "Jim May's grave in Hazelton's cemetery is unmarked, a fact that does not seem fair to his memory," the *Miner* said. "Jim May was a square dealer. Let us give him a square deal."[30] Richard Sargent organized a subscription to raise money to erect the memorial stone over his grave. Fittingly, it remains the grandest of the pioneers' tombstones and one of the few still standing upright.

6

Jack Gillis and His Helpful Grave

1872

For those who like to read about tragic love, Sperry Cline tells a story about a prospector named Jack Gillis.[1] When Jack learned that his girl wouldn't wait for him any longer and had married another, Cline wrote, he committed suicide on a lonely trail in the Omineca Mountains.

Cline arrived in Hazelton in 1904, after service during the Matabele and Boer Wars in South Africa. He was a packer, a carrier of mail to and from the coast, a prospector and, commencing in 1914, twenty-six years a provincial policeman. He became one of the more colourful characters of Hazelton and later wrote about his years in the North.

He wrote that not long after he arrived in Hazelton, one lonely grave out in the wilderness had aroused his curiosity. The graves of most men who died on the trail quickly disappeared into the earth. The grave of Jack Gillis, who had died over thirty years before, was well maintained, however. Someone was repainting the fence posts and refreshing the inscription. Someone was also replacing rotten logs of the enclosing fence. In the bars of Hazelton, Cline pressed old-time prospectors to tell him. Did they remember Gillis from the days of the Omineca Gold Rush? Who was he, anyway? What was his story?

At first reluctant to talk about the matter, the old-timers eventually unwound and told him, but they did so quietly and with respect, speaking of Gillis almost with reverence. They did admit he had shot himself but were reluctant to say more. Eventually, though, Cline persuaded them to tell him the story.

Jack Gillis, they told him, was a man from Prince Edward Island who had fallen in love with a girl of a social station higher than his. She loved him in return. Her parents, though, did not approve of young Jack and forbade the match.

Jack had left Prince Edward Island in the 1850s, determined to make his fortune in the California gold creeks and then return, famous and wealthy, to claim the girl as his bride. He went by schooner to New York and then down to the Panama isthmus, which he walked across. Arriving too late for the California Gold Rush, he went north to the Fraser River in 1858 and then farther north to the Cariboo. He always seemed to have bad luck, being all too often late for the richest pickings. He was one of those people who always seemed to be in the right place at the wrong time. His bad fortune became well known. He grew dour and unsociable. Years passed. Eventually he came to the Omineca. Always he kept the image of his girl in Prince Edward Island alive in his mind and dreamed of making his fortune.

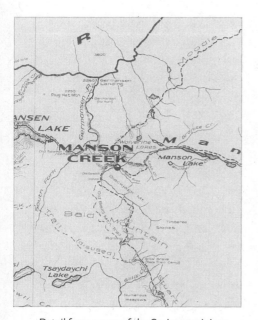

Detail from a map of the Omineca mining district showing Manson Creek, other gold mining centres and Gillis's Grave in the lower quarter, centre. *Topographical Sketch Map of Omineca and Finlay River Basins* (detail), 1917, Northern BC Archives & Special Collections, University of Northern British Columbia

Then, suddenly, against the odds, he found gold. As he was accumulating a fortune of, reportedly, $10,000, he became more sociable, popular even. He talked of returning to Prince Edward Island to claim his bride.

One day in 1871, the old-timers told Cline, Jack Gillis was on the trail not far from Manson Creek, carrying his gold, returning to Prince Edward Island to claim and marry his girl. He and his companions met a man bringing in the mail. There was a letter for Jack with familiar handwriting on the envelope. His companions teased him, saying it was from his bride-to-be and that wedding bells would soon be ringing. They saw him open it. Then Jack trembled violently. He snarled at his companions to stay back, put his gun to his head and pulled the trigger.

His friends buried him at the spot, erected a headboard and built a wooden palisade around the grave. His companions read the letter that had fallen from his disappointed hand. It was indeed from his girl in Prince Edward Island. She had written that, though she still loved him tenderly, she could wait no longer and, in her loneliness, was marrying another.

So great was the sadness of his friends and their respect for his long-lasting fidelity to his girl that they sent Gillis's gold to her. But they would not put their names on the package as senders, because the prospect of receiving a faltering letter of thanks from a heartbroken girl unnerved them.

In honour of his memory, the prospectors maintained his grave over the years. It became a well-known landmark near the junction of the Manson and Pinchbeck trails. In 1897, when William Gordon, suspected of murdering his partner Isaac Jones, was arrested and interrogated in Hazelton, he said he had last seen Jones at Gillis's Grave.[2]

It is a sweet story of many years of single-minded endeavour and disappointed love. It is also a testament to the respect and sentimentality of the mining community.

Prospectors, Cline wrote, did not wear their hearts on their sleeves and were not overtly sentimental, but here was a story that proved their compassionate hearts.

Alas for romance, this story may not be true. In 1971, Cecil Clark, a provincial police inspector, became suspicious and thought he would check the facts. How much did $10,000 in gold weigh? How did Gillis carry it? Something didn't add up. He searched for the papers and found out that the six-man coroner's jury at the time concluded that Gillis had indeed killed himself at that spot in 1871 but had done so in a temporary fit of insanity. The coroner, William Fitzgerald, noted that the letter from Gillis's girl had said nothing that would have led Gillis to kill himself. She had not, he implied, told him she was abandoning him to marry another. Clark was also ungallant enough to doubt whether a girl would wait over a dozen years for her boyfriend to make his fortune in the notoriously uncertain endeavour of prospecting for gold.[3] And what really did happen to the gold Gillis was reportedly bringing out with him?

Clark came closer to the truth, but even he did not tell the full story. For one thing, the shooting happened in 1872. For another, the man's name was Hugh Gillis, although he was commonly called Jack. Born in Prince Edward Island in 1835, he and his brother Benedict had ended up in Quesnel, where Gillis had owned the Occidental Hotel with his partner Thomas Brown since early 1866.

The discovery of gold on Vital Creek had drawn Gillis north. He went to try his prospecting luck in the creeks and also to find a way of relieving successful prospectors of any wealth in gold they might have found. As early as 1870, Gillis opened a saloon in the mining community of Omineca. This, though, may have been no more than a board across two barrels in a lean-to at a shack in a town that some described as a "big town with nothing in it."[4]

The papers from the inquest on Gillis's death tell a more credible story.[5] In August 1872, Gillis and a fellow prospector named George Mitchell rode from Dunkeld just south of Manson Creek to the first pack train camp. This was at Harper's Cattle Camp, seventeen miles south of Dunkeld. Mitchell said Gillis had been uncommunicative on the ride up, giving merely yes and no answers.

On August 19, Gillis was at the camp with Mitchell and a man named Adam McNeily. Before supper that evening, Gillis took a letter from his pocket and read it by the fire. Mitchell testified that Gillis told him the letter was from his sister.

Mitchell called out to him that the supper was getting cold. Gillis replied that it made no difference as it would all be cold shortly. He then put the letter on the fire. After supper, he lit his pipe and walked away from camp for about forty yards. "I saw him with a pair of socks in his hand," Mitchell said, "and after some time he took off his coat and boots. I did not think anything strange in this proceeding as I thought he was going to change his socks."[6]

Gillis called out to Mitchell and told him to tell his brother to telegraph Tom (likely his business partner Thomas Brown) to come home immediately.

Mitchell then saw he had a pistol in his hand. He grasped at once what was happening and moved slowly toward Gillis, asking him what he was intending to do. Gillis said he was going to shoot himself. "For God's sake, Jack," Mitchell said. "Don't shoot yourself."[7] To keep him talking, Mitchell asked him why he was doing it. Gillis said people at Germansen Creek were slandering him. When Gillis said that he would rather die than be slandered, Mitchell said that it meant nothing. Many a good man had been slandered. Mitchell was edging closer, but now Gillis told him to stop. "Jack," Mitchell said, "I would like to say a few words to you before you die, as I have always been good friends with you."[8] Gillis replied that Mitchell was a good man and he was sorry the deed had to be done in his presence, but it had to be done.

Gillis said he had a small amount of gold dust and asked Mitchell to send it to his brother. He then said, "I forgive all my enemies and hope they will forgive me and may God have mercy on my soul."[9]

McNeily, who was also witnessing what was happening, testified, "He then raised the pistol towards his face. Afterwards he took it away from that and placed it by the side of his head and held it there for three or four seconds and fired."[10] Mitchell, who was twenty yards away, then went over and discharged the five loaded chambers of the pistol into the air.

The inquest was held on August 21, 1872. The jury found Gillis had died while labouring under a temporary fit of insanity. No mention was made of any gold he may have been carrying.

Gillis had been thirty-seven years old. Of the approximately $7,000 he owned at his death, $5,000 was tied up in the hotel. He died intestate, and his brother Benedict administered his estate.

But what about the respect for Gillis's Grave? And its careful maintenance? Why would people have chosen to rebuild and repaint this grave but no one else's on the trail? Sperry Cline suggested it was out of respect for Gillis's dedication and fidelity to his girl. A more likely, albeit less romantic, explanation is that the grave became a well-known landmark on the trail and was marked on maps to inform and help travellers know where they were and which trail to take. Conceivably it was maintained as a public good to help travellers.

In his 1954 biography, *Son of the North*, Charles Camsell, the noted geologist and commissioner of the Northwest Territories, told the same story Cline did.[11] The tale told by Sperry Cline seems to have become a legend of the North.

But could it be true? Could it be that the letter Gillis threw in the fire was not in fact from his sister but was indeed from his fiancée, breaking off the engagement? In the tale they told Cline, could the old-time prospectors have merely been embroidering the basic facts of a true story? Was there, after all, somewhere in Prince Edward Island a girl who remembered her long-lost love and repented her letter?

7

Thomas Riley, Barney Devine
and Their Dead Ends

1872 and 1873

Life as a prospector in the Omineca was fraught with perils. For those who had not been lucky in the back-breaking work of digging down to the gold or of washing gravel in a sluice box, merely finding enough food to stay alive was challenge enough.

When David Humphrey, William Cook and Captain A.E.B. Mann, with twelve of their friends, went hunting for mushrooms near their cabins at Manson Creek on June 10, 1872, they were not looking to spice up a juicy meat dish or enliven a soup. They were starving and needed to find something edible to stay alive. The price of food in the store was high, and their earnings from prospecting were low to non-existent. Bringing their harvest of mushrooms back to their cabins, they cooked and ate them. Unfortunately for them, the mushrooms were poisonous. The next day all were violently ill. Humphrey, Cook and Mann died. Humphrey, a man of about fifty, was from Lexington, Kentucky. Apart from the manner of his death, his story was typical. He had gone to California in 1850, moved up north to prospect in the Fraser River in 1858 and later had come farther north to the Omineca.[1]

They faced numerous natural hazards. In the spring of 1873, Peter Toy, a Cornish man, one of the pioneer prospectors of the region (hence the famous gold site at Toy's Bar), and his partner William Southcombe drowned when their heavily laden canoe failed to navigate rapids on the Omineca River.

Some prospectors lost their way in the mountains. In August 1871, George Babington and six others were on their way from Omineca to Hazelton when they missed the trail near Frying Pan Pass. For ten days they blundered around the mountains trying to find the trail. For the last five days they lived on nettles and roots. Separating, one party of four was lucky to stumble onto Edgar Dewdney, at the time surveying for the trail to the Omineca. They lived. The bodies of two of them—Smith and Grant—were found the following April, dead from exhaustion, starvation and the cold.

Accidents—some fatal, some nearly so—and sickness were common. "The health of the district is not at all good," the *Cariboo Sentinel* said of Manson Creek in 1872, "a great many being sick. No doctor here."[2] If the sick or injured man was lucky, there was someone with medical experience close by. Ezra Evans, with his two years of medical school, would have been useful.

Frank Collingsworth was lucky that George Chismore, spending the summer of 1871 in the Omineca, was within reach. Chismore recounted the emergency in his journal:

Just then Ike Stevens came up red hot. He said, "Eight miles up the creek on the first claim below me and two men own it. Frank Collingsworth, one of the Kentucky cavalry men, who served in the Kentucky Hundred, the other is Yanky Jim, who was with Custer. They are partners, love each other, lie awake at nights to tell each other lies about the Civil War and don't think about anything else.

"They were whip-sawing a 14-foot log and Frank was in the pit, Yanky on top. This was their last log, as they had already cut what they needed. They were busy talking about [the] war, and when they started the first cut and came in to the head cross-piece they forgot to fleet the head cross-piece and cut it through. Frank was stooped at the end of the downward stroke, his head almost touching the ground. There was a ragged rock behind raising about a foot there and the sharp edge of the end of the log hit in front of his left eye. It popped his skull like a wet plum-stone out from between your thumb and finger. He lies there in the hot sun with his bare skull as big as your hand sticking out. I've run all the way down and I want you to run back with me, 'cause he don't seem to bleed much nor suffer greatly. Swore he'd get well and wants you."

Among the truck left behind at Tongass was a U.S. pannier, a wonderfully good chest of medicine that grew in the last year of the Civil War, and a fine pair of doctor's saddle-bags. The panier was used by the Telegraph Company, so I was fully familiar with its contents. It was too heavy for me to take, so I filled the saddle-bags and carried them in my blanket. I had a very remarkable pocket-case—I have it yet. Grabbing these, Ike and I set out and made the eight miles in short order.

I found they had some alcohol. Got out my knives, a tenaculum, Torreson forceps, needle-holder, needles and silk, and set to work. The naked skull was ground full of broken twigs, dry sawdust and small gravel. The cut from the bridge of the nose went in a straight line up and over the top of the head as clean as if cut with a knife. The upper left eyelid was ground into eight pieces, like this, and they were all mixed, but the eyelashes remained. The conjunctiva was so bloody that I could see the eyeball, but could not make out the pupil. There was the end of a rough twig sticking out above and with my forceps I pulled it out; it was an eighth of an inch thick, 1¼ inches long.

On the right side of the skull there was an open semi-lunar gash 5 inches long, not connecting with the others (where the root caught him). This wound was attended with so much destruction of tissues that I made no attempt to close it, but left it open for drainage. I hooked my tenaculum into the wreck of the left eyelid and with ease pulled it over below the occipital protuberance. Fortunately, I had a couple of small surgeon's sponges and I made Ike boil them; and thus, with a scalpel and hot water, I sluiced and scraped (luckily) all the foreign bodies. There was but little bleeding, but I never could see that pupil. All this time I was a-studying.

Frank stood it all without a grunt. He said, "Eff you'll luk at my left knee you'll see where hit [it] was shot all ter hell durin' the war, an' I haven't got a limp. I've got a purty gal on old Kentuck dat I'm engaged to. Want you to fix me up so that she'll have me."

I washed the whole thing out with alcohol, put six deep stitches in the straight wound, going right through the whole flap, and it looked fine. I then took an ordinary sewing needle, heated it red-hot in a candle, bent it to the curve of the well eyelid, commenced at the outside, picked, straightened it out by the eyelashes, pierced it in the center, following the cartilage, and went on to the inner canthus. In my card of silks there was some very fine silk. With that I made a figure of 8 over the needle. This seemed to please Frank somehow—of course, he had a miner's hand-glass. With other silk I brought the lower eyelid as near into position as I dared to, because of tension. The ragged wound from the outer canthus to the ear I left open for drainage. Frank growled because of the little V gone in his upper eyelid. I told him to get up and find it and I would put it in. I now applied surgeon's plaster in narrow strips across the brow, first laying a narrow strip of warm gauze the length of the wound; then over all the parts that I hoped for first intention I padded with gauze, kept wet by weak alcohol, until my gauze gave out, then used flour sacks, and wrapped the whole in a roller bandage. I stayed that night. As he was all right next morning, I went to town.[3]

The reality of a prospector's life in the nineteenth century was that it was a hard, exhausting, doubtful business enlivened by the comradeship of fellow prospectors and the ever-present hope of striking it rich. Few did. Many became eccentric. Some went mad. Jack Gillis shot himself in what the jury called a fit of temporary insanity. More likely, though, it was from utter despair. And then there were Thomas Riley and Barney Devine.

In approximately 1842, sixteen-year-old Thomas Riley left his native North Carolina for Missouri. From there he moved to Oakland, California, before he drifted to the goldfields north of the border. He arrived in the Omineca Mountains in 1871. He likely visited Hazelton, the nearest town of any size, to buy supplies, sell a few hard-won ounces of gold dust and have a spree in the bars. In 1872 he was working at the Slate Creek claims but not doing very well. He was drinking heavily.

At about ten in the evening of July 8, 1872, Riley came to see his friend W.B. Robinson. He said he had come across Manson Creek on the log that served as a footbridge. Perhaps giving a warning sign of a troubled mind, he added that "if the water had been deeper he might have had some trouble and he wished to God he could drown himself."[4]

Just before leaving the following morning, Riley told Robinson and another friend, "Boys, perhaps I shall never see both of you together again."[5] He seemed, Robinson said later, perfectly sensible at the time, although he had been drinking. Later that morning he came into the hamlet of Dunkeld and asked someone if he could lie down as he was ill and tired. He went into a tent, was sick and then lay down.

The owner of the tent, Archibald McConnell, was not pleased when he came back and found Riley there. Saying he had never let anyone else sleep in his blankets before, he told Riley to leave. Riley begged to be allowed to stay for a few hours. "Mr. McConnell," he said. "For God Almighty's sake, let me sleep for an hour or two."[6] McConnell relented and told him he could stay. He even offered him some dinner, an offer to which Riley made no reply. McConnell then took his own gun and went out shooting. When he came back three hours later, he found Riley had shot himself dead. Running into the street, McConnell raised the alarm.

George Bent and McConnell went into the tent. They found Riley's body, still holding the revolver in both hands, with his right thumb on the trigger. The shot had gone into the head close to the right temple and out through the top of the head. "Some blood and brains were on the temple," Bent said, "and someone found a piece of skull on the blankets."[7]

The jury concluded he had killed himself in a fit of temporary insanity. Juries, usually made up entirely of prospectors, often came to this conclusion in cases of suicide. It was almost as if they could not bring themselves to accept they were all wasting their own lives by labouring away in the mud and dirt for specks of gold.

Someone who realized this and took desperate action to end it all was in some way invalidating what they were spending their lives doing. Necessarily, therefore, he must be out of his mind. The alternative was unthinkable.

Arthur Wellesley Vowell was the gold commissioner for the Omineca mining community in the early 1870s. An Anglo-Irishman likely named after the Duke of Wellington, another Anglo-Irishman, he later became the superintendent of Indian Affairs for British Columbia. (In October 1918, seriously ill and in great pain, taking advantage of the temporary absence of his nurse, he too shot himself.)

Writing from the Forks of the Skeena in October 1873, Vowell reported that everything at Hazelton was very quiet. But he did write that a man named Barney Devine, who had been mining at Germansen Creek, had become violently insane. The storekeeper there had been obliged to take charge of him and put him under restraint.[8]

This must have presented a great problem. What do you do with someone like this in a small mining community in the wilderness? Eccentricity was one thing and could be tolerated, laughed at and even admired. Violent insanity had to be dealt with.

When Vowell had arrived at Germansen Creek on September 28, Devine had been insane for almost two weeks and was a danger to himself and others. Vowell engaged a man named B. Smyth to take Devine first to Hazelton and then down-river to Port Essington for a fee of $150. He asked Brown, the provincial constable there, to send Devine to Victoria under escort, which he did. The total cost of taking Devine to Victoria was $550.62, a considerable sum of money in those days. This amount included buying clothes for Devine at Hankin's store in Hazelton. There he may have had some violent fit because the expenses included $25 for damage that had been done to a house he had been held in.

Like so many in British Columbia at the time, Barney Devine was an American. Originally from New York, he had moved to Montana to do some mining there before coming north to the Omineca. He had friends in San Francisco, and it was hoped they would be able to help him in his distress. It was all for naught. In the third week of October 1873, Devine died suddenly in the asylum for the insane in Victoria. He was thirty-eight years old.

His death was noticed by his friends in Helena, Montana. He was, the *Daily Independent* said of him the following March, a big-hearted and generous man, and his sudden death while engaged in the active labours of frontier life would be received with much sorrow.[9]

Life as a prospector in the Omineca was tough and the chances of wealth were low. There must have been many wavering close to the line between despair and insanity. The passage of time often adds romance to a story but subtracts hardship and uncertainty; the tragedies are often obscured. The romance of mining did have its dark, tragic side. Did the endless struggle of the prospector's existence bring Devine to the despair that tipped him over the edge?

8

Bishop William Ridley, Jane Ridley and the *Hazelton Queek*

1880–1881

Bishop William Ridley and Jane, his wife, looked around the episcopal palace in Hazelton. This was no more than a drafty shack, without glass in the windows. Since they were going to spend the winter of 1880 here, they set about making it as comfortable as they could. They lit a fire, found some glass for the windows and nailed bark over the cracks in the walls to keep out the rain and snow. A few yards away, the mighty Skeena River flowed swiftly and silently down to where it merged with the Bulkley. Their journey to Hazelton had been a long one. It had taken them through the northwest frontier of India to an English church in Dresden and parishes in Yorkshire. Now, here they were, in a village in the wilds of northern British Columbia.

William Ridley's journey had started many years before. One day in 1859, when he was twenty-three years old and a foreman carpenter in London, he took the plunge. He applied to the Church Missionary Society to be a missionary. To this high calling he would devote the rest of his life.

He was a Devon man, born and bred in Brixham, where his father, Allen, was a stonemason. In those days of red-hot evangelism, young William felt a different call: he wanted to be a missionary and bring less fortunate people to God's grace. He would need to train, of course, and this he did, attending the Church Missionary Society College in Islington. In 1861 he was living in lodgings in Lambeth but still working as a carpenter.

The year 1866 was a momentous one for him. On June 10, he was ordained in the Church of England at Holy Trinity Church in Marylebone. The ordinands that day were given a long sermon on missionary work to stiffen their resolve. Then, on July 14, he married Jane Helmer Heyne, also from Brixham, at St. James's Church in Exeter.

In August, the Church Missionary Society sent him to Peshawar, a frontier town in what was then northwest India. This was reputed to be one of the most dangerous places in the world to be a missionary.[1] "Peshawur [*sic*] is regarded by the Committee [of the Church Missionary Society] as one of the most honourable posts of service in the Indian Mission Field," the *Church Missionary Intelligencer*

said. "It is the rendez-vous of races of the most independent and fiercest character. ... It has been signalized by the early death of many labourers."[2] Honourable,
therefore, because the risk of martyrdom was high. Indeed, several of Ridley's
predecessors had been murdered or physically injured. As a history of the Church
Missionary Society put it:

> Peshawar was proving, as could be foreseen, a Mission-field of singular diffi-
> culty. The Peshawar fever, also, was a serious foe. Three young missionaries
> died there within three years, 1862–1865. ... Ridley's brief spell of service
> among the Afghan is especially interesting to us as exhibiting those qual-
> ities which in later years seemed to fit him eminently for the bishopric of
> Caledonia.[3]

The Ridleys arrived in India on the SS *Hotspur* in January 1867 and soon
went up to Peshawar. When they arrived, the mission house was in the British
cantonments outside the town. But church authorities had wanted at least one
missionary to live in a caravanserai, a walled dwelling for travellers, inside the old
town. When the Ridleys moved into their new mission, they were the only white
people living within the walls. Here they were isolated from their countrymen in
the cantonment, who were loath to risk the dangers of the ride across the old town
to visit them.

William Ridley became principal of a local college[4] and his wife, Jane, "threw
herself energetically into work among the women and girls, and into the study
of the languages. She acquired Urdu and Pushtu sufficiently for her purpose,
and then took up Persian; and to the astonishment of all who heard of it, she
contrived to get into the zenanas [women's quarters] of leading Mohammedans."[5]
She was also the first to organize zenana work, in the form of a women's aid
society in the Punjab. Clearly Jane Ridley was a formidable missionary force in
her own right.

While they were in Peshawar, cholera struck the city with deadly force. Over
two hundred people a day were coming down with the disease, half of whom died.
William Ridley wrote:

> On Tuesday there were more than a hundred cases, of which about half
> proved fatal within a few hours, while many lingered on a day or two. ... The
> cordon [around the old town] makes us all prisoners, so that even if either
> of us were taken ill, we could not send for a doctor. ... I am more a doctor
> (or rather shall I say we, for Mrs. Ridley is the chief doctor) than a padri.
> Mrs. Ridley is now on her rounds, and has just sent for more medicines.[6]

A few days later he wrote, "The despairing cries that constantly assail our ears are heartrending. My wife had a sharp attack, but has been mercifully restored."[7]

He himself was not so lucky. He fell sick. The failure of his health "put an end to their self-sacrificing labours among the Afghans. God had another sphere for them ... among the Indians of British Columbia."[8] William Ridley's ill health forced the couple to return to England, where he could convalesce. They arrived home in January 1870.

When he had recovered his health, the Church Missionary Society sent the Ridleys to the Anglican community in Dresden. He was appointed chaplain to All Saints Church, on the Wiener Strasse. This recently completed church, built in the Early English Gothic style, was either a charming reminder of old England or, depending on your point of view, dreadfully out of place in the beautiful old Saxon city. (During the Second World War, bombs destroyed both church and city.) While they were in Dresden, the Franco-Prussian War was raging. For the good work Jane Ridley did among the wounded Saxon soldiers, the king of Saxony awarded her the bronze cross.

The Ridleys returned to England in early 1872. The church then sent them to the quiet parish of Shelley, in Kirkburton, West Yorkshire. After a year or so there, William Ridley became vicar of the parish of Moldgreen, in Huddersfield. They settled in and made friends, and all was well until the vicar of the neighbouring, larger and better-paid parish of St. Paul's, Huddersfield, died. Ridley then became deeply embroiled in a dispute that could well have come straight from a novel of clerical intrigue by Anthony Trollope.

The scandal was this. Rev. William Calvert in Huddersfield had the right to appoint vicars to the parishes of both Moldgreen and St. Paul's. He had a brother who was looking for a parish. Why not move Ridley to St. Paul's and put the brother into Moldgreen? This, accordingly, Calvert did. This high-handed action upset not only the parishioners of Moldgreen, who felt robbed of a competent and popular preacher, but also the parishioners at St. Paul's, who had their own candidate and who angrily complained they had not been consulted. This, they said, was simony (the buying or selling of church positions by some form of inducement) and bribery! What favours, in addition to the higher stipend, had been given to Ridley to persuade him to move? None at all, protested Mr. Calvert. The parishioners' candidate was too young (he was thirty) and did not speak loudly enough. Ridley, he said, was far better qualified for St. Paul's. Meetings were held. Delegations were dispatched hither and yon. Furious letters were sent to the newspapers. "I say that Mr. Ridley is deliberately coming amongst us against our protests," a speaker said at one meeting, "and against our expressed determination to uphold the interests of the Church in their integrity; and that he ought not, as a Christian minister, to place himself upon us when he knows he has not our confidence. (Cheers) ... The vicar's brother was decidedly unfit. (Hear! Hear!)"[9] To no avail. Ridley stayed and seemed to overcome most of the hostility to him. In a way, this was all good practice for his coming conflict in northern British Columbia.

Ridley weathered the storm and settled down. Jane Ridley continued her work to help Indian women, founding the first Home Association of the Zenana Missionary Society in Yorkshire. As might be expected of her, she was active with the local Sunday schools and other good work in the parish. When she left, the Sunday school teachers organized a collection and bought her a travelling clock. The Mothers' Meeting gave her a handsome leather bag.

In early 1879, the church appointed William Ridley bishop of the new diocese of Caledonia in northern British Columbia.[10] For good measure, the archbishop of Canterbury conferred a doctorate of divinity on him. In the presence of six bishops and other church dignitaries, he was consecrated as a bishop in St. Paul's Cathedral on July 25, 1879. While Ridley and the two others consecrated with him were changing into their episcopal vestments, the choir sang John Stainer's "How Beautiful Are the Mountains."[11] Ridley might have thought this was appropriate, bearing in mind where he was going.

The Ridleys left Liverpool for New York on September 13, crossed the United States to San Francisco and reached Victoria on October 4. After staying with Chief Justice Matthew Baillie Begbie for a week while consulting Bishop George Hills about the new diocese, Ridley and his wife headed north to Metlakatla.[12]

Even before he left England, Ridley knew he would a need a steamboat to visit the Indigenous villages scattered up and down the coast. He had started raising money before leaving and he arrived with almost £1,000. On November 3, 1879, newly arrived on the coast, he wrote, "I find it will be impossible to build my steamer without at least 1,400 L [pounds], and bringing the machinery from Victoria. In the meantime I am using canoes and it is no joke, I assure you. About a week ago we were as nearly lost as saved men could be. ... How I longed for my steamer! Unless I get one, a new Bishop will soon be wanted, for the risk in these frail crafts is tremendous, and a short career the probable consequence."[13] He soon did acquire the steamer he so fervently desired, and he named it *Evangeline*.

The senior Anglican in northern British Columbia at the time was the controversial missionary William Duncan. He came from Yorkshire and had also attended the Church Missionary Society school in Islington, although a few years before Ridley. At first Duncan had based himself at Fort Simpson, where he had learned Tsimshian from Arthur Wellington Clah. He later moved to nearby Metlakatla and there set up a godly community. In 1879 alone, he and his followers built or nearly completed eighty-eight buildings. The church he built there was the largest in British Columbia at the time.

Here the brilliant fire of missionary zeal burned brightly—perhaps too brightly. There was a dark side. He designed and enforced rules to keep the parishioners on the straight and narrow path as he saw it, which meant a strict regime of legislated behaviour that denied Indigenous people their ancient culture. He set up sawmills and farms. He was also a magistrate who exercised his powers freely enough to cause controversy in Victoria. His Indigenous constables enforced the strict rules vigorously. However, the community thrived. Ridley's first impressions were good, or so he said. "Metlakatla has not disappointed me," he wrote in February 1880. "The situation is excellent."[14] This calm did not last long.

Duncan had not been appointed bishop to the new diocese because he had never been ordained. Since that problem could have been remedied easily enough, there may have been another reason. The church missionary leadership was becoming increasingly concerned about Duncan's opinions and conduct. The much-lauded Duncan, valiantly working to convert Indigenous people, was showing alarming signs of sliding away from Anglican orthodoxy. Not for him were the anthems and liturgy, the bells and incense and the rich brocaded vestments of High Church Anglicanism. Hymns and the Bible were enough. His non-observance of the sacrament of Holy Communion and adoption of other Low Church practices had alarmed the mission authorities in London. Almost certainly, they instructed Ridley to bring Duncan and his Indigenous flock back to the Anglican fold.

Conflict between Duncan and Ridley was inevitable from the start. Both men were strong, intolerant and given to authoritarianism. Duncan was sliding ever deeper into Low Church Anglicanism. He was not about to give up his control and bend his knee to the new bishop.

Ridley was determined to restore Anglican standards. He required observance of the liturgy, proper baptisms, the wearing of vestments and the celebration of Holy Communion. Duncan thought his Indigenous parishioners did not want or need this. To offer them Christ's blood and body in the Communion could encourage them to believe cannibalism was acceptable. Not to mention the harm the alcohol of the Communion wine would do as it touched their lips. Ridley required that he be addressed as "my lord." Duncan said he had spent ten years teaching his flock there was only one Lord, and it was not Ridley. This, Constance Cox commented many years later, led to an unseemly fist fight between the two clerics.[15] All the elements of conflict were there: differences about the observance of their faith, a struggle for power and a profound personality clash. Both sides had outspoken advocates and supporters, who did not water their wine with mealy-mouthed platitudes. The fight was on.

Bishop William Ridley, luxuriantly bearded, seated on the far left, and companions on a vessel that may be the *Evangeline*. The body language suggests that his wife Jane, may be the one sitting in the centre of the photograph. Image A-02434 courtesy of the Royal BC Museum and Archives

Ridley had visited Hazelton in May 1880, and he decided to return and spend the winter there. By this time, Hazelton had settled down into its routines of total isolation during winter and a passing stream of prospectors on the river in summer. The village itself had a permanent population of less than twenty. But this was swelled in winter by approximately twenty prospectors seeking respite from the harshness of winter in the Omineca. Ridley bought a cabin to stop the inimical—by this he likely meant the Methodists—from establishing a foothold there.

Not long before, the Methodist Church had sent a missionary named Mathieson to establish a mission in Hazelton. When he proved a disappointment and left, the Anglicans moved in. One of the reasons Ridley spent the winter of 1880 in Hazelton—apart from seeking a rest from Duncan's obstructions—likely was to strengthen the Anglican hold on what was obviously going to be an important place.

Another Anglican missionary lived close by. This was Robert Tomlinson, Low Church like Duncan, though easier to deal with. He lived at Ankitlas, a farm a few miles up the Skeena River, not too far from Kispiox. Ridley wanted Tomlinson to move into Hazelton. This led to another row. It also led Tomlinson to leave the Anglican Church and, later, to set up his own strict religious community at Meanskinisht (later named Cedarvale) down the river. This strict community was known up and down the river, not always with goodwill, as the City of God. So strict was Sabbath observance there that if a steamer dropped off the mailbag on a Sunday. no one was allowed to touch it until Monday.

Ridley described his time in Hazelton in the ensuing winter in several letters. His account shows the sharp and not always laudable end of the missionary ethos. He wrote:

I shall describe my winter's work as a winter campaign. It was preceded by seven months of seafaring among the many maritime tribes of Indians. Last May (1880) I paid my first visit to the inland tribes of Indians. It was a novel experience, and much pleasanter than tossing about the open sea in a "dugout," as canoes are called. Oh, for the comparative luxury of my stout steam launch! My voyage up lasted a fortnight. Fourteen days breasting the rapid Kshia or Skeena River; fourteen days without destruction amid fine scenery; thrice fourteen camps beneath forest trees beside a river, in some places two miles broad, dotted with innumerable islands. Working from dawn to sunset, often soused, as sailors say, by the angry-looking rapids, we enjoyed our hard-earned rest each night. With branches from the same friendly cedar that spread its arms over us, our bed was soon made. ... I saw no time should be lost when I came here [Hazelton] in the spring. As I could send no teacher I changed my own plans, and, instead of settling in my newly-built house at Fort Simpson, came up here, and though ill-prepared, began operations in the heart of the enemy's country. Mrs. Ridley came, too, and is the first Englishwoman who has navigated the Skeena. Horrors and calamities were predicted, but, happily, were falsified by the event. ...

My first operation was to open a day-school. So the battle began. My pupils were my infantry. Few or many, I drudged away daily at A, B, C, and 1, 2, 3. The school grew—nearly two hundred attended. The medicine-men, who are the priests of this heathenism, took alarm. ... After loud talking they withdrew, and ever after kept their distance. This also seemed to encourage the pupils. It intensified the hatred of the enemy. When the school-bell was rung through the village, out would rush one of the foe on the ringer. But ring, ring, ring goes the bell daily, and in flock my infantry. They have done famous havoc in the enemy's ranks. Bolts of truth have been shot into their camp. The three B's have been taught. The first class have read half through the Second Book, First Series, and the writing of some is remarkably good. While the teaching proceeded the background would be filled by interested and wondering spectators. The pictorial Bible lesson was a great attraction. The school has been a marked success. I have great faith in my infantry. ...

Young men gathered round me. An undercurrent of rebellion against the heathen abominations became apparent. The old men complained of their loss of influence. Indications of a better state of things grew clearer. The

William Ridley, bishop of Caledonia. Image A-09452 courtesy of the Royal BC Museum and Archives

dog-eating rites were performed less boldly. The time had come, I thought, for a bold step on my side. I invited the four chief men of each Indian confederacy, and thirty-two responded favourably and came to my feast. After the eating and drinking came the speaking. I addressed them, and seven responded. The older orators announced their resolve to finish their course on the old lines. The younger demurred. This was most promising for the Gospel. The children first, then the young men, and these secured, the old men must follow the younger.[16]

Ridley related his experiences in Hazelton for the *Church Missionary Gleaner*, a missionary journal published in London:

> The community here is mixed. The Indians have worked for the gold-min-ers during the summer, and both live here during the winter. This steady employment has told advantageously on the Indian's character. ... As a rule the miners have paid them well and taught them the value of labour. Hence these people ... have, through the material advantages they had enjoyed, risen in the scale, and now have better houses than their neighbours, bet-ter food and better clothing. They are therefore healthier, stronger ... and the proportion of children greater. Contact with the whites therefore has not produced the deplorable results that one too often hears of. Now that a Mission has been established here, and stress laid upon education, this community of Indians is likely to advance rapidly. Their progress is stirring up envious feelings among the other tribes of this nation. Deputations have come to me begging me to send them teachers, but we cannot support them if we had them.
>
> Our services have been crowded by attentive congregations, especially the regular daily evening service. The miners, too, come, and I rejoice to see them, not only for their own but for the sake of the Indians, on whom they exercise much influence. When in the spring they left for the mines, it was a pleasant sight. In returning, they looked worn and weather-beaten. When they started, all looked smart. The white men with braided leggings and ornamented snow-shoes, and the Indians with streamers fluttering from their caps of ermine, marten and other furs looked picturesque; even the dogs harnessed to the birch-wood sleighs seemed proud of their tinkling bells and gay adornments.
>
> Never before was Sunday kept on the long marches. I had given prayer and hymn-books to some of the whites, and suggested that one of them should minister to the rest, but none ventured. The Indians had prayers every day and spent the Sunday in a most profitable manner. The whites attended the service, and though they could not understand the prayers, they joined in the hymns and encouraged the Indians.
>
> I had not appointed any leader; but J—, a catechumen [a Christian convert under instruction before baptism], last winter a dog-eater, came forward as a natural leader, and said the prayers, and exhorted the listen-ers. He is a splendid fellow: square built, of great muscular strength, having a large head, and intelligent, though unhandsome, face, this man cannot but attract attention. During the summer he paid a visit to Hazelton, and

"Raising the First Pole at the Village of Getanmaksh," by Helen Kate Woods, from the January 29, 1881, edition of the *Hazelton Queek*. After a fire in approximately 1875, the village was moved from its site close to the confluence of the Skeena and Bulkley Rivers. Gitanmaax is the village on the bench. The buildings on the right are in Hazelton. The cemetery is on the bluff above them.

the days he spent here could not be quiet. His attentions to Mrs. Ridley, then here alone, were almost comical. He hung about her all day. The clock would not go fast enough to hasten school or service-time, that he might ring the bell and gather in the people. He was the terror of the gamblers, and hated of medicine-men. ... It was he who conducted the service on the miners' march.[17]

Ridley's neighbours at Hazelton included Thomas Hankin, who, with his wife, lived in a farm called Roseberry. The Gitxsan village of Gitanmaax, between Hazelton and the point where the two rivers merged—the one Chismore would have known—had burned down a few years before. The villagers had moved to the bench above Hazelton, where they constructed new buildings and erected new totem poles.

The isolation of winter was long. How to ward off boredom? What better way than self-improvement? On Tuesday evenings, therefore, Jane Ridley opened the episcopal palace in Hazelton for a social evening of reading, music and conviviality.

Helen Kate Woods was the sister-in-law of Robert Tomlinson. She had come up from Victoria with her brother Edward in the spring before the snows were gone. They had hiked in over a grease trail from the Nass and down into Kispiox—not an easy journey at the best of times. She spent the year helping her sister with

Helen Kate Woods's drawing of the Skeena from the Christmas 1880 edition of the *Hazelton Queek*, showing the village of Hazelton on the left. Almost a mile downriver it joins the Bulkley River. Image PDP01680 courtesy of the Royal BC Museum and Archives

her four young children. Edward was going to work on the farm. When not busy at Ankitlas, Helen took her sketchbook and drew scenes of the surrounding area. To her we owe the first drawings of Hazelton, Gitanmaax, the bridge at Hagwilget and the community at Ankitlas.

The Ridleys and others in the community came up with the idea of publishing a small local newspaper, which they called the *Hazelton Queek*. (*Queek* was the Indigenous people's name for the whistling mountain marmot.) Usually only two handwritten pages, distributed free, it was copied out by the bishop on a gelatin press. He and his team produced about a dozen copies of each edition. The first edition was dated December 18, 1880, and the last, March 12, 1881. "It was published every Saturday morning and distributed among the residents for miles around," the *Victoria Daily Times* said later. "Copy had to be in the hands of the printer on or before Thursday of each week, as printing a paper was no easy matter. The office of the *Hazelton Queek* was in the bishop's residence, the drawing room being the press room, and C.W.D. [Charles] Clifford, now M.P.P. [member of provincial parliament], was chief scribe and press man. ... It was printed by the gelatine process. First the paper had to be written by hand, then transferred to the gelatine and the required number struck off."[18]

In a note with the only surviving copy of the *Queek*, in the BC Archives, Helen Kate Woods wrote, "This social evening [Jane Ridley's social evenings] developed into a desire for a weekly paper. Both the Bp. and Mrs. R. were very talented and had taken many sketches locally. Mrs R. and I going out together, sketching up the Haguilket [Hagwilget] Valley. There was no news coming in for the winter months from the outside world. We were absolutely cut off till spring would come. So everyone was expected to help in gathering items of interest, a riddle, a story, anything. My brother sent weather readings from our mission station. I contributed a few sketches, for our paper was an illustrated one, and we looked forward to receiving it on Sat[urday]."[19]

The *Hazelton Queek* started with a flourish with the following notice on Saturday, December 11, 1880:

Notice

It has been proposed by several members of this Community to start a weekly paper and that it shall be named the *Hazelton Queek*. All contributors and correspondence will be most acceptable and as it is proposed to issue the first number on Saturday 18th inst. all communications will please be sent to the office not later than Thursday night. Also we announce that Mr. Chas. Clifford has undertaken the office and duties of Editorship. The "Local Gem" department will be in the able hands of Mr. C. [Charles] Stevens.

Our "foreign correspondence" will be under the management of Mr. H.G. Warburton, whose well known accuracy and despatch on all news etc will be surety of obtaining the first possible news from abroad. The new line of wire just finished will much aid in this matter.

Sketches from Indian life and notes of travels will occasionally appear from the Graphic pen of Mr. Thos. Hankin, whose well-known ability in this delightful department will ensure amusement to our readers and offer advantages to subscribers and advertisers not excelled if equalled on the Pacific Coast.

Its political tone will be liberal in the extreme and its moral aim will be, if possible, in a quiet and unassuming way to do what good it can.

His Lordship the Bishop, having kindly offered to lend his multiplex steam printing press, regularity in the issue can thus be relied upon. His Lordship has also promised to become a frequent contributor.

Hazelton Queek Offices

The editors did not, it appears, take themselves too seriously. The following extracts are from several editions.

December 24, 1880:

The Honest Miner

He is a most interesting and peculiar animal, not described in natural history. Very shy and generally conscious of his own social differences. ... He is a great one to form a good idea of a man's character at the first glance. His close and continued interest with all sorts and conditions of man has given him great proficiency in this respect. He loves gold not for its own sake, who so lavish as he when he has it but for what he thinks he can get for it. He cannot understand how a man with, say, a million can be anything but perfectly happy. He has always a pet scheme of what he will do when he makes his pile and how he will spend it. His idea of a pile varies from five thousand dollars to a million and a half. ...

He puts not his trust in banks and he thinks they are all got up for the express purpose of getting a man's money and then breaking. He often has an idea that he could make lots of money in the wholesale liquor business. He is invariably of a sanguine temperament. ... He cannot afford to save. He should sell out sometime to someone who can. He has been the pioneer of whatever civilization the people on this coast can lay claim to. He is only at home and only seen to advantage in the mountains and in a civilized community he is an anomaly.

January 1, 1881:

Summary of Foreign Affairs in Geographical Order

Beginning with the United States on the Pacific we find them foremost on the road to civilization, via Panama. Here Europe is prepared to operate on the backbone of America. Lesseps' water cure will paralyze the Monroe doctrine and leave the Falkland Islands to be rediscovered by future generations.

France, having lost her Rhine provinces, has restored the balance of power by annexing Tahiti. She steers badly and appears likely to collide.

Spain has pacified Cuba and vexed her kings. Well for Italy if she bursts all her big guns. The poor people would be richer without them. Austria is ready for a trip southward but it will not improve her constitution. Since Germany has owned Metz her debt has grown. The population of Siberia has also grown since the lavish use of the dynamite in Russia. Holland is too independent for Germany and Belgium for France. Ireland has the same aims but no allies. The United Kingdom has no taste for the fine arts of New World politics.

Home Again

British Columbia is as large as Great Britain and some think of greater importance. After Hazelton, New Westminster is likely to become the most influential city in the Province. The *Queek* has turned the earth upside down.

On Christmas Eve Mrs. Ridley very kindly invited everybody to dinner. It is needless to add that it was thoroughly enjoyed. The guests afterwards adjourned to the school house where a Christmas tree laden with presents had been prepared for the Schoolchildren. After distributing the presents, the Children and Visitors dispersed, highly pleased with the evening's entertainment. At a later hour, the school choir promenaded the town singing beautifully a Christmas carol. The effect in the clear, cold air was very pleasing.

Mr. [A. Henry] Owen, while skating the other day, broke through the ice and had a narrow escape from drowning. Fortunately he was enabled after great exertion to regain the solid ice and thus escaped with only the inconvenience of a thorough wetting.

Mr. McIntosh and family and Mr. Kossuth came up from their place at Kit-wan-gar [Gitwangak] this week. They are the guests of Mr. Alfred Sampare. Mr. William Keynton who resides about seven miles down the river also paid a flying visit. Some kind person on Christmas Night relieved Mr. [Charles] Rolles of a clothes line and a pair of drawers, perhaps it was the Gov.

On Christmas Day Mr. [Amos "Charley"] Youmans gave a dinner to a party of friends, which we hear was a perfect success. The Christmas festivities at Rosebery farm [where Thomas Hankin lived] were in the usual Good Old English style. The Indians ... in their own way do seem to be enjoying themselves.

An interesting discussion took place at the usual Thursday evening meeting on the mountain and valley formations of British Columbia. Some curious information was elicited. The proceedings terminated with a humorous recitation by Mr. Warburton.

An original poem by Mr. Owen, an essay by Mr. Hankin and all advertisements, are unavoidably crowded out of this issue.

January 8, 1881:

The usual Thursday evening meeting was not well attended. The subject for discussion mentioned in our leader today was proposed for next Thursday evening and it is to be hoped that the debaters will muster strong on both sides. Mr. Hankin gave two readings, the first being on "Newspapers" in which attention was directed to the faults of newspaper writing and management. Everyone felt that there is only one paper in existence where adverse criticism is unmerited. That paper is the *Queek*. The next subject was "Love" treated (we suppose) in a way which gives a good idea of the tender passion. Indeed the accomplished reader and several of the audience implied as much as they acknowledged to having been "there themselves." Mr. Clifford gave an entirely new recitation entitled "Lord William's Daughter." The proceedings terminated with a most interesting description of a trip from Manson Creek to the Yukon, the Omineca, Peace and Mackenzie Rivers, given by Mr. [Frederick] Harte.

January 15, 1881:

On Thursday evening Mrs. Ridley gave a reading to a small but appreciative audience. Several influential members were "conspicuous by their absence." For their own sakes this is to be regretted, as they missed a great treat. Their non-attendance was so strange a phenomenon that we can only account for it by supposing that the study of the *Queek* and the Thursday evenings wit combats have been so great a mental strain that rest was absolutely necessary. This is what we have feared. Last summer we were nearly worn out physically by hard labour, and now our brains are giving way under a surfeit of intellectual good things. Hoping to counter-act this, we have occasionally thrown off in the *Queek* a few light trifles, the efflorescence, so to say, of our wit. We acknowledge that the disease has taken a more serious form than we had anticipated, and, in order to check it effectually, we intend next week to be so outrageously funny that with the mental reaction will disappear all traces of the disease.

We were informed by Mr. [Edward] Woods that at Antiklast [Ankitlas] the mercury was frozen on 8th, 9th, 10th and 11th of December, last year and that up to the 10th inst., the coldest this year has been 4 below 0.

The Skeena just above the town was frozen across last Wednesday night for the first time this winter.

Notwithstanding all the influences brought to bear by the Medicine Men against the Missionary Work, Bishop Ridley has already over forty scholars daily attending his school. This fact speaks volumes.

At our office may be seen plans for the erection of paper mills. Tomorrow, inking manufactories, wire and glue, scissors and paste works with all the other main accessories of the large publishing trade to be conducted on the Skeena and its tributaries.

Our best hopes are about to be realized. A statue of the pioneer of the press in these regions is to be erected on the summit of the adjacent mountain. Powerful telescopes will be distributed among our numerous readers, who will hand them down as heirlooms to their children. Thus the *Queek* will never be forgotten. We shall look calmly down on the busy crowds of happy beings that will look up to us as the progenitor of the noblest race of men evolved from the obscurity of the dark past. One slight glance through a telescope will inspire the dullest mind with luxuriant thought.

There was a time when we thought of modestly withdrawing from literature. We almost feared we should fail to provoke even criticism. Conscious that the press was but feebly served by our poor efforts we struggled on until the latent talent lying then waste in every direction demanded a hearing. Competition put us on our mettle. We spurred our writers with promises of large salaries for their best productions. The plan succeeded. Now we cannot walk or ride or even drive without meeting men and also women with brains too large for their bodies. Literature has acquired a mighty impulse. Minds over-filled with culture and originality will now be eased of their throbbing treasure. The general public will revel in the brilliant strain of genius sparkling on all sides. They will pity the generations that were proud of Bacon, Shakespeare, Milton and Newton and clapping their telescopes to their eyes will exclaim that we owe all our advantages to yonder *Queek*.

January 22, 1881:

Tenders will be received up to the 29th inst. for the erection of a statue in front of the *Queek* office emblematic of "Wisdom Crying in the Wilderness, and No Man Regarding It." The lowest or any tender not necessarily accepted.

The following is a list of the miners at present wintering at Hazelton and in the vicinity, viz: Albert Gale, H. [Henry] Warburton, Henry Owen, A. McIntosh, Dan McDonald, G.P. Hathaway, Kossuth, F. Harte, G.W. Terry, C. Stevens, Alec McDonald, Chas. Rolles, Wm. Keynton and C.W.D. Clifford.[20]
    We intended giving a short Biographical sketch of each of the above pioneers, interspersed with characteristic anecdotes, but our space is so limited that we are impelled reluctantly to forego a task, which would be at once a pleasure to ourselves, and an acquisition to the biography of the present century.

The time is drawing nigh when some of us at least will have to abandon the luxurious ease of this life for the arduous duties of mining. Assuredly, one of our greatest privations in the mines is a want of books. We are entirely shut out from what Dr. Johnson calls "the endearing elegance of female friendship" and reading is really the only humanizing influence that we have within our reach. Miners as a rule are reading men, but they are too negligent and careless to provide for themselves mental pabulum. [Pabulum: that which nourishes and sustains the mind or soul. Food for thought.] The consequence is that, with the exception of a few sickening novels, there is hardly a book to date on Manson Creek.

January 29, 1881:

We are still in the heart of winter, yet some are making preparations for the journey to the mines. The quiet time is nearly ended. Work awaits us. Hope and uncertainty lie beyond. Success no man can command. We may, however, try to deserve it. Then even if missed, we shall not reproach ourselves. The present winter has been an unusually pleasant one. We are bound to acknowledge a feeling of regret at the approaching break-up of our community. This cold season will be remembered with much pleasure. At the same time no millionaire will think of settling on the banks of the Skeena and therefore we hope to bid them an early farewell.

Queeks in general hibernate. This one has been busy all during the summer. Once or twice we hope to wake up, to look around the world, to set it right and then retire to our hole until the tramp of feet returning from the mines rouses us to renewed action. Doubtless our readers will await our reappearance with impatience. We hope to dream pleasantly of their success all through the summer and share their happiness during many a winter to come, each happier and better than the last.

To the Editor of the *Hazelton Queek*.
Before another week shall have passed, several of your readers will have taken their departure for the scenes of their respective labours. Allow me in this (and, I'm sorry to add) last issue of the *Queek* under its present management to be means of tendering to Bishop Ridley and to Mrs. Ridley, our sincere thanks for the many kindnesses, and evident interest taken in the welfare and amusement of all. I feel sure I am but echoing the feelings of your readers when I say that Hazelton began a new and healthful existence which dated from the arrival of His Lordship Bishop Ridley and his truly kind lady. The Thursday evening meetings were a treat to all who attended them. The fact of Mr. Clifford retiring from the editorship of the *Queek* will cause it doubtless to lose many of its supporters, but let us hope that it will take a new lease and that its whistlings will still continue to edify and amuse the Hazeltonians. T.H. [Thomas Hankin], The Roseberry Farm.

The Editor, in resigning into abler hands the management of the *Queek* does so, not with any doubts as to its future, but with a sincere feeling of regret at quitting a task which to him has been an unmitigated pleasure. He desires to thank the contributors one and all but more especially Bishop Ridley whose sketches and articles have been the main attraction. In fact the *Queek* without his assistance would, we are afraid, be very much like the play of *Hamlet* without the Prince of Denmark. Our heart is too full and we have no room to write more, so Au revoir.

The end of winter brought the end of the *Hazelton Queek*. Miners left Hazelton to prospect in the Omineca Mountains. The gelatin printing press broke. And the bishop and his wife returned to the coast. Waxing lyrical, Ridley described the breakup of the ice on the river:

The breaking up this past spring I was fortunate enough to witness. It was not the immediate action of the sun that effected it, but the south wind and the consequent down-pour of ice-cold water from the mountains, where the snows lie fathoms deep. The floods uplift the ice by slow degrees till the weight of water starts the ponderous mass that winter laid on the river's bosom. I have seen the rivers of Germany break up, but the scene was tame compared with the tumult on these swift rivers of North America.

I was on the ice when the movement first took place. It moves! What moves? The banks seem to glide up stream. Then came a slight tremor beneath my feet, and I sprang to the shore. The sensations were like those produced by shocks of earthquakes. The stone-like surface I had often walked on was in motion bank to bank. At no great distance the channel narrows, and the greater breadth of ice from above was here caught in a vice. The river is in agony—groaning, gurgling, sighing, surging, tilting, hissing, roaring deep and loud like subterranean thunder. What can ever dislodge this piled up mass? The flood is rising at the rear foot by foot. Crack, crack, crack! Look! There go the trees falling inward. The forest king, that has drunk life from the river at its roots, is quivering. There it lurches! Down, down, flat on the ground without axe or tempest, all its roots now exposed to the ice in motion. ... At last, with a sullen groan rising in a terrific roar, away goes the stupendous obstruction, and down sinks the river as if to rest after its splendid victory. Then succeeds the ministry of the south wind; then triumphs the gracious sun in his royal progress northwards. As the baffled ice king retreats, the snow-clad heights are melted with the joy of freedom. The tears trickling from under the snow-fringe that swell the cascades that furrow the mountain's face. Down they roll, swelling the river until its volume sweeps away all obstacles, and leaves it ready to bear the traveler seaward.

So is the Gospel ministry dissolving hard hearts around me; uplifting the dread incubus drawn over them by Satan, and settling free the streams of faith and love that remove all barriers between man and rest in God.[21]

When Ridley returned to the coast that spring, he had to deal with Duncan. The breach between the two men was now irreparable. The *Daily British Colonist* reported that their hostilities continued with little probability of a settlement.[22] The Anglican Church believed that the sacrament of Holy Communion was central to its faith. If Duncan would not permit his parishioners to take Communion, he could no longer work for the Church Missionary Society. He would not change his ways. Consequently, Ridley gave Duncan a letter dated September 29, 1881, terminating his employment with the society. "His work is worthy to be held in remembrance. But the man has slowly changed," he wrote. "He no longer remains an ornament to the missionary cause. Instead of developing the noble work he reared, he is damaging it."[23]

The strife between the two factions in Metlakatla intensified. Duncan's adherents were in the large majority, and they openly defied Ridley in every way possible. In October 1883, Duncan's followers tore down buildings that Ridley's followers were constructing and took the pieces as far away as they could. They harassed Ridley and prevented his adherents from going about their business.[24] They even threatened violence. The Indian commissioner went up and ordered Duncan and his followers to obey Ridley. They wouldn't. Conflict continued and became an internationally noticed scandal in the church. (Faraway Peshawar may have seemed a peaceful memory to the Ridleys at this point!)

Ridley installed a new missionary in Hazelton. Soon, though, this man's wife fell ill, and they had to return to England to allow her to convalesce. On a moment's notice, Jane Ridley agreed to remain in Hazelton to take charge of the mission there. Her husband wrote, "As soon as navigation on the river was resumed, I left Mrs. Ridley behind to do what she could, and right well she carried on the Mission for months single-handed."[25]

On December 14, 1883, William Ridley left Metlakatla and went to Ottawa—down to Victoria, train to Chicago and then north—to seek the assistance of Prime Minister John Macdonald in dealing with Duncan. Macdonald was supportive but refused to interfere in what was a religious dispute. So Ridley went on to London to justify his case to his superiors in the Church Missionary Society. Meanwhile, Jane Ridley did not know her husband had gone to England. She ably managed the mission at Hazelton throughout that winter.

In 1884, the province set up a commission of inquiry to investigate the goings-on at Metlakatla. Members of the commission, one of whom was Andrew Elliott, a former premier of the province, arrived there in early November, heard the evidence and delivered a report in December that required the Duncan faction to obey the law. This order was ignored. Strife continued.

Finally, Duncan felt he had endured Bishop Ridley and his High Church interference for long enough. On August 7, 1887, he left Metlakatla with approximately eight hundred followers in a convoy of canoes and set up a community he called New Metlakatla across the border in Alaska. Even this did not stop the conflict. A party from New Metlakatla came back to Old Metlakatla in October and desecrated the church, smashing all the windows and almost destroying it.[26] Ill feelings persisted for a long time.

Jane Ridley was an invaluable assistant to her husband. She worked with him on learning the Indigenous languages and translating the New Testament and

Prayer Book. Together they recorded five Indigenous languages, which hitherto were oral languages, in written form..[27]

Falling sick, Jane died in 1896. In two pages of Victorian deathbed detail, Bishop Ridley wrote of her death: "My dear wife had long been ailing. One evening in November, 1896, before bed-time she showed great signs of physical distress, and we tried to carry her upstairs to her bedroom but she fainted in our arms. I ordered a bed to be made up for her where we were and there we laid her. ... She passed from that night of exhaustion, and her eyes became bright and her conversation became full of animation and spiritual profit. Next day (Tuesday) crowds of Indians hung around her bed and she was delighted. ... That night another attack came on and we again thought she was dying. ... From that time onward all work in the village was suspended. ... Every ten minutes messengers passed from the bedside to the supplicating crowds repeating her actual condition. ... Many souls found the light during her death struggle. And so, in this glorious manner, my dear wife entered into the presence of her Lord."[28] Ridley continued his mission alone and lonely.

The conflict between Duncan's adherents and Ridley's did not end. In July 1901, the church at Old Metlakatla burned down. Many suspected that followers of Duncan had set the blaze.

Ridley resigned in 1904. He then went home to England, going first to Japan and then on to Australia, where he arrived in the last week of February. His intention—and conceivably his mandate—was to inspect the missionary work in the countries he visited.

He spent six months in Australia, extending his stay from June to November. He travelled widely—Sydney, Melbourne, Brisbane, Bendigo, Tasmania. He spent most of May and June in New Zealand. Wherever he went, he preached and lectured—in churches and cathedrals, in YMCA halls, city halls and schools. He told them about the state of the missionary work in Japan, for which he had high hopes. He described his experiences in British Columbia: the gospel being spread among the Indigenous people, the frost in his beard, his cooking and the sturdy self-reliance of the people. He seems to have been a great success in Australia. When he was leaving, the archbishop of Sydney told him how sorry they were that he was going and that his visit had given much pleasure. On his way home he spent time in India inspecting the missions there, doubtless remembering the time he had spent in Peshawar thirty years before.[29]

He arrived back in England in September 1905. Here in his last years, he involved himself in the work of the Church Missionary Society, attending conferences, giving talks and preaching sermons. He wrote a third book, which he titled

From the Four Winds. He also wrote letters to the *Times* to raise money for the work of the British Columbia Church Aid Society.

And he boasted of his cooking. He said he had already been doing his own mending and washing for twenty-five years, and cooking was a good activity for a lonely man. He told a church missionary meeting in Torquay, "I do my own cooking. Yes, I can even make yeast." Amid laughter, he told them proudly he could bake bread. He was, the *Daily Mail* said, a very domesticated bishop.[30]

In 1908 the Church Missionary Society found him a position as rector of the small Dorsetshire parish of Compton Valence, where his brother Christopher lived. Here, in 1911, after a lifetime of unwavering service to his missionary calling, he died.

9

Richard Loring and the Mystery
of the Swedish Balloon

1896

On July 3, 1896, Richard Loring, the Indian agent in Hazelton since 1889, wrote to Arthur Vowell, his superior in Victoria. "Sir, I have the honour to report that this day at 7:35 p.m. (local time) an object by description in the shape of a balloon, was seen by a boy about four miles to the west of here, latitude 55.15, longitude 127.40. ... The boy's description of the balloon and its actions left no doubt as to its reality."[1]

So, what was it? It was certainly a mysterious flying object. Loring was sure he knew what it was. To him, it was obviously Professor Andrée's balloon from Sweden.

Richard Loring was solid, conscientious and not given to flights of fancy. He had been born in Dresden, Saxony, in July 1852. His family, he wrote, had gone there from England several generations before. He was educated in Leipzig and then at a military school in Dresden. Arriving in New York in 1874 to visit relatives, he stayed for a few years and then went west to Colorado. In 1882, after spending five years mining in that state and one year in California, he came north to British Columbia. After a stint in mining, he found work on Vancouver Island as a foreman on the construction of the Esquimalt and Nanaimo Railway. Later he found work with the British Columbia Provincial Police as a special constable. In 1888, he was one of the police squad that came to Hazelton to search for the accused murderer Kamalmuk (Kitwancool Jim), but he was not present when Kamalmuk was shot dead.[2] During his time in Hazelton, he met Margaret, the widow of Thomas Hankin, who had died a few years before. Romance bloomed. They were married at the Cedar Hill church in Victoria on August 29, 1889. With his bride, he then returned to Hazelton as Indian agent for the new Babine District. They settled into a house on the lip of the bluff in the Gitanmaax reserve. From there the Lorings could literally overlook Hazelton.

Loring said that in Saxony he had been a baron—Baron von Wilkie or Wilke—but he had stopped using his title when he joined the police. Fifty years later his stepdaughter Constance Cox said his full name was Alfred Richard Ernest Loring, Byron von Wilkie, but there is no independent confirmation of this.[3]

Loring had been on the lookout for Professor Andrée's balloon all summer. In May 1896, Joseph Pope, undersecretary of state for Canada, had published a notice in newspapers advising Canadians that the government of the king of Sweden and Norway was sending a balloon expedition to the North Pole in the interests of science. Authorities in Victoria reissued this notice in the early summer. The Hudson's Bay Company also put the word out. Canadians were asked to give the balloonists all possible assistance after they had crossed the North Pole and floated over Canadian territory. They were also asked to report any sightings to the authorities. Loring took note.

Richard Ernest Loring, Indian agent at Hazelton from 1889 to 1921. Image A-04364 courtesy of the Royal BC Museum and Archives

Professor Salomon August Andrée was an engineer and examiner-in-chief of the Swedish Patent Office. When it came to balloons, he was the Swedish expert and main booster, having flown numerous balloons in the Baltic, albeit with mixed success. Sweden was lagging behind Norway in Arctic exploration and wanted to catch up. Andrée now believed he had perfected special drag ropes for steering his new hydrogen balloon. He intended to fly to the Arctic and be the first man to reach the North Pole. The balloon would be carrying Andrée and two crew members, Nils Ekholm and Nils Strindberg. His sponsors included King Oscar II, who donated £1,730, and Alfred Nobel—of dynamite and the Nobel Prize fame—who donated £3,410. National prestige was at stake. Sweden's heart swelled with patriotic pride, nationalism and expectation. Andrée was the expert and appeared to know what he was doing. What could go wrong?

When the object appeared in the skies of the Upper Skeena, there was great excitement. The first sighting was made by a local boy. This was confirmed by a second sighting made by Ghail, a Gitxsan Chief from Kispiox. Loring knew what he had to do. He picked up his pen and reported it:

Professor Salomon Andrée's balloon that Richard Loring thought had floated over the North Pole and over the Upper Skeena. Wikimedia Commons

In an—at the time—strong NNWly wind, it was seen to emerge from out of a heavy bank of white clouds, sailing in an intermediate clear space in semi-circular line, to disappear in another at an altitude of about four hundred feet above the timberline on the mountain. It had a black appearance, having been seen between the setting sun. The boy's description of the balloon and its actions left no doubt as to its reality and is no doubt the Andrée balloon reported to have left Spitzbergen for the North Pole on or about the 1st inst.

Again on the 10th inst., it was reported to me by Ghail, the head chief at Kits-pioux [Kispiox] that, while trapping with a party of Indians on Blackwater Lake, above the headwaters of the Skeena, an object resembling a balloon and then displaying two very bright lights was also seen by them on the evening of the 3rd inst.

Ghail, whom you know, is a trustworthy man and his statement must be credited. The Indians on the Skeena were made aware they were liable to see, during the beginning of this month, a balloon going north and of the purpose of its occupants, etc.[4]

Significantly, Ghail had been out for several weeks on the hunting trail and was unaware of the sighting made by the boy. These were, therefore, independent sightings. But just as significantly, Loring had previously alerted local residents to be on the lookout for the balloon.

The newspapers published Loring's reports. There had in fact been other sightings of the balloon, including several more around Victoria and also several near Winnipeg.[5] The Swedish authorities were informed.

However, it soon became clear that what they had seen could not have been Andrée's balloon. It was impossible. Professor Andrée had never left Sweden. In addition to other problems, Andrée and his companions had relied on the winds to take them where they wanted to go. The winds had not co-operated. In mid-August the intrepid—or foolhardy—explorers let the hydrogen out of the balloon and gave up the attempt for the year.

The following year Andrée repeated his attempt. He was so sure that his project would be successful that he ignored several warning signs. His drag ropes, so critical to the success of the project, did not work as well as he anticipated. Moreover, the balloon itself, new from its manufacturer in France, had not been properly tested and developed leaks. Nevertheless, Andrée and two others set out. They were never seen alive again. Their fate was one of the riddles of Arctic exploration until their frozen bodies were found in 1930 on White Island in Svalbard, Norway.

What, then, had been seen over Hazelton in 1896? It could not have been Professor Andrée's balloon. So, what was it? Some might be tempted to believe it was an unidentified flying object with a mysterious out-of-this-world origin. More cynical people might think those with fertile imaginations knowing what they were looking for might have mistaken a cloud for Professor Andrée's balloon.

10

Father Morice and His Trembling Knees

1885–1905

Father Adrien-Gabriel Morice had a serious personal problem. He was standing on the north side of the Bulkley River at the Hagwilget Canyon, four miles upriver from Hazelton. On the south side stood the expectant congregation of Indigenous Catholic faithful in the Wet'suwet'en village there. He was due to preach to them shortly. He stared at the rickety bridge. The prospect of having to cross it again filled him with deep dismay. But how could he let his parishioners down? Exhorting him to cross, they stared at him and he stared back. What to do?

Father Morice had been the Oblate Catholic priest in the Bulkley Valley since 1885. He ministered to the spiritual needs of the Wet'suwet'en and Sekani Indigenous Peoples, as such needs were decided by him. He was based at Fort St. James at the southern end of Stuart Lake, the trading post established by Simon Fraser in 1806. But he spent much of his time travelling around his huge parish. As he himself modestly wrote, "he crossed by boat, on horseback or on foot, practically the whole width of British Columbia, from the mouth of the Skeena up to Hazelton, thence to Babine on foot."[1] This necessitated crossing bridges over many of the rushing streams and rivers. He hated this part of his job.

The Gitxsan and Wet'suwet'en First Nations were skilful bridge builders. They had constructed many bridges across rivers and streams. When he was in the area in 1870, George Chismore was one of the first to write about them. There were at least fifteen recorded bridges, including the ones over the Skeena at Kuldo, across the Bulkley at Witset (Moricetown), across the Babine River at Kisgegas, and across the Cranberry, Sustut and Suskwa Rivers. Undoubtedly many more went unrecorded.

The bridge across the canyon at Hagwilget is the most famous, being the most recent in a series of bridges at this spot. Although there had been bridges at Hagwilget long before there were written records, it is probable they had been rebuilt and repaired numerous times over the years. With a shore-to-shore span of 146 feet and a width of 6 feet, it was approximately 50 feet above the river. Until a low-level bridge was built closer to Hazelton in 1906 and the high-level bridge was built at Hagwilget in 1913, there were no other bridges across the Bulkley River at the western end of the canyon. There was, to be sure, a bridge at Witset twenty-four

A photograph of the First Nations bridge at Hagwilget taken by Charles Horetzky in 1872. Image P1453 courtesy of the Bulkley Valley Museum

miles upriver. And it is possible that Indigenous people had built other bridges between Hagwilget and Witset.

These bridges may have been marvels of early Indigenous construction, but crossing them was not for the faint of heart. In his memoir *Fifty Years in Western Canada*, Father Morice described the bridge at Hagwilget, which he was now trying to calm his nerves to cross. It was, he wrote, made of three slender logs joined one to another, with heavy stones piled on each end. No nails were used. Ropes made of cedar bark held it together and provided a handrail. Reportedly, twenty to thirty years before, the Indigenous people had strengthened it by using steel wire left behind when the Western Union Telegraph project was abandoned.

Writing in the third person, Father Morice said:

The worst part of this was that so frail was the primitive bridge which resulted from that assemblage that, as soon as you set foot over it, it started to shake. You could not advance three or four steps on it without causing the whole thing to swing in a most ominous manner over the angry billows of the rapid. The necessity of watching a point to tread on forced you to look at it and exposed you to the danger of fatal dizziness. Father Morice had already passed it several times, painfully crawling on hands and knees with perspiration on his brow, and had finally sworn never to attempt again such a perilous venture when, having been called to that village, where he was eagerly awaited, he was assured that the famous bridge had been steadied and could be crossed without much difficulty.[2]

Father Morice was born in France in 1859 and, like William Ridley, felt the call to be a missionary. "This is what I want!", he wrote. "To work and suffer for souls, to battle among, and conquer, the lowly of America, that is my vocation."[3] He was not a good student, though, and perversely took pride in his low marks. When he was in training for the priesthood at Autun in France, he had been, his superior later said, disciplined for his vanity, ambition and insubordination, but he had been allowed to continue because he was intelligent and had a flair for languages.[4] This presciently foretold the life he would lead.

Although undoubtedly a brilliant scholar, Father Morice was a difficult man to have any dealings with. The entry about him in the *Dictionary of Canadian Biography* comments that clearly he should never have been ordained at all, let alone as an Oblate priest.[5]

Father Morice came to British Columbia in 1880 to complete his training. He was troublesome from the start. He did not obey the orders of his superiors. He was pugnacious. He quarrelled with his equals and was demanding of his subordinates. He translated his perverse objections into active disobedience, even, allegedly, deliberately ringing the church bells at the wrong time to confuse congregants. The *Dictionary of Canadian Biography* paints a damning picture of his insubordination, quarrels and obstinacy. In 1885, his superiors, conceivably to get him as far away as possible from the southern part of the province—out of sight, out of mind?—sent him north, first to Williams Lake and then to Fort St. James. There he remained until 1903, ministering to his flock and shepherding them into the Roman Catholic fold.

What Father Morice was good at was linguistics. No one doubted his brilliance in this field. He became an expert in the Indigenous languages of the region, preferring to deal with Indigenous people in their own tongue. Mean-spirited folk said this was so his parishioners would not learn English. This, they said, meant that he was able to control them in a way that other missionaries, less able to speak local languages, could not. He established a printing press in a building behind the church, which, if Bishop William Ridley's printing of the *Queek* counts as the first, was probably the second printing press in central and northern British Columbia. From there he published tracts, dictionaries and prayer books in Indigenous languages. Arguably, he spent more time on his publications and scholarship than on his ministry. He devised a way of transcribing Indigenous languages. He compiled dictionaries and books on their grammar. He wrote numerous books on linguistics and cartography. Soon he became widely acknowledged as a scholar of the first order. His *History of the Northern Interior of British Columbia* and *The Carrier Language* remain classics.

Father Morice had a high opinion of his own intelligence and abilities, and he did not hesitate to let people know this. One whole chapter of his memoir was called "Benefactor." In this, writing in the third person, he said:

> A special chapter to show Father Morice as a benefactor of his people may seem more or less out of place and in the l ght of useless redundance here. Are not all missionaries public benefactors? Why, then, this attempt at pointing out what is to most readers a matter of course? The answer is easy. Father Morice did for his Indians what no other missionary has done for his. … The prodigious influence which our missionary's mastery of his people's language and his endless exertions in their behalf, as well as his successful interventions with the powers that be, gained for him, shows him to us in the light of a unique benefactor in the secular field, in which, it is safe to say that very few, if any, other clergymen ever outdid him.[6]

He was vain to the point of narcissism. In his memoirs he was forever repeating compliments paid him. Admittedly a good cartographer, he recorded that one eminent surveyor wrote to him, "With other land surveyors of British Columbia ... I have a deep appreciation of the splendid work which you have done in our northern country. ... We are all in your debt, sir."[7] Writing of his own literary efforts, he said, "The country owes him a debt of gratitude for quite a series of works whose value cannot but get better appreciated as years roll by. Our author is somewhat of a stylist, either in French or in English, and, as we have already seen, his manner of writing usually generates an interest which does not lag."[8]

By virtue of his position as the priest in a district in which Roman Catholicism had taken a deep hold, as well as of his knowledge of local languages and his strong personality, he achieved a dominant role in the governance of the Indigenous Peoples in the North—at least those south and east of Hagwilget. Beyond that line lay the land of the Protestants. He was autocratic. He refused confession to Indigenous people who missed his sermons, something his church definitely did not allow priests to do. He imposed the controversial Durieu system of governance on Indigenous people. Bishop Pierre Paul Durieu was the Catholic bishop of New Westminster between 1890 and 1899. His system of discipline was achieved by strict rules that were backed by corporal punishment for transgression. Local Indigenous policemen enforced his dictates. These required Indigenous parishioners to obey four rules: not to drink or gamble, not to consult shamans or *halayt*, not to hold potlatches and not to perform traditional dances. Since these were traditional and much-loved occupations, the injunction not to indulge in them was a heavy one.

By 1900, much had changed in Hazelton since the days of Thomas Hankin and the miners of the Omineca Gold Rush. The town had been resurveyed, and lots auctioned off. For six months of the year, sternwheelers arrived as regularly as the river allowed. For the other six months, winter conditions made the river unnavigable. The telegraph to the Yukon had been completed and a branch line went through Hazelton to Port Simpson on the coast. The town was the centre of the mule-train business in the North. In the 1890s Richard Sargent, the leading merchant in town for the next several decades, had arrived to work for the Hudson's Bay Company. James Kirby, the first resident policeman, arrived in the spring of 1900. Dr. Horace Wrinch, the first doctor to live in the northern interior, arrived in the autumn of that year and was planning to build a hospital. And the missionaries had come: the Anglicans in Hazelton, where Rev. John Field had built St. Peter's Church; the Salvation Army in Glen Vowell; and the Methodists in most of the surrounding villages.

In 1902, Father Morice wrote to the Methodist missions board in Toronto and laid down his conditions for permitting his Indigenous parishioners at Hagwilget to subscribe for the hospital that the Methodist Dr. Wrinch was building between Hazelton and Hagwilget. He may have thought that medical care in a Methodist hospital would pose a risk to their immortal souls or, more to the point, lead to a diminution of his authority over them. The missions board passed that ball to Wrinch to deal with, which presumably he did because the Hazelton Hospital register shows Roman Catholics being admitted to the hospital from its inception. The annual report of the hospital, for example, shows that in 1906, out of seventy-five patients treated, fifteen were Roman Catholic. Since Father Morice had left the district in 1903, Dr. Wrinch would have found his successor, Father Nicolas Coccola, easier to deal with.

When crossing streams and shallow rivers, Father Morice was reputed to order Indigenous men to carry him over. That would not be possible at Hagwilget. The canyon was too deep and too wide. The river was too swift and too powerful. There was no alternative. He would have to cross that bridge. In his defence, many others shared his feelings. Even Sperry Cline, not a timorous soul by any means, said crossing it was an ordeal and always walked his horse over.

Saint or sinner, Adrien-Gabriel Morice had no head for heights. He had crossed this bridge at Hagwilget on his hands and knees a couple of times and had sworn never to cross it again. But here he was, having to do just that. He wrote, again in the third person:

> Once arrived there, however, the missionary realized that it was the same old rickety structure, and at once expressed his displeasure that he should have been brought in front of a place which he could not reach—just across almost the whole population of the village had congregated, the men with rifle in hand ready to salute his arrival on their side, and were shouting out to him their best encouragements. Two of them came across, as if to show how easily this could be done and how solid was their bridge. They offered to help him on to the village, nay, almost forced their services on him, one of them walking over it immediately ahead of him, the other just behind. But when the white man commenced to feel the swinging of the old thing to the right and to the left, he knew that dizziness was going to have the better of him. "Back! Back! I cannot do it," he cried out.
>
> But his guides would not go back, and, on the contrary, tried to coax him on. They had, however, to yield to his entreaties, when presently a little man with no aristocratic features ... ran in from the other side, and offered to pack the priest over. Instantly Father Morice thought of the man whom [French tightrope walker Charles] Blondin carried on his shoulders across Niagara Falls, and shuddered. ... All the bystanders averred that, despite appearances, the little wiry man was serious and could do it, having already taken across that same bridge on his broad back that most unwieldy of burdens, a one hundred and fifty pound barrel of sugar! Father Morice was ungenerous enough to refuse to add to his laurels and, to the disgust of the crowd, he preferred to ride ten good miles round, and reached at dusk the village, whence all enthusiasm seemed to have gone.[9]

In 1906, too late to be of any assistance to Father Morice, the government built a low-level bridge across the Bulkley River between Hazelton and the Indigenous bridge at Hagwilget. This was located where Two Mile Creek joins the Skeena. It was capable of taking any wagon that could negotiate the steep slopes and difficult bends, but it was unpopular. The problem was not the bridge itself—though it was too narrow—but the approach roads, which were steep, winding and, in winter, icy.

In 1913, a private entrepreneur built a bridge across the canyon at its top; this was the Craddock bridge.

By this time the Indigenous bridge was badly in need of repairs. The *Omineca Herald* noted:

Citizens Association Should Procure
Permission to Preserve Historic Relic

A few nights ago, the matter of repairing the old Indian bridge which crosses the Bulkley River at Hagwilget was under discussion among some of the citizens. It is only a small matter at present to renew one or two pillars and the bridge would be made good for a number of years yet and at the same time the appearance would be in no wise affected. It is acknowledged on all sides that this bridge with its historic value is an important asset to the town when the tourists begin coming through. The Indian bridge, with what it represents in native ingenuity and the extreme labour required by the primitive methods employed, represents to the tourists one of the wonders of the world, and they will come thousands of miles to see it.

This is one of the most important matters connected with the attractions of New Hazelton and there is no other organisation in the district to look after this than the Citizens Association. Steps should be taken at once to secure permission to repair the structure and retain it for its historic value.[10]

Several attempts were made to secure money to do this, but nothing came of them. The bridge collapsed into the river in August 1917. "The old historic suspension bridge ... collapsed last Sunday morning and now floats in the waters of the Hagwilget Canyon, held by cables on which it was suspended for more than twenty years."[11]

Although much admired by some, Father Morice was controversial all his life. The passage of time has not improved his reputation. He argued with everyone. He never did follow orders. His superiors criticized him for naming so many places after himself—Moricetown, the Morice River and Morice Mountain. He spent stretches of time away from his parish. He spent 1896 studying in France, admittedly with the approval of his superiors. He spent the winter of 1899 in New Westminster. The *Dictionary of Canadian Biography* notes, "By the fall of 1903, his neglect of his priestly duties, his failure to teach English, his autocratic manner and the increasingly audacious demands he made on the Hudson's Bay Company had combined to bring him down."[12] One of his assistant priests accused him of treating his Indigenous charges as if they were slaves, "while in matters of spiritual development he allowed them to fall behind converts elsewhere."[13]

His Oblate superiors finally had enough. They couldn't ignore the complaints any longer. He was too much of a problem. But with his scholarship, a powerful personality and a printing press, Father Morice had many influential people prepared to stand up for him. In November 1903, his Oblate superiors ordered him back to Vancouver. He accused them of persecuting him. In 1905, they moved him to Kamloops, where he provoked a fight with fellow priests in which he was severely beaten.[14] Not knowing what to do with this troublesome priest, the authorities then sent him to Manitoba, where, in St. Boniface, he spent the rest of his life.

Father Adrien-Gabriel Morice, the controversial Oblate priest in the Bulkley Valley.

Here, despite increasing recognition of his undoubted achievements as a linguist and cartographer, he continued to be a major headache for all around him until his death in April 1938.

11

James Kirby and Mexican
Tom, the Hazelton Bully

1900

On October 3, 1879, fourteen-year-old James Kirby was playing his French horn in the regimental band in Portsmouth, England, welcoming heroes home.[1] The transport ship had docked and the Second Battalion of the Twenty-Fourth Regiment of Foot, flush with glory after the valiant stand at the Battle of Rorke's Drift in the Anglo-Zulu War, started to disembark.

In grand imperial style, the band struck up "See, the Conquering Hero Comes" and then "Rolling Home to Dear Old England." The regiment disembarked to cheers, cannon salutes, speeches and a rousing welcome by the Duke of Cambridge, the commander-in-chief of the army. They came back battered, proud and with eleven Victoria Crosses. "A day never to be forgotten," Kirby wrote in his memoirs, "as the Regiment was in a deplorable condition, their clothes all patched up in places and holes everywhere. Head gear all shapes, colours and sizes. Then so many of them having curios, assegais, and shields and what they called Nob Carries [knobkerries], a stick with a big knob on one end of it."[2] The band played them through the cheering, flag-waving crowds lining the streets to their barracks. The last tune they played was "Warwickshire Lads and Lassies." It was a long way from the small frontier town of Hazelton on the Skeena River, where Kirby was to live for almost twenty years.

James Kirby was born in Rochester, in Kent, on February 25, 1865. There is a mystery about his parentage. His death certificate says that his father's name was Jessi Kirby and his mother's name was unknown. In his memoirs, however, he says his father's name was Colonel Hendrie, which hints at illegitimacy, and that his mother's name was Jessie.[3] He was brought up by his Uncle Horace, a foreman at the Turkey Paper Mill, near Maidstone. They lived in an old huntsman's cottage outside the gates of the lands of a local dignitary. Being adventurous, young James ran away to join the army.

He said he wanted to enlist after seeing a parade of the mounted Kentish yeomanry with their flashing cuirasses and military panache. He was, consequently, easy prey for the recruiting sergeant who took him into the Twenty-Fourth Regiment of Foot on May 28, 1879. He was only fourteen years old, but he was registered as fifteen so he could draw an adult's pay. The regiment, renamed the South Wales Borderers two years later, had its base at Brecon, in Wales. After training as a bandsman at the military band school at Kneller Hall, Kirby was sent to Portsmouth to greet the main body of his regiment on its arrival back in England.

With his regiment, Kirby was then sent to India, where he spent seven years. His career in the army, moving from one cantonment to another, would not have been much different from that of many other young soldiers in the imperial service at the time. He was impressed by the many cobra snakes that were so plentiful wherever he was stationed. Snakes were one danger. Dacoits (bandits) were another. And another was sickness. One time, when he was recovering from a bout of near-fatal dysentery, the popular commander-in-chief, Lord Roberts (known universally as Bobs), visited the men in hospital. Kirby wrote he was surprised by how small a man the great hero was.[4] As a bandsman he occasionally played for Lord Roberts's levees and social occasions, where he would have seen the British Raj in all its rich pageantry—the scarlet uniforms, the medals and gold braid, the feathers and finery of the ladies and the gorgeous colours of the bejewelled rajas and princes.

Kirby later went with his regiment to Burma (now Myanmar) and took part in the Second Burma War. He was with C Company when it captured the rebel leader, which led to the end of the war. He was in Burma in March 1879 when Rudyard Kipling visited the regiment, inspiring him to write the verses in the famous ballad "On the Road to Mandalay." Kirby wrote that Kipling composed them there when visiting the officers and troops. Kirby recalled that he and his comrades sang the ballad as they worked building roads and hunting for dacoits.[5]

In 1889 he applied for transfer back to England and returned on the SS *Orentes*, arriving home on Christmas Eve. Since they were still in their Indian Army uniforms—marked by white helmets with puggrees (headbands)—he and the twenty-three men he was in charge of almost froze to death. He took part in the grand review of the army by the kaiser on Wimbledon Common during his state visit to England in July 1891. The soldiers were furious because they paraded in heavy rain while the officers wore great rain capes. "I shall never forget the look on the Kaiser's face," Kirby wrote. "What a stern one and how proud he looked in his Eagle helmet (all silver it looked like)."[6]

After leaving the army early in 1892, Kirby packed his bags and embarked on the SS *Sardinian* for Canada. He was going to join his uncle, who was running a hotel at Metlakatla on the northern coast of British Columbia. After his arrival, Charles Todd, the Indian agent on the coast, gave him work as a cook, deckhand, pilot, bottle-washer and special constable. Kirby said he had never cooked as much as a potato in his life, but his aunt gave him lessons and he managed somehow.

James Kirby, first resident policeman in Hazelton. Image P2083 courtesy of the Bulkley Valley Museum

His work as a special constable soon led to his joining the British Columbia Provincial Police as a regular constable.

Conscientious and able, he had numerous adventures enforcing the law. One encounter was with the gangster Soapy Smith (Jefferson Randolph Smith), who was on his way north to the Yukon on the steamer *Corona*. The men and women of his gang had been making a nuisance of themselves on board and bothering the passengers. When the ship ran aground without loss of life on Lawyer Islands, just off the mouth of the Skeena River, the captain put everyone ashore, including Smith and his gang. Kirby did not like Smith, and so he ran them all out of the country by putting them on the next boat going north to Skagway. There Smith became famous for his misdeeds as the gangster who took over and terrorized the town during the Klondike Gold Rush, before being shot to death in what became known as the Shootout on Juneau Wharf in 1898.

Kirby had numerous crimes to deal with in these years on the coast. He recounted one robbery in his memoirs:

The next important case was burglary of several stores on the Skeena. This again was a corker, as none of the stores seem to know when their respective stores were robbed. All they knew [was] that certain goods were missing. So what could I do? I simply had to wait and see. So one day I saw a friend of mine come down the Oxtal [Ecstall] River in his sloop towing a fish boat behind him. This was nothing unusual, but events proved otherwise for as I was standing in front of the hotel talking to Mr. Cunningham, a week or so later, facing the river, we saw a sloop sailing round Point Lambert about five or six miles away towing what seemed to be a boom of logs, as it or they were low in the water, coming in towards Essington so as to keep to with the tide. The old man got his telescope and said, why it's B—, I wonder what he is towing. When he got within a mile or so, we could see it was a boat loaded with something very heavily laden. He passed right by of us plainly in sight, about half a mile, and went up the Oxtal River. I did not think much about it till later in the afternoon, when it struck me like a flash that he might be the man we were after: viz—the store robber.

I made up my mind at once and gave the information necessary to obtain a search warrant and warrant to arrest, keeping everything to myself and the J.P., and went and got one Simon Wallace, an Indian constable absolutely trustworthy, and getting a few supplies etc. left that night very quickly, about midnight, just as dark as could be, myself pulling the oars and Simon steering (he knowing every inch of the Oxtal River) and proceeded to cross the said river to get on the other side. B— the man we were after lived with a Norwegian family, a boat builder about eighteen miles up this river, and it would be just about daybreak when we should arrive there. But on getting to the other side about 6 miles upriver, I saw a light in a logger's cabin about 50 yards from the bank and decided to see who was there.

So, leaving Simon in the boat to watch, I approached and knocked on the door and who should open the door but our man himself. I arrested him and on his pleading to let him go up to his home to get a change of clothes and begging me not to let the family know of his arrest as he was engaged to one of the girls ... I promised to let him explain to said family himself as to why and wherefore he had to go down with me that morning to Essington.

We had a cup of coffee and the old boat builder took me round to show me all his out houses and keeping my eyes open (Simon staying with the boat) I noticed ... a lot of iktas [Chinook Jargon for stuff, things] in the hay loft. Might be a real place to hide things, particularly in one place of the hay. I saw the butt of a gun and also noticed other things lying around that did not seem in place for a farm. So on the turn of the tide I took my man B— down to Essington and locked him up, and, getting a trustworthy special sworn in, returned with the flood tide accompanied by two men in another boat, still keeping Simon with me. We arrived in due course at Mr. O—'s farm again and on searching the house and outhouse found enough of goods, dry goods, rifles, shot guns, knives, forks, spoons, suits of clothes, boom chains, anchors to set up a good-sized store. We filled the extra boat and half of my police boat and brought the whole of it down, and sent to my chief John Flewin, all information as to what I had done.

Meanwhile news had travelled to all the canneries as to my capture. Then, getting word that the chief had arrived at Claxton Cannery about 9 miles down the Skeena River, I had a special constable sworn in to guard the prisoner and lockup, and went down to bring the chief constable up, as he had no boat with him. I arrived at Claxton and wanted to return on the turn of the tide, but the chief said I had better have a night's rest and return on the flood tide in the morning. I had been rushing things for three or four days with little or no sleep and lots of boat pulling.

So next morning I returned, taking the cannery manager a Mr. Robertson with us, he having lost a lot of goods from his store and being one of the informers. We arrived in due course and on landing the people were surprised to find that it was Mr. Robertson who was with us, and not B—, the prisoner, who had made his escape from the lock-up that morning, while the special constable had gone to order their breakfast. Of course this was a surprise to me as well as to the chief. He, the prisoner, had been assisted by some person on the outside, for, on searching the lockup we found a one-inch file which had been worn down so as to use it as a screw driver, but someone would have to help from the outside. Therefore we concluded that assistance had been given and a boat had been stolen from the beach, belonging to one Indian. That finished that case until a report had been received about two months later that an American steamer had picked up a man and a small skiff and had taken them to the Yukon. On identification, the goods were returned to the owners.[7]

In early 1900, Kirby was posted to Hazelton and came upriver. "And what a crowd!" he wrote. "The whole tribe of Indians and all the white people were on the bank to meet the boat and Captain Bonser tooting for all he was worth, it being the first boat of the year."[8] That August, he returned to Port Essington to marry Annie Goodman in the parlour of Cunningham's hotel.

In Hazelton, he had to deal with a not uncommon situation when a policeman first comes to an unpoliced town: how to deal with the town bully, in this case, Mexican Tom.

In his memoirs, Kirby wrote of this first challenge:

I was soon acquainted with Dick Sargent, J.P., and Ed Stephenson and Rev. John Field and all the white people, including the Indian agent R.E. Loring. ... I also met lots of old time miners: Jim May, Joe Lyon, Ezra Evans, Charles McKinnon, old man Keynton and many others.

I might state here that the Hudson's Bay store at this time was still in a stockade, that is, built like a fort with walls all around, about 10 to 12 feet high, with the 4 corners built for protection and built with logs all about 4 to 6 feet square etc. The street was not surveyed yet and was occupied by half a dozen or so of Chinese cabins right where Main Street should be. It was not long before the streets were surveyed and cleared of all obstacles, cabins included. In fact, one old timer, Gus Lacroix, had his garden right across the street.

I was invited to batch with the two justices, Sargent and Stevenson. One day during luncheon hour, a person whom the justices were already wise to, who had the townspeople scared out of their wits (as this man had frequently taken over the town by walking up the main street shooting off a couple of revolvers that he carried, as well as Bowie knifes carried in his belt, by name Mexican Tom), walked into the cabin and was invited to take a cup of tea with us. He was a big man, way over 6 foot and heavy built. He undid his belt and, before sitting down, was introduced by Sargent to me, as the provincial constable just arrived. He sized me up for a few minutes then took his seat. He asked me lots of questions and finally asked me what I intended to do. So, without beating about the bush, I told him I was taking over the charge of the town as far as Law and Order was concerned. He had a kind of grin on his face that I did not like, so I began right then to watch him closely and soon made up my mind that he was a big windbag, and would soon prove so.

So as soon as luncheon was over, he got up, put on his belt with two revolvers and Bowie knives, and I warned him that he was liable for carrying concealed weapons, but he just laughed at me and went out onto the street. I followed him but had nothing but my handcuffs with me. So after he was a good way over and on the street, I went up to him and arrested him for carrying concealed weapons, and my hunch proved right for he immediately wilted, and I took the weapons from him and locked him up.

He was tried that afternoon before the said two justices, and he was fined and the weapons confiscated. The court was filled right up with townspeople and when he, Mexican Tom, left the court, he was booed by all and what a change in a man. He who had scared the town for so long was just a poor miserable boob, and ever after when spouting out his bazoo or wind, the crowd or some of them would say, "Look out Tom, here comes the constable," and he would become a lamb again.[9]

While Kirby was in Hazelton, he saw the town grow as settlers, prospectors and later railway workers arrived. Doubtless he was present when St. Peter's Anglican Church was opened in 1900. The new telegraph line to the Yukon, which arrived in Hazelton that year, brought the outside world much closer. Hazelton Hospital, which opened in 1904, kept the town the centre of the district and provided a measure of medical security for local residents. Miners, telegraph operators and surveyors for government projects and the planned railway all presaged an increase in everything—mining activity, railway work, farming, new settlers and the growing presence of government authorities. With this, though, came an increase in crime and an increase in the potential for conflict between the Indigenous, mainly Gitxsan, and non-Indigenous people.

Generally speaking, there was a huge racial and cultural divide between Indigenous and non-Indigenous people. On one side was the unchallengeable assumption of racial superiority and the instruments of power; on the other, what must have been a sense of loss, of cultural fragmentation and resentment. Yet the two groups needed to get on together. Before 1900, when the non-Indigenous people were still in a minority, there was coexistence, with both sides needing each other and in many cases respecting each other's cultures.

After 1900, the potential for trouble grew. Often-justified Gitxsan grievances increased. They were no longer in the majority. Surveyors came to plan the railway lines that were to cross their lands, and workers arrived to smash their way through the landscape to build them. Non-Indigenous people flooded into the district, waving bits of government-issued paper that gave them rights to land the Gitxsan people believed was theirs. Fishery officers started enforcing new fishery laws and taking down Gitxsan, Wet'suwet'en and Babine weirs. Prospectors roamed over the creeks and valleys. More settlers and newcomers meant more liquor, leading to increased alcohol abuse. Much of the mutual understanding and willingness to coexist was weakened by more overt racism and discrimination. Discontent rose. Friction increased.

Kirby had his hands full. He had the liquor laws to enforce. He also had to deal with the numerous minor infractions of the law that beset authorities. There were several serious crimes. One of these was the famous and sensational Gunanoot affair.

Kirby was the only policeman in Hazelton in 1906 when Simon Gunanoot was accused of the murders of Alex MacIntosh and Max LeClair. Kirby vigorously led the search for the murderer for a week. Then the chief of police in Victoria replaced him with a constable named Harry Berryman, who mismanaged the search until relieved of his responsibilities. But by then it was too late. Gunanoot had vanished into the wilderness and remained at large for thirteen years. In 1919, he gave himself up to Sperry Cline, who by then was the only police constable in town. Gunanoot was tried for the murder in Vancouver and acquitted. Gunanoot's defence counsel unfairly attacked Kirby's character, accusing him of stupidity and of mismanaging the search.

As the only policeman in Hazelton until early 1908, Kirby on occasion felt alone and almost ignored. In June 1904, he wrote plaintively to the acting police chief in Victoria:

James Kirby celebrating his one hundredth birthday on February 25, 1965, at a dinner at the Smithers Restaurant. Image P7479 courtesy of the Bulkley Valley Museum

Dear Sir, Will you kindly oblige me by sending to me a holster for my revolver #35. I have not had one yet and cannot get one in this town and I should be very much obliged if you could let me have one pair of handcuffs. I have only one pair and as it is possible that I may have to send a special constable out to the Bulkley Valley (where there is a great rush of people this year) I should very much need another pair.[10]

Kirby's wife fell sick. Short of money to pay her medical bills, he was careless—let us be kind here—with his expenses, which he had to repay. This was discovered after he had retired from the police in 1909. He became the mining recorder in town. Leaving Hazelton in 1918, he moved to nearby Smithers, where he worked as the mining recorder until he retired in 1931. He became a community leader, a member of the Legion and a charter member of the Omineca Lodge No. 92 of the Masons. In 1922, he donated three lots of land in Smithers for a hospital and served on the hospital board. His first wife, Annie, died in 1921. In 1924, his seventeen-year-old son, Ernest, tragically drowned in Tatalaska Lake.

To honour his son's memory, Kirby started handing out peppermints, his son's favourite candy. In February 1965, the *Northern Sentinel* reported that "Mr. Kirby lives by himself, does his own cooking and walks downtown every day for his mail, waving to friends and distributing peppermints."[11] He was said to credit his long life to that daily walk. "Even on sub-zero days he wore only a suit, sweater underneath and a good scarf," Winnie Robinson wrote. "Everyone, friend or stranger would be greeted with 'Here's a pep,' an English peppermint—the flat kind. He bought them by the carton. ... Sometimes the 'peps' were warm and sticky, sometimes a bit fuzzy from the wooly sweater pocket but always they were a sincere greeting from a friendly old timer. ... His spring flowers were always the first to bloom, on the sunny slope by his house on 9th Avenue North."[12]

In 1965, when Kirby reached one hundred years old, the Masons and the ladies of the Anglican church organized a tea for him at his home. That March he was able to blow out the hundred candles on the birthday cake at the dinner the Masons organized for him. The *Interior News* reported he could still read without glasses and, apart for an occasional dizzy spell, could still get around well. He said he was happy to be independent and enjoyed watching people coming and going along Ninth Avenue, where he lived. His mind, the newspaper said, was still sharp and his memory clear.[13] It could have taken him back to the pioneer days of Hazelton when Jim May, Ezra Evans and the packer Cataline paced the trails to the Omineca and even further back to his early days in the British Army in India in the 1880s. Later in 1965, he died.

There are still people alive today who remember James Kirby.

12

Horace and Alice Wrinch and Their Arrival in Kispiox

September 1900

Finally they had arrived. They were in Kispiox, standing on the stony banks of the Skeena River. They were alone with each other, a newly married couple, embarking on their lifelong mission. The moment that Dr. Horace Wrinch helped his wife, Alice, out of the canoe at Kispiox, their lives were divided into a before and an after. Before, they were medical professionals in the busy metropolis of Toronto; after, they were medical missionaries in a quiet frontier town in northern British Columbia. Their new lives now began.

They would have felt very much on their own. Their families and friends were in Ontario, thousands of miles away. Their new friends, Revs. Robert Whittington and Dennis Jennings, had returned to Port Essington at the mouth of the Skeena.

Here in Kispiox, a few miles upriver from Hazelton, the only person they knew was the Methodist minister, Rev. William Pierce, whom they had met once or twice in Ontario when Pierce had been touring and preaching. A powerful and charismatic preacher, Pierce was half Tsimshian. When his mother died soon after his birth, his grandparents banished the Scottish father and brought the child up on the coast. Pierce took credit for persuading Wrinch to come to the Upper Skeena.[1]

Apart from Pierce's often bedridden wife, Horace and Alice were the only non-Indigenous people in the village of over three hundred. Their knowledge of local languages would have been rudimentary at best. Although they may have learned some Chinook Jargon from books on the long train journey from Toronto, the Gitxsan language of the people around them now would have been incomprehensible.

Gitxsan villagers helped them up the riverbank and unloaded their luggage close to where George Chismore had landed over thirty years before. Their luggage included the portable organ and the sewing machine Alice had brought with her from Toronto. The Kispiox River, shallow but fast flowing, bubbled over the stones and joined the mighty Skeena at this spot. The two rivers merged close to where Western Union had built its now long-burned-down supply base, Fort Stager. It was very quiet. Along the riverbank was the village with its array of storytelling totem poles. (It would later be moved farther from the river after flooding.)

Here and there in the branches of the trees, bald eagles, with their white heads, watched for fish.

Here their dreams of medical missionary work and the anticipation of doing God's will—everything they had been working toward for the last few years—ended. The door to their old lives had closed firmly and irrevocably. Toronto would already have seemed a lifetime ago! Now they could only look forward. Their mission was to provide medical services for the Indigenous and non-Indigenous people on the Upper Skeena. Furthermore, they wanted to build a hospital, which—if they could do it—would be the first in the northern interior of the province.

Horace would be the first resident doctor and Alice the first resident nurse in an area that stretched to Edmonton in the east and from Atlin near the Yukon border south to the Cariboo. To be sure, medical men had visited Hazelton before. George Chismore had passed through in 1866, 1870 and again in 1871, but he had stayed only a short time on each occasion. Richard Loring—the Indian agent—and the missionaries had for many years provided medical care to the best of their respective abilities. Dr. Alfred Bolton had been busy with medical work on the coast. At Meanskinisht, the City of God, downriver, Rev. Robert Tomlinson also provided much-needed medical care. Although Tomlinson had taken medical training in Dublin, he was not a qualified doctor or surgeon, either in Ireland or in British Columbia. However, his training was good enough that, when he was based on the Nass River in 1868, he had ambitions of building a mission hospital.

Horace and Alice's journey had started in Toronto in mid-July. In some ways, though, it began when they first decided to become medical missionaries. Born in 1866, Horace had spent most of his early life farming, first when growing up on a farm in England and then later in Halton County, Ontario. In the early 1890s he heard the call to become a medical missionary. To this end, in 1899, he qualified as a doctor and surgeon at Trinity Medical College in Toronto, winning top honours. He turned down offers of a good career in Toronto to come to Hazelton as a medical missionary. On June 16, 1900, a few weeks before he left Ontario, he married Alice Breckon, the daughter of a neighbour in Halton. A qualified teacher and trained nurse, she shared his religious fervour and practical ability.[2]

Horace and Alice journeyed across the vast spaces of Ontario and the prairies to Vancouver. They took a small steamer up the coast to Port Essington, where they arrived on August 27, 1900. After spending a week there and at Port Simpson seeing people—among whom would have been the Anglican missionary William Hogan and May, his nineteen-year-old daughter, as well as the aging William Duncan—they then boarded the sternwheeler *Monte Cristo* for the journey upriver to Hazelton. From there Horace and Alice carried on to Kispiox, either going all the way by canoe or, more likely, going as far as they could by wagon and then crossing over the Skeena by canoe.

Travelling with Horace and Alice upriver from the coast was Rev. Robert Whittington, the new superintendent for missions for British Columbia, and Rev. Dennis Jennings, a missionary based at Port Essington. Charles French, the Hudson's Bay Company factor at Babine, and his wife, Jenette, were among their fellow passengers. With them also was the Newfoundland puppy that Rev. Smith Stanley Osterhout had given Horace in Port Simpson. Horace said he was hoping to train it to pull a sled.

Horace and Alice Wrinch on their wedding day in Halton, Ontario, June 16, 1900. Image courtesy of the author

Any journey up the Skeena was an adventure. Even in the months between May and October, it was a torrent of fast-moving, usually (but not always) shallow waters, with roving sand and gravel bars and fierce contrary currents, of sharp bends, of dangerous rapids and narrow canyons, rocks and islets. Steamers often had to pull themselves through the canyons using long hawsers attached to ringbolts hammered into the rocks. In the 180 miles from Hazelton to the coast, the river dropped over 800 feet. Depending on conditions, going up could take a sternwheeler between six and twenty days. Going down could take as little as one day.

Whittington later described this journey with Horace up the Skeena:

On Monday, Bro[ther] Jennings, Dr. and Mrs. Wrinch and myself started up the Skeena for Kish-py-ax [Kispiox]. For six days and a half we stemmed the rapid current, twenty-nine times the steel wire hawser three thousand feet long was used to pull us through the worst places, and three times it snapped and left us whirling down stream to smoother water. Nerve tension as great sometimes as hawser tension. A sail up the Skeena must always be one of thrilling interest.

Visited all our work on the Upper Skeena, and on Wednesday, September 5, in the early morning, started down river again. What a mad rush, landscape whirling all around us, now shooting a rapid, sometimes

The Skeena River steamer *Inlander* coming through Kitselas Canyon. Image P1912 courtesy of the Bulkley Valley Museum

The SS *Hazelton* attaching a line to the rock to pull itself through a difficult spot on the Skeena River. Image D-01864 courtesy of the Royal BC Museum and Archives

bumping the bottom, but always flying swiftly along. The upward toil of six and one-half days was retraced in a downward rush of one. The Skeena is the sail of a lifetime.[3]

He later added, "So great was the fascination that all day long the passengers stood at the front of the boat watching the straining hawser as it wound us slowly up past these whirling rapids."[4]

The *Monte Cristo* arrived in Hazelton on September 2 or 3, 1900. The arrival of the steamer was always a big day in town. It brought mail, supplies of food and liquor, old friends and new faces. The crew would have lowered the gangplank across the rocks to the bank, and then disembarking passengers would have crossed to the dry land in front of the stores and warehouses. A crowd of

Gitxsan residents, settlers, children, traders and a cacophony of barking dogs would have greeted them. At this time Hazelton had a population of approximately forty non-Indigenous people, although there were always many prospectors and others passing through. Approximately three hundred Gitxsan people lived in Gitanmaax, the village on the bench above the town. The Gitxsan reserve there enclosed Hazelton on three sides. The Skeena River ran along the fourth.

Horace and Alice spent the first couple of weeks with the lay preacher Robert Cole. He lived across the Bulkley River on land owned by the Methodist Church on Mission Point. This was the place where, before he had moved across the river to found Hazelton, Thomas Hankin had lived over thirty years before. Here Horace and Alice could get their bearings and become acquainted with the residents of Hazelton. They would have been aware that many people in town were impatient with missionaries, seeing them as troublemakers, not to be trusted. Building a hospital would be impossible without their moral and financial help.

Horace was determined to build a hospital as soon as he could. He and Whittington, before he went back downriver, looked around the district for a suitable site. They could not decide on anywhere at the time, but both thought there should not be a problem in starting construction the following year. This turned out to be overly optimistic.

After they moved to Kispiox, Horace and Alice rented a house from a Gitxsan lay preacher named Edward Sexsmith. Here, in a lean-to beside the house, Horace established his medical office. He performed surgeries either on the kitchen table or in the patient's own home. He often performed surgeries on a door he took with him to provide a reliably flat surface. He surrounded the surgical area with sheets soaked in carbolic to keep it as antiseptic as possible.[5]

Horace described this house in Kispiox to friends back in Ontario:

> At present Mrs. Wrinch and I are living in an Indian log house. Please don't conclude from this statement that we are in a shanty too low for one to stand upright in, or that we have to cock over a log fire made on the ground in the middle of the floor in the one room in the house. In some few Indian houses this would be true. But ours is somewhat more pretentious than that. We have it divided into four rooms, and have a loft above, which is most useful as a store room, and have also two (small) cellars under the floor. Altogether we are (although somewhat cramped for space) very comfortable; and very much more so than I expected we could be until we had built our own home. Now we shall have time to look round for the most suitable place for our house, and can build it more at our convenience than if we were camping out until we could get into it.[6]

Horace and Alice Wrinch in their travelling clothes soon after they arrived in Kispiox. Image courtesy of the author

Dr. Horace Wrinch at work. Image courtesy of the author

Not long after their arrival, Horace received an urgent message from Charles French at Fort Babine, sixty-eight miles east of Hazelton. French had travelled upriver with the Wrinches and had obviously spread word of the arrival of a doctor. A group of Indigenous people there were sick. They had asked French to see if the new doctor could come to help them. Could he come at once? Well, yes. How could he not? But it would be a two-to-three-day journey and a hard one at that.

Horace described this trip to his friend Rev. Egerton Roswell Doxsee at Albert College, his old school in Ontario. He wrote that after receiving the call he had found a guide, a saddle horse for each of them and a third horse to carry the tent, provisions, cooking apparatus, axe and medicines. He said he doubted they could reach Babine in two days on horseback.[7]

Kispiox. Image P0754 courtesy of the Bulkley Valley Museum

They started late on a Tuesday morning because one of the horses had to be shod before they could leave. After swimming the horses across the river, they reloaded the pack horse, saddled the other horses and set out. That first day, Horace said, they made good time. By about 6:00 p.m. the following day, Wednesday, they were looking for a good place to camp. They came round a point from which they could see, beyond a band of spruce or balsam, a large valley with a lake winding along it. They could just distinguish some horses at its upper end, which they realized must be Fort Babine. They were undecided about whether to camp. The guide estimated the distance at about three or four miles. Horace, an experienced horseman from his time on the farm in Ontario, thought it looked like more. However, he deferred to the guide, who he assumed knew the land well, and they decided to finish their journey that night.

Horace wrote that he did not relish that ride in the dark, having to avoid stumps, stones, branches and mudholes. They just had to let the horses find their own way through the trees. By nine-thirty they were outside the palisade of the Hudson's Bay Company post and did full justice to the supper given them. The actual distance, they now learned, had been eight miles.

Horace tended to the patients and left medicine for them. After giving the horses a day's rest, he and his guide started back. On their way home, they shot half a dozen grouse. On the Saturday it was raining heavily, and the horses started slipping over the wet trail. Since the horses preferred to ride on the side of the trail, where the path was not so muddy, the riders became very wet as they brushed past the branches and trees. By five that Saturday evening, they had arrived on the opposite side of the river from Kispiox. Now they had to swim the horses across the river. Not, said the doctor, a journey he wanted to make every week.[8]

The Wrinches settled into their new home, meeting people and making friends. One of these would have been Simon Gunanoot, a well-respected trapper, who kept the store in town. Alice worked in the Sunday school and started community health work. She also taught sewing to Gitxsan women. Mrs. Wrinch, Rev. Pierce wrote, held a church picnic in the snow on December 28.[9] At the time of their arrival, over half of the approximately three hundred inhabitants of Kispiox were described as being Christian. Horace helped Pierce build the new Methodist church, which, when it opened at the end of 1901, had space for four hundred worshippers.

Horace walked to Hazelton and back once a week to dispense medical care. This was a distance of approximately ten miles each way, depending on whether he went by water, by dogsled over ice or on foot. It was actually easier in winter because walking on the flat ice of the river was better than climbing up and down hills. If he went by horse, he would have had to swim the horse across at least one river, which was not really practical, so he usually walked. The Newfoundland dog that Rev. Osterhout had given him made itself useful carrying medical supplies on its back. Dogs were commonly used as pack animals in Hazelton at that time.

Very soon, Horace was turning his thoughts to a hospital. At this point, he had no land and no money. All his supplies—building materials, medicines and food—would have to be brought up the river when it was navigable. But he was determined to build a hospital. And build it he did.

He raised money. He selected and acquired a suitable site, and in 1902 he and Alice moved from Kispiox to a rented house in Hazelton. This was more convenient for Horace to supervise the construction first of their family home and then of the hospital. While the hospital was being built, they opened their own home for surgeries and as a place of convalescence. In the year between completion of their home and the opening of the new hospital, thirty-one patients lived with them, seventeen of whom were Indigenous people. The patients shared meals with the family, played with the couple's two young children and sang hymns around Alice's organ.

The Hazelton Hospital, which opened in the autumn of 1904, was the first hospital in the northern interior of the province. Horace established a training school for nurses and a hospital farm in the hospital grounds to provide food for the patients, for staff and for their growing family. With the river being closed to steamer traffic for half the year and with no roads or rail, this farm was essential for the operation of the hospital.

Horace would stay in Hazelton until 1936, becoming a much-loved community leader. As a member of the legislature in Victoria in the 1920s, he became known as a champion for public health insurance. Alice, his dedicated companion in all his endeavours, had their first child in the autumn of 1900 and went on to have four more children in the next dozen years. In 1923, after having been a source of strength to him and to the community for over twenty years, she died of cancer and was buried in the cemetery on the top of the bluff overlooking Hazelton.

When Horace died in October 1939, the *Vancouver Sun* described him as the most beloved man in northern British Columbia.[10] The Hazelton Hospital, renamed Wrinch Memorial Hospital after his death, remains as a tribute to his years of dedicated service.

13

Sperry Cline and the Suspended Corpse

1904

A traveller on the trail between Hazelton and the telegraph cabin of Kuldo on a snowy day in the last days of December 1904 would have received a shock. There, hanging from a branch, was a corpse. Beneath it was a fire, being tended by a young man the traveller might have recognized as Sperry Cline, who then would have had some explaining to do.

Fourteen-year-old Sperry Cline from Elgin County, Ontario, was in England in late 1895 or early 1896. How and why he was there is not entirely clear. Cecil Clark, a fellow policeman, who knew him, said he had travelled there on a cattle boat, perhaps as a worker. Since Cline had grown up on the farm of his father, Jonas, this explanation is as good as any. Young Sperry, who had been christened Jonas Perry—hence the Sperry—was on the loose in the urban wilderness of London in the 1890s. Any stories about his time there are, regrettably, lost in the dust of history.

Sometime in 1896, Cline found his way to South Africa, where he took a job with the British South Africa Company. He joined the British South Africa Police, the paramilitary police force this company operated. With this force, he took part in the Second Matabele War. What he did in this conflict—called by many the first war for independence in what is now Zimbabwe—is not known, but this force did help relieve the besieged city of Bulawayo and defeat the Matabele warriors in the Matobo Hills. After the war ended in 1897, it appears he went back to London and did—who knows what? But by the end of December 1899, he was ready for another adventure.

By 1900, the Boer War was raging. The Canadian government raised a regiment, largely composed of cowboys and members of the North-West Mounted Police, to assist the imperial government in London. Cline enlisted in London with the Second Canadian Mounted Rifles on December 26, 1899. His enlistment papers recorded that he was five foot nine, with an intelligence described as fair and a temperament described as sanguine. He had a fair complexion, brown hair, blue eyes and good teeth. He was just what the army wanted.

When the main body of his regiment arrived in England from Canada on February 21, 1900, Cline joined it and then sailed with it to South Africa, arriving in Cape Town one month later. The force soon saw action. He was likely present at the fierce engagement at Leliefontein on November 7. So sharp was the action on this day that three Victoria Crosses were won by Cline's battalion. The British press gave much praise to the Canadian troops. On November 8, Lord Roberts, the commander-in-chief (James Kirby's "Bobs" from his time in India), wrote in his official report, "The rear on the return march was defended by Colonel [François-Louis] Lessard with the Canadian Dragoons and two Royal Canadian guns. ... No praise is too high for the devoted gallantry these troops showed in keeping the enemy off the infantry and the convoys. In the afternoon an event unpreced-ented in this war, I believe, occurred. Some 200 mounted Boers suddenly charged the rearguard to within 70 yards of it. Then they were stopped by the Canadian Dragoons."[1] Though obviously a much smaller and less famous engagement than the battle on Vimy Ridge, Leliefontein can be considered an early building block of Canadian national identity. A grateful British government awarded Cline the Queen's Medal for service in the war, with clasps for the Cape Colony, the Orange Free State and the Transvaal.

When the regiment returned to Canada in 1901, Cline came with it. He left the army on January 10 of that year. Now at loose ends in Ontario, he had likely seen too much of the world to want to settle down to farm like his father, Jonas. Tragedy then befell his family. For whatever reason, Jonas walked along the Michigan Central line and was killed by a train. Sometime in that same year of 1901, Cline, still seeking adventure, came west to British Columbia.

Conceivably, the fever of gold had infected his imagination, as it had for so many others, because he first went north, either to the Yukon or to a mining town such as Atlin. Returning to Vancouver in 1902, he was looking for a job when a man approached him. Cline described what happened:

> I remained for a part of the winter in Vancouver, having put up at an hotel that was frequented by mining men. One morning a man who had been at the hotel for several days was seated by me at table and during the meal remarked that he had noticed that I always ate a very hearty breakfast [and] then proceeded to ask if I wanted a job. I found that he was from Ottawa and was head of a mining company which had been working a lease in the Omineca for several years. He was preparing to take a crew of men into that district for the summer and was waiting for them to arrive at Ashcroft from Ottawa. I enquired as to why he was interested in my appetite—perhaps I might prove too expensive to board. He replied that a man who always ate a good breakfast could be relied upon to stay with him on the trail.
>
> He later explained that the crew would walk from Ashcroft to Quesnel while he went on ahead to make arrangements for further travel. He also explained that the wages would be two dollars and fifty cents per day to

commence at the time we started actual work at the mine. I was getting low on funds and accepted his offer.

The walk up the Cariboo Road was a pleasant experience. We stopped at night at the old road houses where we met many of the original miners of the Cariboo and by the time we reached Quesnel I had become fascinated with the country and its people.

From Quesnel to Manson Creek we pulled our supplies and outfits on toboggans, teamed up two men to one toboggan. The inhabitants of the Omineca were all men such as I have described and I came to know many of them intimately and the more I got to know of them the greater became my admiration for them.[2]

With a population of no more than forty non-Indigenous people, Hazelton was the nearest big town to Manson Creek. Cline would have visited the town for supplies and recreation and likely to spend the winter. He became acquainted with the men of the North—packers such as Cataline and prospectors such as Jim May, Joe Lyon and Ezra Evans. With his experience and his rough and ready competence, Cline was a useful man to have around. He settled in Hazelton.

When the news of a young man's death on the telegraph line at Kuldo arrived in Hazelton on Christmas Day in 1904, Edward Hicks Beach, the local coroner, realized he would have to hold an inquest. Someone, though, had to bring the body back to town through the sixty miles of snowy forest in the northern winter. He asked Cline to do it.

Hicks Beach was a young, well-educated and well-connected Englishman who had started out to reach the Klondike on the Skeena route a few years before but had given up and stayed in Hazelton. One of the few professional men in town at the time, he was, in addition to being the coroner, also a magistrate, notary public, insurance salesman and real estate agent. Possibly he was a remittance man, one of those sons of England supplied with regular payments of money from home.

Cline, sworn in as a special constable for the job, set out for Kuldo on Boxing Day, accompanied by Tommy Hughes and John MacIntosh. Hughes was being sent out to replace the dead man as the telegraph operator. MacIntosh was an experienced dog musher and knew the trails.

The telegraph line from the south to the Yukon had been completed in 1901. Every thirty miles there were cabins for the operators, who worked in pairs. The operators were completely isolated, especially in the long, cold winters. Pack trains such as the one run by the famous packer Cataline brought them their supplies. Some telegraph operators drank too much. A few went mad from the isolation.

A short time before Christmas, someone had taken a supply of liquor to one of the cabins on the line. The telegraph operators prepared for a Christmas celebration. On Christmas Eve, the young operator at Kuldo had gone to the next cabin to collect his bottle of Christmas cheer, had drunk far too much and, on the way back to his own cabin, had perished in the snow. Cline noted wryly that the dead man was unaccustomed to drinking.[3]

Cline's job was to put the corpse on a toboggan and bring it back to Hazelton for the inquest. The body, though, had been discovered face down in the snow, frozen solid, spread-eagled, with arms and legs stretched in an awkward position. This made carrying him on a low toboggan through the forest in deep snow impossible.

Cline and his companion realized they had to try something else. They located a suitable tree and passed a rope over a branch. Then they hoisted the body up and lit a fire under it to thaw it. This took fourteen hours. Cline said he was grateful no one had come across them while they were doing it. After they thought the body was sufficiently thawed, they rearranged the limbs comfortably at attention and loaded it back on the toboggan, where it froze solid again. Cline arrived in Hazelton and delivered the refrozen corpse to the coroner. Dr. Horace Wrinch, the only doctor in town, performed the autopsy. Both coroner and doctor commented on the oddly unnatural pose of the body but did not ask questions. Dr. Wrinch merely noted the remarkable quantity of alcohol in the young man's body.

The inquest was held in the old log building that served as police office, jail and courthouse. Hicks Beach asked Cline to collect six men for the coroner's jury. He chose six of the oldest Omineca miners wintering in Hazelton, thinking they could make good use of the small stipend for their services as well as having the satisfaction of being useful to the community. The jurors took their duties seriously. They combed their grey hair, trimmed their beards and arrived for their duties in their Sunday-best clothes. Ezra Evans, the soft-spoken old miner from Caernarfon, was their foreman. Jim May and Joe Lyon were likely also on the jury.

The evidence was given. The coroner addressed the jury on what he thought was an open-and-shut case. The man was drunk and died in the snow. What could be clearer? The jury retired to a room in the nearby hotel to deliberate in private. After a time, it returned and announced its verdict. The man, it declared, had died of natural causes. This caused consternation—Cline's word—in court. No one was more astounded than the coroner, who thereupon admonished the jury for coming to a verdict that not only contradicted the presented evidence but was also at variance with his instructions to them. Why, he asked, testily, had they come to such an irrational verdict?

From left to right, Chief Constable John Kelly, Simon Gunanoot, Constable Sperry Cline and Inspector Thomas W.S. Parsons in 1919. Gunanoot had recently surrendered to Sperry Cline and would soon face trial for the 1906 murder of Alex MacIntosh. Image B-04313 courtesy of the Royal BC Museum and Archives

The foreman of the jury informed him that in their view it was quite natural for a man to get drunk at Christmas. And so—death by natural causes. With what he considered a frivolous explanation, Hicks Beach had to be content.

Cline, however, knew the jury had performed its duties with care and seriousness. A few months later, he asked Ezra Evans what the real reason for the verdict had been. Evans told him that the dead man had an old mother living in eastern Canada. Rather than have her think that her son had died as a result of drinking "and thereby break her heart,"[4] Evans said, they preferred she spend the rest of her days believing her son had died doing his duty as a hero in the wilderness.

For the next ten years Cline knocked around Hazelton doing some packing, some mining and some mail carrying to and from the coast. He also did some prospecting. In 1911 he announced he had struck a worthwhile project—ore with silver lead and high-grade copper—in his Silver Pick project on Nine Mile Mountain, but nothing seemed to come of that. He was even a pilot on a river boat, although, as he cheerfully admitted, he had no knowledge whatsoever of the shoals, sandbars and rocks of the Lower Skeena. His nickname was Dutch because he used so many Afrikaans words he had acquired when he was in South Africa.

Cline, it has to be admitted, was scruffy. On account of his unshaven face, uncombed hair, shirt open to his waist and unlaced boots with his trousers tucked in the top, he looked, Cecil Clark wrote, like a stocky scarecrow that had escaped from a farmer's field.[5] When he later joined the British Columbia Provincial

Police, it seems he reformed and tolerated the uniform. Conceivably, though, it was Euphemia, a nurse at Hazelton Hospital, whom he married in 1913, who achieved that sartorial miracle.

In 1914, a gang of seven Russian robbers tried to rob the Union Bank in New Hazelton. The citizens saw them, surrounded the bank with their rifles and in the ensuing shootout shot three dead. Cline was sworn in as a special constable in the posse that went to find the remaining four robbers in the woods, three of whom were wounded and brought in. He then joined the police force as a regular constable in the Hazelton detachment. His wide experience and sturdy common sense stood him in good stead. This helped him negotiate the surrender to justice of the accused murderer Simon Gunanoot in 1919.

Sperry Cline later in life. Image F-02731 courtesy of the Royal BC Museum and Archives

Nor was the Kuldo telegraph operator the only body he brought back. In 1922 he made a round trip of fifteen days to recover the body of a man named Murdock at the fifth telegraph cabin.

Sperry Cline left Hazelton in 1926 but remained a member of the provincial police. Cline was stationed first in Chemainus, then in Smithers and later in Powell River. After he retired in 1946, he often wrote about his time in Hazelton and the North.

Cline was adventurous, cheerful and competent at almost anything he turned his hand to. He practised many trades. He had started as a policeman in South Africa and ended as a policeman in British Columbia. In between he had been a miner, a river pilot, a packer, a mail carrier and a resourceful corpse retriever.

14

Mr. Sargent, Mr. Loring and Their Bitter Feud

1899–1904

N ot all was harmony and Christian goodwill among the residents in Hazelton. For at least half a dozen years at the turn of the twentieth century, a bitter dispute divided the community. The roots lay partly in a clash between federal and provincial authorities, partly in religion, but mainly in personalities. Although it is hard to assess when it started and when it ended, the ongoing battle stretched at least from 1899 to 1904, with early 1900 apparently being the epicentre.

On one side was Richard Loring, the Indian agent with magisterial powers under the Indian Act. Loring was a federal employee, Low Church, with deep roots in the Hazelton community. A Saxon, conscientious and hard-working, he wrote about the personal conflict to his boss in Victoria, Arthur Vowell, who was the superintendent of Indian Affairs for the province. Since we have more letters of complaint from Loring than from his opponent, it is tempting to believe his side of the story presents a more accurate picture.

On the other side was Richard Sargent. Born in Prince Edward Island in 1873, Sargent had come across the country in the late 1870s to Qu'Appelle, where his father had been appointed an Anglican minister. In 1891, the Hudson's Bay Company hired young Sargent and sent him to the west coast as an apprentice clerk. Company archives indicate that he spent five years on the coast at Port Simpson and Masset before coming to Hazelton in 1896 to take over the management of the Hudson's Bay Company store. When he arrived, Hazelton had a population of approximately eighteen, mainly composed of Loring's blended family, Rev. John Field and his wife, and prospectors such as Jim May, Ezra Evans and Joe Lyon.

Sargent managed the Company's store until May 1900, when he resigned and went into business in town with a partner. Meanwhile he had been appointed the postmaster, a position he held until 1927. In 1898, over the objections of Vowell, who had met him and thought him unsuitable for the job, the provincial government appointed him a magistrate, a position he held until 1902.[1]

Variously described in the Hudson's Bay Company records as "young, clever and steady" and "bright, capable and too independent," Sargent was younger than Loring.[2] As a young bachelor in town, he was not noticeably tethered to domesticity. Loring's letters paint a picture of an irresponsible young man, given to wildness. Once, Sargent, a magistrate himself, was even convicted of being drunk and disorderly.[3] Loring wrote that Sargent, a strong Anglican, was supported by Rev. John Field, the Anglican minister in town.

Loring believed Sargent sold liquor illegally to Gitxsan drinkers and sold liquor to whites knowing it was going to be resold illegally. For his part, Sargent had little respect for Loring and made no secret of it. Loring, who took such conflict to heart, remonstrated with Sargent, who laughed at him. At one time, he wrote that he was not on speaking terms with Sargent.[4] Every time he mailed a letter of complaint about Sargent to Vowell, he would have had to take it to the post office in Sargent's store to mail it. This must at times have been awkward.

A glimpse of Loring's problems can be seen in his letter to Robert Tomlinson, downriver at Meanskinisht. Loring was writing after midnight, when his family was away from home:

Richard Strong Sargent, the adversary of Richard Loring. Sargent later became a highly respected citizen and community leader in Hazelton. Image D-07019 courtesy of the Royal BC Museum and Archives

Things are getting here from bad to worse. ... The getting of the JP-ship [JP meaning justice of the peace] (and the liquor license) was accomplished by getting the signature of every drunken ruffian passing through here, actually within the store, which were anything but good sense. I have noticed petition after petition being signed by strangers in transit, under free and unlimited application of liquor.

The license for the latter must have been obtained under circumstances other than existing, and regardless of stipulations regarding the statutes, requiring, inter alia, hotel and dining-rooms, beds, stable-room, etc. etc. I am convinced, beyond a doubt, that not a single signature was got here, unless it be of Mr. and Mrs. Field. The latter two are at any time prepared to see the country sink into calamity, so long as Mr. Sargent is thereby served. Those desire the end desire the means. In front and about the neighborhood of their house the lowest and most degrading spectacles are almost daily on exhibition. ...

Mr. [Robert] Cole has seen, through a field-glass, departing canoes pass his place wherein strangers handed the bottle around the Indian crew. I am here now, if present affairs were to remain, merely a check on the very worst. ...

Like occurrences could scarcely transpire without notice before a C.M.S. [Church Missionary Society] mission establishment in every remotest part in the darkest of Africa. ... Anything pertaining thereto is passively countenanced, sub rosa, hidden under a cloud of subterfuges and confined to chuckling over the difficulties. ... The Indian population will bear me out in everything occurred, whilst the know-all here, with courteous pretense, simper amiable denials of all obvious facts, and will be loaded down with "don't remembers," etc., in contrast with the exceeding minuteness of particulars about other matters. ... One would prefer the wolf that does not disguise itself in sheep's clothing, or in also persistently seeking fault on one's part. ... I find it far too frequent that when the troubles of the day have ended, worse than those, those of the night begin. ...

The defamatory declamations against me by countrymen to whom this town, and recollections thereof, consists of no more than having spent a night or two here of drunkenness and debauchery, were too readily accepted by the authorities at Victoria without corroboration, excepting that of their companions. Mainly, in that I breached my authority in upholding law and order, regarding which I always take particular care to disarm criticism and forestall complaint. ...

During December '97, everybody was left mightily disturbed by the, at all times, firing of guns, tooting of horns, rattling stones in coal-oil tins, name-calling, the ringing of the bell—which by the way is C.M.S.'s property—the latter, at least, could have been stopped as contributing to the pandemonium if Mr. Field had made simply a single objection. And, my constable, Frank Pugh, was shot at from inside of the H.B.C.'s stockade at 11:30 p.m. on the night of the 18th of the same month while tolling the bell on the death of Lucy (Tom Lagh's wife) a member of that church. ...

After "Messrs." Sargent's and Devereux's leaving here on December 22 and during their absence till the 31st, Devereux, at Babine, tore down my notices on the approaches of the bridge spanning Babine Lake to which the present J.P. was a consenting party. Mr. [Charles] French begged me to send these notices to keep the Indians from horse-racing thereon. On Mr. French's remonstrations for the actions he was met with a rebuke from Mr. Sargent. ...

It is my purpose to draw attention to these facts only to show to what an extent they convey a policy of reckless insolences, treacherous antagonism and insensate hostility, the strength marked with evil tendencies to be safely treated with leniency. ...

The incongruity, the absurdity of trusting such illimitable power to those who are incapable of an idea beyond that of selfish indulgence of their lust, that of propensity for mischief and whose very instincts are base. ...

Of paramount necessity such disgraceful state of affairs can only be made to disappear by a fundamental attack on the evil and removal of their causes. ... The assertions made by me are not audacious and can be proved point by point.

I am, at present, writing like in a fever born of desperation. My family is at the ranch. My heart feels the sting of bitterness. I am alone past midnight—the idea comes to mind of all the wrongs, of late years, experienced. I find driven in upon myself. In that I know your sympathies are with me, and trust, combining a defensive as well as an offensive alliance in all communications of this sort.[5]

In another letter Loring states that the "contumacious [wilfully disobedient] conduct of Mr. Sargent ... is without parallel and precedent in treacherous antagonism. On several occasions, I came to Mr. Sargent's rescue, and his very existence here I made possible but past favours seem as nothing compared with the satisfying of personal spite."[6]

Richard Sargent knew his enemy. When he heard that a petition was being circulated in Hazelton asking that his liquor licence be cancelled, he had his own petition prepared and signed. On January 9, 1900, he submitted it to the attorney general:

We, the undersigned white residents of Hazelton, having been informed that a petition is afoot in this neighbourhood praying for the withdrawal of the liquor license held by the Hudson's Bay Company at Hazelton and at the same time reflecting discreditably on the character of Mr. R.S. Sargent our highly esteemed Justice of the Peace; and having unsuccessfully sought to get sight of the document we beg to make the following statement for your information and guidance in case said petition should reach you,

1. We believe and have every opportunity of knowing that the licence has not been abused, but on the contrary has been most carefully handled and having never heard of a single instance showing the opposite, and that the

conduct of the people both white and Indians during the time that the licence has been in force, compares not unfavourably with that of the time preceding. We hear that it is alleged in the petition referred to above that drunkenness is on the increase among the Indians and is attributed to the existence of said licence. This we utterly deny and further affirm that the liquor if any that finds its way to the Indians is not worth mentioning. One resident affirms that he was shown the petition and, having refused to support it, was requested to keep it secret.

2. We have great pleasure in testifying to Mr. R.S. Sargent's integrity, high sense of honour, love of justice and congratulate the Provincial Government in having men of his stamp representing it on the bench of justice. The population of Hazelton is twenty and we, the supporters of this, number, as you will see below, and yet the petition has been withheld from us. We leave you to draw your own inference from this.

Any communication in regard to the above may be addressed to C.J. Morison, Hazelton, BC.[7]

The signatories included John Field (Clerk in Holy Orders), Charles Morison, W.J. Larkworthy, Charles Paquett, a couple of others and about a dozen prospectors, one of whom was Ezra Evans. Charles Morison was George Chismore's friend from as long ago as 1866.

A correspondent who called himself Bystander, but sounds as if it could well be Richard Sargent himself, wrote a letter to the Victoria *Daily Colonist* in February 1900 complaining that Loring's actions were entirely unjustified and illegal.[8] The residents of Hazelton, he wrote, were scandalized by Loring's behaviour. The newspaper published a note the following day putting as much distance as it could between itself and that letter and cautioning letter writers to check their facts before mailing their letters to the newspaper for publication. Clearly someone had spoken to the paper and informed it that, as Indian agent, Loring had every right to act the way he did.

Sargent also wrote about an incident resulting from the presence of two magistrates in town, one federally appointed and one provincially appointed. Loring had arrested a man for selling liquor illegally on the Gitanmaax reserve and put him in a lock-up on his own property. Sargent, a provincial magistrate, objected to this alleged encroachment on his authority. He wrote:

On the night of the 23 inst. a white man happened to be on the Indian Reserve in one of the houses. The man was arrested by Indians sent by the Indian agent for the purpose and conveyed to a *private lock-up* on the agent's premises, tried next morning in the agent's house *in private*, the prisoner having asked and been refused permission to send for one or more of his friends, and, after being urged to plead guilty, was sentenced to two months' imprisonment or a fine of $100. All this was done without a reference to me whatever, although the attorney-general had instructed the agent to refer all criminal matters to the Justices of the Peace. ...

I at once determined to look into the matter and asked several of the residents of the town to accompany me to the agent's house. We expressed our surprise at such secret proceedings and informed him that we were of the opinion that he had acted illegally and that the man should be released, pointing out at the same time that if he wished to bring the man to justice a proper course was open to him. The agent after demurring slightly released the prisoner.

It would seem that after I refused to receive a prisoner from Mr. Loring, whom he had condemned to six months hard labour (of this case I have already communicated with you) a *private jail* has been set up in the agent's premises.

The course pursued by Mr. Loring in this matter is, I take it, in direct opposition to the wishes and instructions of the Provincial Government. Can it be possible that Mr. Loring does not clearly understand what a criminal matter is or that he doubts the Provincial Government's right to send in its local officers?

Before the appointment of Mr. [Edward] Stephenson and myself took place, the feeling of the people here was anything but in sympathy with Mr. Loring's high-handedness and overruling way of doing things, of which the case when he sent some Indians down into the town of Hazelton to lock up some white men, against when there had been no complaint, is sufficient proof.

I have been greatly harassed by Mr. Loring's actions lately and trust that this will be the last time I will be competent to report to yourself of his interference.

The man before referred to as being privately locked-up, tried and condemned, has since complained to me desiring legal proceedings against Mr. Loring but I told him that I would first refer the matter to the attorney-general. Please instruct me as to what steps I am to take in case the man complaining insists on my acting on his information.

I cannot understand what is prompting Mr. Loring to such open disregard and, I think, I may say, contempt of the instructions of the Provincial Government.[9]

Serious allegations indeed. Loring wrote to Vowell about his side of the story, which perhaps sounds more credible:

One Charles Paquett (white) of here has for over a year past been continually committing himself against the Indian Act, by vending Indians, bringing in innumerable instances liquor on the reserve. He, Chas. Paquett, several times also threatened the lives of Indians in the Hudson's Bay, for informing me on his doings. George Moore (Indian) came to me with charges, substantiated by others, of that nature, and again the Indian constable Long Charlie (Hagwilget). The latter was threatened by the said Paquett in a violent and boisterous manner in that establishment, to be shot, like a dog, on the 9th inst. and claims within the hearing of Mr. R.S. Sargent, J.P.

On the morning 12:30 of the 24th inst., I was awakened by knocking on my door and on seeing what was wanted, found an Indian constable, Jim Robinson, with others, having the said Charles Paquett in charge for being found drunk in an Indian woman's house on the reserve and having previously assaulted an Indian, Simon Peter Moat, by striking him in the face without provocation.

I had said Charles Paquett confined during the night in a dwelling back of my house, which I then had converted into a lock-up at the expense of $34 out of private means.

I arranged the trial of the said Charles Paquett for 10 a.m. of the same day (24th inst.) whereat I imposed, after the plea of guilty, on him (Paquett) a sentence of two (2) months of confinement or a fine of $105, according to one leading part of Section 99 of the Indian Act. ...

On the same Paquett's representation that Rev. Mr. Field and others would pay his fine, I allowed him to send a note to one Billy Stuart. At 12:55 thereafter, I was startled by a violent ringing of my door-bell by my step-son Thomas Hankin. The latter stated that Rev. Mr. Field [was] rushing in the greatest excitement from cabin to cabin getting up a party to rescue the said Charles Paquett. A party of eight (8) white men headed by Mr. Field and Mr. Sargent arrived almost simultaneously with my step-son.

On inquiring the party's errand, I was asked by Mr. Sargent if I had Paquett in my charge, to which I replied in the affirmative. Mr. Sargent said, in a very trembling condition, that he demanded the immediate release of the said Paquett. I acceded to the demand under protest. A copy of my letter of the 24th inst. to Mr. Sargent, bearing on the matter, I have the honour to append.

I am not heretofore known to give in to a wrong but acted on the judgement a demonstration would effect on the Indians under the deplorable condition of their affairs, especially of late. There are consequent thereof now Indians who are awaiting the first opportunity of seeing a blow struck. With the better class and law-abiding of Indians it required all my ingenuity to avert a conflict during and after the meeting-house swindle perpetrated on them. That instance, for one, stands in violation of Section 111 of the Indian Act. With the common impression prevailing among the Indians that there is, really, a law for the whites and none for them, their hatred of the former such as they are—becomes under the circumstances more and more apparent. Up to the present writing, the Indians are yet standing about in groups as to the possible outcome of it all. … On the afternoon of the 27 inst. Mr. Henry Martin, schoolteacher, pro temp., at Kispiox came to my office informing that the infection of conspiracy against me, and engendered here, is being spread at Kispiox.[10]

Sargent took the battle to higher authorities. In May 1900, he wrote to the attorney general:

Complaint of the Interference of Mr. Agent Loring in Criminal Matters
This business has been allowed to run much too far. Where is Loring getting his backing from? Does the Indian Department prompt him in his continuous interference with the Justices of the Peace of this neighbourhood? My letter of 27 January last pointed out to you very clearly that Mr. Loring had taken matters into his own hands and made provision for a secret lock-up and had tried a white man secretly. Do you wish this kind of thing to be continued. Am I, a Justice of the Peace, to allow such irregular proceedings as these to be continued? Has not Mr. Agent Loring been told on three distinct and several occasions to refer all complaints of a criminal nature to the Justice of Peace of the neighbourhood? In answer to this last question I would refer you to your three letters respectively—18 October, 1898, 17 November 1899 and 28 July 1900. Definite instructions will be much thankfully received.[11]

Hazelton was largely an Anglican town and had been since Bishop William Ridley's visit in 1880. The neighbouring villages of Kispiox and Gitsegukla were Methodist. Across the Bulkley River at Hagwilget were the Roman Catholics, and here Father Adrien-Gabriel Morice still held sway. Because there was no

Methodist church in Hazelton, the few Gitxsan Methodists there built a meeting house. When it was finished, a group of Anglicans led by Sargent and Rev. Field physically ejected the builders and owners and took possession of it for the Anglicans. The ejection notice pinned to the door was in Sargent's handwriting. Loring commented how unjust this was and that there had to be consequences for the violators, but there weren't any. The Gitxsan Methodists then promptly joined the Salvation Army.[12]

Loring was so annoyed with Rev. Field and his support of Sargent that he wrote a letter of complaint about him to the Church Missionary Society in London. "Mr. Field's indifference as to the Indian's moral character," he wrote, "has become notorious. ... With conciliatory intention as to the fact of the matter I repaired to see Mr. Field and received for my pains a torrent of laughter, indifference, and the reply, no one can remove me from here, not even the Bishop."[13]

This dispute reached up to the ministerial level in Ottawa, which reviewed the evidence and came down on the side of Loring. In July, John Douglas McLean, deputy minister of Indian Affairs, wrote to George Maxwell, a federal member of Parliament. Clearly, Sargent had been trying to pull Tory strings to fight back. McLean wrote:

> I beg leave to return herewith the letter from Mr. R.S. Sargent, J.P. of Victoria, B.C. in which he makes certain complaints about Mr. R.E. Loring, Indian Agent at Hazelton. I may state in this relation that the complaints referred to were carefully investigated some time ago, and from the result of this enquiry there would appear to be no doubt whatever that Mr. Loring has performed his duties faithfully both towards the Indians and the Department. There is evidence that he has endeavoured to suppress the liquor traffic among the Indians, and altogether has had a hard task to keep matters in order. Under the circumstances I hardly think there is any ground for making any further enquiries into Mr. Loring's conduct in connection with the discharge of his official duties.[14]

The dispute between the two men rumbled on through 1902, 1903 and 1904. In 1902, Edward C. Stephenson, Sargent's fellow magistrate, refused to sit on the bench with him any longer, citing his unseemly actions.[15] A briefing memorandum for the federal deputy minister of Indian Affairs that year described Sargent as anything but an estimable character. There was clear evidence, the memorandum stated, that Sargent had been trying to thwart Loring's attempts to suppress the illegal liquor trade.[16]

In September 1902, Sargent's business was in trouble. Some of his cheques had bounced.[17] His partner left the business. With a mortgage on his property and not much money coming in, it looked as though the end of his business was in sight. This was the lowest moment. But he survived.

There was no ultimate winner in the dispute. Neither Loring nor Sargent succeeded in having the other replaced. They had to live together in the same small community, isolated from the outside world for six months of the year. Both appear to have come to terms with coexistence. They may not likely have become friends or even friendly, but they had to work together. They both sat, for example, on the Hazelton Hospital board, which oversaw the administration of the hospital and the nurse training school.

Richard Loring retired as Indian agent in 1920 and went to live in Victoria. He died on October 6, 1934, and is buried in the Royal Oak cemetery.

Rev. John Field remained in Hazelton until 1917, when he retired for health reasons and moved to Duncan, on Vancouver Island. He left Hazelton with the reputation of a genial saint, always with a good word for everybody. When he died the following year, his obituary in the *Omineca Miner* said he was "universally respected and most highly esteemed by all, irrespective of race or creed."[18] Richard Sargent went to Duncan for his funeral. At the memorial service in Hazelton, Dr. Horace Wrinch gave the eulogy.

During the years in which the authorities were searching for Simon Gunanoot, the accused double murderer, the police strongly suspected that Sargent knew a lot more than he was willing to reveal. It was known, for example, that he bought furs from Gunanoot through middlemen such as George Beirnes. Many suspected that Sargent knew very well the whereabouts of Gunanoot and Peter Himadam, who had also gone into hiding. In 1909, the Pinkerton's operatives engaged by the police to hunt for the outlaw wrote of Sargent:

It is quite evident that Sargent knows, or at least has a very good idea of, the hiding place of these two Indians, but which information will take time to get. Sargent has a large trade with the Indians, and especially the Kispiox Indians, and this being the fact it will be hard to gain anything which would be a detriment to Simon and Peter.[19]

In September 1911, Sargent married Emily Barbeau in the Catholic church in Prince Rupert. The wedding took place before friends and family at 7:00 a.m., the early hour doubtless to enable them to catch the steamer down the coast for their honeymoon in Vancouver and Seattle. Marriage perhaps helped calm Sargent down. He became one of the leading businessmen in the district, respectable and respected. He settled down into being a community leader, chairing the hospital board and presiding at dances and other local events. Remaining in Hazelton, he prospered and opened additional stores in Telkwa and then Smithers. With political aspirations, he ran as a Tory candidate in the 1924 provincial election, losing to the Liberal candidate, Dr. Horace Wrinch. Richard Sargent died in Hazelton in August 1944, a much loved and revered pioneer, all memories of the wilder young man having been long forgotten.

15

Sperry Cline and the Winter Mail

1904–1912

"Some of the pioneers travel fifty miles for their mail instead of having it brought to their doors by a uniformed carrier," the *Omineca Herald* complained in September 1908. "They are not asking [for] any sympathy because they are pioneering in this country, nor do they complain of their lot. All they want is simple justice in the matter of a mail service, which is being denied them."[1]

If residents in the big cities could have mail deliveries two, three, four or more times each day, surely it was not unreasonable, the residents of the Upper Skeena maintained, to ask the government to provide more than two mail deliveries each winter. It was true. Between October and May, mail arrived in Hazelton only twice, although this number did creep slowly upward. Even then, the mail carriers would not take parcels or large packages.

For six months of every year Hazelton was isolated. Except for those twice-a-winter mail deliveries, it was largely deprived not only of mail but also of supplies, which had to be in town by the end of September. This included drugs and supplies for the hospital, basic food stores and liquor. This was not a theoretical problem. The sinking of the *Mount Royal* and other riverine disasters at the end of the season in 1907 led to scarcity and high prices for food. By the following April the bars had run out of cigarettes, tobacco, beer and whisky. Not for nothing, therefore, did the paddle steamer *Distributor* bring up to Hazelton 105 barrels of beer that September, with another 100 barrels waiting in Kitselas.

The problem was the Skeena River. In summer, the sternwheelers brought upriver the mail and supplies. In winter, ice and dangerous waters closed the river to navigation. Patrons in the bars of Hazelton placed bets on what exact day in spring the first steamer would arrive, bringing the mail, supplies, new faces and old friends. Usually it arrived in the first week of May. Between the end of sternwheeler navigation in October and the freeze-up, the mail, to be sure, could occasionally be brought upriver by canoe. Sometimes this intermediate period lasted until Christmas. But the river was unreliable and often dangerous. Sperry Cline wrote that the tides and westerly gales made the ice for the first thirty miles up the Skeena particularly untrustworthy.[2] On March 19, 1904, for example, the *Skeena River News* reported that the river was a sheet of solid ice and that gales had polished the surface to a slippery state, making it treacherous to travel on.

By about 1904, mail deliveries had increased from two to four each winter, and they later became even more frequent. Between deliveries the mail piled up in the post office storage rooms in Port Essington or Kitimat. At one point over a thousand pounds of mail destined for Hazelton and the Bulkley Valley was waiting in Port Essington.

Sometimes packers brought the mail on foot over a grease trail from the Nass River. Dr. Horace Wrinch described one such mail delivery in 1901, his first winter there:

> This winter mail has to be carried in by trail from Naas [Nass] Harbor, about one hundred and fifty miles. It takes the men about five to ten days to come over (according to the condition of the trail), and as they have to carry provisions with them the mail matter is limited to fifty pounds. This fifty pounds has to be divided between the people of Hazelton, Kishpiax [Kispiox], Kishgagass [Kisgegas], Babine, Kitwanga [Gitwangak], Memokimosht [Meanskinisht], and several other places beyond, so you can see each person cannot get much. However, they can generally bring all the letters and a few of the papers. So don't conclude from this that it will be no use writing until spring.[3]

In addition to being one of the leading merchants in town, Richard Sargent, Richard Loring's adversary, was the postmaster in Hazelton. He had the job of organizing carriage of the mail to and from the coast. Just after Christmas 1905, Sargent asked Sperry Cline to make an emergency mail run of the 160 miles to Kitimat.

Cline later said this particular journey was the hardest one he ever experienced. He and his partner Gus Rosenthal left Hazelton with the mail and a six-dog toboggan soon after New Year's. Cline said this was a job for two people. One went ahead on snowshoes with a heavy pole to break the trail, and the other handled the toboggan and dogs. Thaw had set in, and they had to test the soft snow and break ice every step of the way. Later, at the Lakelse portage, a heavy snowfall made progress even slower.

They stopped well before darkness each night to allow them to set up camp. They then had to cut down two or more trees, place them side by side and build a fire on the fallen trunks. This was called rafting. A fire not built in this way would thaw the deep snow and become useless for both heating and cooking. Another reason for rafting was to keep the fire burning all night to keep the wolves at bay. Wolves were always out there, Cline said, often quite close. Once, Cline saw the reflection of their eyes in a circle around his camp. He made it a practice to move the dogs close to the fire for protection. He said that on one such occasion he found the dogs' coats had become scorched.

Mail carriers, Prince Rupert to Hazelton. Image courtesy of the author

They travelled as lightly as they could, but with an ample supply of dog food, dried salmon, rice and grease. Where possible, they camped close to one or more of the communities along the route.

When they reached Kitimat Arm, they had to find a boat to cross to the village. Cline said Sargent hadn't given them instructions regarding to whom they should deliver the mail. They assumed it was the local store and so they took the mail there. Having successfully delivered it, they came back up the river to Hazelton to find they had been scheduled to make two more mail runs that winter.

The amount of mail to be carried inevitably increased as the population in the district grew. The government began awarding contracts to carry the mail on a regular basis for the whole winter instead of on a trip-by-trip basis. George Beirnes and Barney Mulvaney, packers in Hazelton, won a contract. However, they caught gold fever for a new strike on the Ingenika River, so they handed the job over to Cline and went prospecting instead.

Cline sometimes found it difficult to find a partner because so many men had also gone prospecting to the Ingenika. He teamed up with Joe Brown, a Gitxsan man from Gitsegukla, and never regretted his decision. Brown was an expert canoeman, Cline said, excellent with dogs and one of "nature's gentlemen." Brown and Cline became lifelong friends. Their first trip together was by canoe to Port Essington. After that they went on the Kitimat route.

Cline commented on the increase in the number of people using the trails. Sometimes cheechakos (Chinook Jargon for "newcomers") had no idea what they

Hazelton's winter mail arriving. Image P6947 courtesy of the Bulkley Valley Museum

were doing and made travel difficult for others. Some did not use snowshoes and as a result punched knee-deep holes in the snow with their boots, making sled travel difficult. Some made their camps on the trail itself, which presented annoying barriers for other travellers. Cline said sometimes it was humour alone that kept him going.

One of the dangers of running sleds in the snow, Cline related, was that snow fell on top of vegetation, often as much as twelve to fifteen feet above the ground, forming a thick crust indistinguishable from the trail. In the spring, the warm water at ground level thawed the snow beneath the crust. In such conditions, the toboggan, six dogs and two men could sometimes be travelling on a surface that fell away under them, leaving them floundering in oozy mud and slush, the mailbags spilled out and the dogs snarling in a tangle of spilled mailbags and ropes.

On one of their mail runs, Cline and his partner arrived at a camp at Onion Lake one morning. The chief surveyor summoned them to his tent, where he was lounging in bed. He told them to stay in camp until after dinner because he had important letters for them to take. Cline waited, not without some impatience at the man's high-handedness, and set out later with the man's letters. They were approaching Kitimat when they were hailed by a lad of about eighteen on the trail behind them. When he had gathered his breath, he told them the chief surveyor had committed suicide immediately after they had left. The second-in-command had sent him to ask them to register the death. Why, the lad complained petulantly, couldn't he have done it sooner and saved him the bother of his trip?

On January 1, 1910, the *Omineca Herald* notified its readers that Barney Mulvaney (back from prospecting and not noticeably richer) and Sperry Cline were carrying the mail between Prince Rupert, the new terminus of the Grand Trunk Pacific Railway on the coast, and the Kitselas Canyon. It also noted that the Hazelton post office was by now receiving six thousand letters a month from the outside and sending four thousand out. George Beirnes (obviously also recovered from his gold fever) then brought it on up to Hazelton. Mulvaney and Beirnes then joined forces to take the mail on to construction camps.

Eventually, the time came when mail was delivered to Hazelton twice a week. Beirnes remained at Hazelton to handle the purchasing of dogs and equipment, while Mulvaney stayed in Prince Rupert to handle the dispatching and delivery.[4] Usually there was one driver in charge of each outfit, which comprised two to four dog teams. On the way down, the teams were left at Telegraph Point while the driver went on with the mail to Prince Rupert to collect the mailbag to take back to Hazelton. The increasing demand led to the award of a second contract to carry the mail. This one went to Charles Sterritt and Charles Clifford. At the peak, Cline said, there were at least seven dog teams engaged on the river carrying the mail.

Occasionally the Hazelton Hospital asked the mail carrier to take a patient from the hospital to the coast for specialized treatment. Until mid-1914, the hospital did not have an X-ray machine, nor indeed the electricity to power one. Usually someone from the hospital accompanied the patient.

On one occasion the police asked Cline to take a man with mental health challenges to the coast. From there he would be escorted to Vancouver for appropriate medical treatment. Unlike the more violent Barney Devine in 1871, this man was very personable and willing to help. On the journey, Cline and his charge became quite good pals. Cline related how scruffy and dishevelled they both became, with unshaven faces and straggly beards. (Cline was never a tidy dresser at the best of times.) He suggested they both spruce themselves up with a shave and a haircut at the local barber's shop while they waited for the steamer. Meeting the steamer captain on the way there, Cline learned they had better hurry. There would be only enough time for one of them to have his hair cut, but which one? Cline's companion suggested it should be him because he wanted to look his best when admitted to the hospital. If he looked smart, he reasoned, the doctors there might give him better treatment. Cline acquiesced.

When the still-scruffy Cline went to deliver his charge to the police station, the man, now spruce and respectable, stepped up to the desk and announced, "Well, here he is. I brought him down from Hazelton."[5] Laughing at the joke, Cline reached for the committal papers but found he had left his satchel with the papers inside at the barber's shop. Less humorously, he found that the policeman believed the better groomed of the two men was the custodian. Cline saw himself being taken down to the coast and, protestations of sanity notwithstanding, held indefinitely in a mental hospital. The mistake was cleared up only when the local chief constable arrived and identified Cline.

Times were changing fast. After Wiggs O'Neill started a gas boat service between Port Essington and Telegraph Point in 1908, carriers took the mail from Hazelton to Telegraph Point by dog team and then by O'Neill's boat service to Port Essington. From there they took the mail on to Prince Rupert.[6] In 1906 the Grand Trunk Pacific commenced building a railway line from Prince Rupert, past Hazelton and on to the prairies to the east. It wouldn't arrive in Hazelton for a few years, but as it came closer, the activity—surveying, food supply, workers, managers, blasting, gravel collection and laying—increased. New towns such as Telkwa and the railway towns of Terrace and Smithers were established and quickly grew. New stations also grew up—Vanarsdol, Skeena Crossing, Carnaby, Tramville and New Hazelton.

This was the time of the Hazelton mining boom and the settlement of the Bulkley Valley. Newcomers with a set purpose were coming into the district. Some of them were farmers and ranchers; others were miners and prospectors. Many were government workers. The hundreds of labourers helping to build the railroad brought their own problems of liquor use and racial animosities. Boomers arrived, men looking to make money in any business venture they could. There were also "tinhorn gamblers and outright crooks," as Cline noted, as well as numerous remittance men from England.

As the railway approached, the glory days of the winter mail run started to come to an end. Trains carried the mail as far as the railhead. When it was clear that the railway would not come into Hazelton, the new towns of New Hazelton and South Hazelton grew up south of the river. In 1912, when the first scheduled service started, the winter mail run from Hazelton to the coast finally came to an end. The railway changed everything.

16

George McKenzie, the Missing
Medicine Chest and Runaway Dogs

1906

I f you have walked for miles through snow in temperatures of sixty degrees below zero, knowing you have frostbite in your toes, and if you have managed to stagger back to your shack, you would probably reach for the medicine chest as soon as you could. So, doubtless, did George McKenzie that day in early 1906. However, there was a problem. Where was it?

Thirty-three years old, McKenzie was an experienced frontier man and no stranger to its often life-threatening challenges. As a wilderness man, he knew what he was doing. Had he not once walked on snowshoes from the Omineca Mountains to Port Essington, a trek of 440 miles?

His home was in Greenwood, a town near the southern border of the province, where, in one of his many occupations, he had been a driver on the West Fork stagecoach.[1] In July 1903, he was driving the stage when a huge wind brought down trees all around him, knocking him off the stage and leaving him concussed on the ground. The stage then continued on its way until it ran into a telephone pole in the main street of Greenwood and broke apart.

In April 1905, he left Greenwood with a partner to drive fifty horses north to Hazelton. Their journey, which would take two months, took them through Osoyoos and up the Cariboo Road. McKenzie planned to sell the horses in Hazelton and then go four hundred miles farther north to join his prospecting partners, who had been trapping there all winter.

He had also made numerous prospecting expeditions into the Omineca Mountains. On one of these explorations, he had discovered some placer gold and had tucked the location away in his memory, expecting to return one day.

On January 13, 1906, he was prospecting in the mountains forty miles north of Manson Creek with his partners Dan Sullivan and a man named Thone (possibly John Thorn).[2] He left a fellow prospector named Charles Newman in charge of his camp and went to walk through the deep snow to find the site where he had previously found the placer gold. In the sixty-five-below temperatures, his feet started to freeze. Realizing the danger of frostbite, he returned to camp.

The problem was that Dan Sullivan had taken the medicine chest to his own camp four miles away. Would Charley go to get it? No, Charley wouldn't. Although Charley Newman tried to look after McKenzie as best he could, cooking for him and dressing his feet, for some inexplicable reason he refused to go to Sullivan to retrieve the urgently needed medicine chest.

George McKenzie suffered for eight weeks, eating salt meat. A passing Indigenous hunter, seeing how badly McKenzie was suffering and "responding to the dictates of simple humanity,"[3] volunteered to fetch the much-needed medicine chest. By the time it arrived, six of McKenzie's teeth were falling out and the flesh was peeling off his toes. He had scurvy. It was now clear to them all that his life was in danger. There was only one thing to do. They had to take him to the hospital in Hazelton two hundred miles away as quickly as they could.

On March 25, Sullivan, Thone and two Indigenous men strapped McKenzie to a stretcher on a dogsled and set out.

The journey to the hospital was through a frozen hell. The dogs were wild and almost unmanageable. Numerous times the handlers lost control of the team, which ran away with the sled, bumping around over logs and the rugged terrain. The *Boundary Creek Times* reported:

> If the dogs broke away from their Indian guides and ran away once, they must have done so a dozen times. There, lashed to the sled, he was dragged at a flying pace over the rough trail, the sled bumping against fallen logs, bounding over dangerous places and at times half capsized, with the half senseless man dragging in the snow. Several times when night came, he despaired of surviving until morning, and for the last twenty miles of that terrible journey he was too weak to ride on a sled, but had to be carried on a stretcher between the two pack horses.[4]

When they arrived at the Hazelton Hospital on April 5, after a journey of eleven days, McKenzie was nearly dead.

Dr. Allison Rolls treated him on his arrival. When Dr. Horace Wrinch, who had been away in the East on an extended trip, arrived back, he helped Rolls give McKenzie the treatment he needed. They had to amputate four of McKenzie's toes. But he survived. He was discharged on May 26 with a hospital bill for fifteen dollars. He was the 123rd patient in the still relatively new hospital. "Few men," the *Boundary Creek Times* said of McKenzie, "could have passed through half what he has done and survived to tell the tale."[5]

17

Constance Cox and the Nurses of Hazelton Hospital

1905–1932

One day in 1892, twelve-year-old Constance Hankin held a chloroform-soaked cloth over the face of a badly injured man until he lost consciousness. Richard Loring, her stepfather, then took the saw and amputated the man's leg. She was not a nurse and he was not a doctor, but the deed had to be done.

Before the arrival of Dr. Horace Wrinch in 1900, there was no resident doctor in the interior of northern British Columbia. One of Loring's duties as Indian agent was to provide medical care to the Gitxsan and Wet'suwet'en peoples to the best of his ability. In reports to Arthur Vowell, the superintendent of Indian Affairs for the province, Loring often listed the names of the Gitxsan and Wet'suwet'en people he had vaccinated against measles and other diseases. With no formal medical training, he also performed simple surgeries. Constance assisted him in some medical duties, learning first aid and basic nursing alongside him. Her qualification was experience, not education.

Loring was not alone. Most missionaries had medicine chests and gave such care as they could. Although not a qualified doctor, the Irish missionary Robert Tomlinson had received some medical training in Dublin, and he dispensed medical as well as religious care at Meanskinisht. Father Adrien-Gabriel Morice across the Bulkley River provided medical care for the Wet'suwet'en people. The wives of the missionaries also provided medical care. Unfortunately, their stories were not often recorded. Bishop William Ridley's wife, Jane, for example, had experience nursing during the cholera epidemic in Peshawar and tending wounded soldiers in Dresden. In an emergency, everyone did what they could. If Dr. Wrinch was going to build a hospital, though, he would require qualified nurses.

Constance was the daughter of Thomas Hankin and Margaret MacAulay, who was half Tlingit. Born on September 27, 1880, she was allegedly the first non-Indigenous birth in Hazelton. Her father is said to have sponsored a $3,000 potlatch to introduce her to the Gitxsan community. Four years after Hankin's death in 1885, Margaret married Richard Loring, the recently appointed Indian agent, in Victoria.

Numerous stories are told about Constance, some more substantiated than others. In the winter of 1888, the Gitxsan people observed that their non-Indigenous neighbours had not fallen sick during the measles epidemic that was killing so many of them. Some maintained that the settlers were putting measles germs into the sugar given them. In this *Guns, Germs and Steel* moment, non-Indigenous people were likely saved from infection by the immunity built up over many centuries. Constance recounted that her mother painted her face with spots to convince their Gitxsan neighbours that she too had the measles.[1]

Alice Wrinch was the first qualified nurse to live in the district. Settling first in Kispiox, she assisted her husband in his duties there. Much of Dr. Wrinch's work, though, was in Hazelton, ten or so miles away. Busy with her own work in the community and church, Alice would not have been able to accompany him often. Moreover, in 1901 she became pregnant, which would have made the journey to and from Hazelton arduous, perhaps dangerous. When she arrived in 1900, she was already thirty. In the next dozen years, she gave birth to five children.

Dr. Wrinch clearly needed someone living in Hazelton to assist him on his medical visits there. He found Constance Hankin. One of her first major operations was to assist the doctor in removing a cancer from the breast of her own mother, Margaret. This took place on October 21, 1901. Because this was going to be major surgery, Dr. Wrinch asked Dr. Thomas Wilson to come up from Port Essington to assist in the operation. The two doctors arranged a rehearsal the day before so Constance would know what to do.

Before the operation, as was his custom, Dr. Wrinch knelt and prayed for God's blessing on their work. "A human life is placed in our hands," Constance recalled him saying. "We must have God's help if we are to do our best work. Let us pray together."[2]

Constance said Dr. Wrinch spoke quietly, but his voice was "like thunder" to her.[3] She did not want to let him down. There was no laughing or irreverence in his operating room. He could well have felt in the room the presence of God, who had created the body he was about to cut open. The operation on Constance's mother was successful. "In conclusion," Loring wrote a few days later, "I here must not omit that Mrs. Loring, on 21st inst., underwent the operation in removing the cancer from her right breast by Drs. Wrinch and Wilson, and is, thank God, doing well at present writing."[4]

"Dr. Wrinch himself really did most of the nursing," Constance said. "He could go without sleep for 24 hours."[5] She recounted that he used to do surgeries in people's homes. Later in life she related that nearly every operation required some carpentry. To provide a reliably flat and stable surface for operating on, "he had just a door propped up with two trestles. And when the question came for a patient to have his head lowered, he propped the feet up with a bit of cord wood. He used the stable for his dispensary. And he packed the door and the trestles around with him."[6]

When Dr. Wrinch and his family moved to a rented house in Hazelton, Constance's workload likely increased. Moreover, Alice, already busy with her community work and one infant, soon was expecting another child. Constance continued her work with the doctor for almost two years while he was building the family home in the new hospital compound.

Wrinch knew he would need qualified nurses for the new hospital. Constance was no doubt practical and useful, but she was not formally qualified. He reached out to his friends in the Women's Missionary Society in Toronto

Matron and nurses of Hazelton Hospital in approximately 1905–1906. Image courtesy of the author

for help. They recruited Anne Sherwood, a good Methodist with a missionary fervour of her own, to come to work in the new hospital. She arrived from Ontario in the autumn of 1902 and stayed for two years. Soon to arrive also was seventeen-year-old Helen Deane, who came from Vancouver to learn how to be a nurse. When Anne Sherwood left, Helen Bone took her place as lady superintendent.

Helen Bone had been Alice's roommate at Grace Hospital in Toronto when they were both training to be nurses. She was not a stranger to the rougher side of nursing. For a year or so, she had been a nurse at a small hospital in the mining town of Atlin near the Yukon border. She once accompanied Dr. Wrinch downriver to deal with a man who turned out to be suffering from acute appendicitis. After spending the night locating a canoe, the two set off downriver at first light. Later that day, the surgery accomplished, Dr. Wrinch returned to Hazelton, taking five days to get back upriver, leaving Helen with the patient to return later.

When Helen Bone left on account of ill health, Claire Hollingsworth became lady superintendent, and after her, Marie Broughton. In 1912, May Hogan, the daughter of the missionary William Hogan, became matron and lady superintendent. She stayed with the hospital in various capacities until 1936.

The problem of how to hire and retain nurses remained. The Wrinches knew the hospital needed a steady and reliable supply of nurses. Living in an isolated frontier community was not easy. After a year or so, nurses tended to leave, either to get married or to return home.

How then to staff the hospital? Both Wrinches had experience with nurse training schools. After Dr. Wrinch had qualified as a doctor and surgeon in 1899, he had worked for almost a year as house surgeon and intern at St. Michael's Hospital in Toronto, which had its own nurse training school. Alice was a qualified nurse and had been superintendent of Grace Hospital in Toronto for a year while her fiancé finished his own medical training. Why not set up a nurse training school at Hazelton Hospital? This would solve the problem. Nurses would stay at the hospital for at least three years, learn their trade and work at the hospital. It would, in effect, be an apprenticeship program, beneficial to all parties.

The nurse training school at Hazelton Hospital was established in 1905. Tiny Hazelton, with approximately fifty non-Indigenous and about three hundred Gitxsan inhabitants, had a nurse training school before St. Paul's Hospital in Vancouver, which opened its school in 1907. (Vancouver General Hospital had set up its training school for nurses in 1898.)

The Women's Missionary Society, which had recruited Anne Sherwood, was instrumental in finding nurses and student nurses for the hospital. Most usefully, the society also paid their salaries.

Writing in the *Canadian Nurse* in 1907, an unidentified nurse at the Hazelton Hospital said:

> Two years ago the Hazelton Hospital was opened. It is a wooden building, prettily painted green, containing twenty rooms besides an attic and furnace cellar. This year the finances permitted improvements in the shape of the installation of a complete system of waterworks and disposal of sewerage on the septic tank system; also an acetylene gas plant, and the addition of an ice house and store house. The staff consists of the medical superintendent, a graduate nurse in charge, with two assistants, one in the housekeeping department and one in the nursing. Also a boy for the outdoor department: for the patients have what are considered in Hazelton real luxuries, fresh eggs, vegetables and milk. … There is no other hospital nearer than two hundred miles, and to the south, north and east within many hundred miles, so that many of the patients, especially white patients, miners and others, travel many miles. Some have walked upwards of two hundred miles, others ridden on horses and others still more helpless have been carried on stretchers. In winter, mails only reach us once a month and then mainly letters, very few periodicals or papers get through.

Hazelton Hospital about 1909. Nurses lived in rooms on the top floor until a nurses' residence was built in 1926. Image courtesy of the author

From October to May there are classes for the nurses, Clara Weeks' textbook on nursing being used. Lessons are also given in anatomy and materia medica. This year the nurses are taking up cooking, using as textbook "The Boston Cooking School Cook Book." The scenery around the Hazelton Hospital is very beautiful, surrounded on all sides by snowy-capped mountains, some near and some in the far distance, whilst as for climate, it is second to none. Miss Bone (Gold Medalist of Grace Hospital, Toronto) is head nurse in this interesting hospital.[7]

Trainee nurses studied and were graded on topics that included deportment, health, materia medica, theory of nursing, anatomy, physiology, obstetrics, surgery, pathology, dietetics, bandaging and bacteriology. Not every student survived the rigours of the program. Some left—or were asked to leave—early.

In the 1906 version of the rules and regulations of the hospital, Dr. Wrinch set down the duties and salary of the staff:

3. Duties of Staff

The Medical Superintendent shall, in addition to the duties ordinarily devolving upon his office, also perform the duties of Secretary and Treasurer of the hospital.

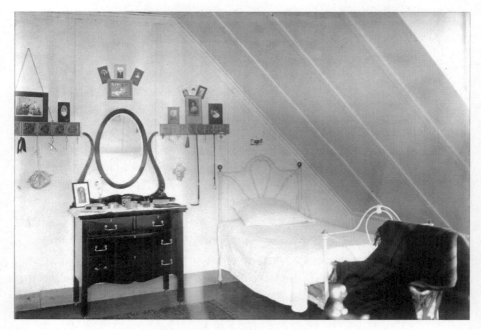

A nurse's room at the Hazelton Hospital. Image courtesy of the author

The Lady Superintendent shall direct the work of nursing, give instruction to the nurses in training and have oversight as well of the housekeeping department of the hospital.

The Nurses in Training shall work under direction of the Lady Superintendent, complying cheerfully with whatever shall be required of them. Their course of training shall be three years, at the end of which time, if their work and attainments are found satisfactory, they shall be awarded a diploma certifying to their proficiency.

The Housekeeper, with whatever assistance can be found necessary, shall perform the duties of the housekeeping and culinary department, in consultation with, and under the direction of the Lady Superintendent.

4. Salaries of Staff

The Medical Superintendent shall receive no salary from the funds of the hospital.

The Lady Superintendent shall receive $400 per annum, with an allowance for travelling expenses to Victoria at reasonable intervals.

The Nurses in training shall receive—for the first year, $125, for the second year $175, and for the third year $225.

The staff of the Hazelton Hospital in 1911–1912. Top row, left to right: Connie Goddard (later Falconer) Chowk (laundryman), Violet Bird (housekeeper), Laura Adams, Marg Crawford, Fred Goddard (farmer and handyman), George T. Crowe (janitor). Middle row: Amy Grist, Harris, Gertrude Martin. Front row: Dr. Horace Wrinch, May Hogan (matron), Dr. C.G. MacLean. Image courtesy of the author

For Nurses in Training the hospital will pay travelling expenses from their starting point to Hazelton, if not farther than Victoria; and will pay return expenses to the same point if they complete their three years term of training. Any candidate for position as Nurse in Training, who comes from a point more distant than Victoria, will if necessary be allowed an advance on salary to meet these additional travelling expenses. Deductions, extending over a reasonable length of time, will be made from salary to reimburse the hospital for these advances for travelling expenses over and above the amount allowed from Victoria to Hazelton.

The salary of the Housekeeper shall be at the discretion of the Medical Superintendent and Lady Superintendent.

The Lady Superintendent, the nurses in training, shall have residence, board, and laundry, in, and at the expense of, the hospital.[8]

So who were they, these nurses from over a century ago? The first to graduate was Annie Lawrence from Seaforth, Ontario; she entered the nursing school on

May 1, 1905, and graduated in May 1908. Euphemia Anderson, a Presbyterian girl fresh from Dumfries in Scotland, graduated on June 1, 1910. The 1908 hospital annual report said of her that she was "not many years from Scotland" and had "already well demonstrated the fact that in choosing this exacting work she [had] not mistaken her calling."[9] In 1913, Euphemia married Sperry Cline in St. Andrew's Church in Vancouver, with Helen Bone as a witness.

Laura Moore from Toronto graduated in 1911; Jessie McDonald from Seymour Street in Vancouver, in 1912; and Gertrude Martin, a Methodist girl from St. John's, Newfoundland, in May 1913. Amy Grist, who came from Victoria, graduated in April 1914.

The training school register noted that Ella Bates from Frankford, Ontario, was "interested in her duties" and "appeared willing to take correction" but could not assume responsibility.[10] Nevertheless, she graduated in 1922. Kathleen White, a Roman Catholic girl from Vancouver, did not fare well. Her work was recorded as not satisfactory and she left after one year. Ruth Bolivar's work, on the other hand, was considered to be very satisfactory. She was bright and quick in performing her duties. Janet Ford was another one reported as being bright and willing to learn.

Elizabeth Nock, who was recorded in her first year as resenting correction, improved but, the record says, she had no executive ability. She was thorough but slow. She took charge of the diet in the kitchen for a month in the summer of 1921. By her second and third years, she had pulled her socks up. She was recorded now as being "very thorough" and showed "considerable improvement in performing duties. Both in ward duties and studies she had pleasing manners with patients."[11] She graduated in 1924 and went to run the new nursing home in Telkwa.

Dr. Wrinch and the hospital community celebrated nurses when they graduated. There was usually a dinner for the graduate, attended by staff, nurses and members of the hospital board. Ruth Bolivar, for example, graduated in 1924. Dr. Wrinch usually gave the address, but at the time of her graduation, he was making his maiden speech in the legislature in Victoria and could not attend the ceremony. Consequently, as chairman of the hospital board, "R.S. Sargent presented the diploma and Mrs. Anne Mathieson [the lady superintendent] presented the pin, heard the Obligation, and presented the graduate with a bouquet of magnificent 'mums on behalf of the nursing staff. A round of cheers was given and the exercises [graduation ceremonies] were brought to a close with the 'Maple Leaf' and 'National Anthem.'"[12]

The nurses lived on the top floor of the 1904 hospital. By 1925, everyone agreed this was no longer suitable. The hospital was crowded, and the risk of fire to the wooden building was a continuing worry. To everyone's relief, a new residence for nurses was proposed, approved and funded. By January 1926, it was erected and ready for painting. "The new residence," the *Omineca Herald* said when it was completed, "is a handsome structure, not so much from the outside appearance as from the interior finish and furnishings. There is nothing lacking that would add to the comfort and happiness of the nurses, and this will in turn reflect on the nurses' services to the patients in hospital."[13] This building, later extended, survives as the Wrinch Residence.

By the end of the First World War, nursing standards and requirements were changing. Many in the big cities felt that the training in the nursing schools of small rural hospitals did not provide adequate experience. The enactment of the Nurses Registration Act in 1919 led to an agreement between the Hazelton Hospital and Vancouver General Hospital whereby nurses completed the last year of their training in Vancouver. There they acquitted themselves well.

The Hazelton Hospital nurse training school continued to train nurses until the financial pressures of the Depression led to the announcement of its closure in August 1932. Doris Robinson was the last nurse to graduate. In her final examinations, she headed the list of results for the entire province.

When they graduated, most nurses left to return home or move to other jobs. On occasion, the *Omineca Herald* noted their progress in life. Helen Bone was appointed superintendent of public school nurses in south Vancouver in 1912. She died of cancer in 1919. In 1917, Claire Hollingsworth was a victim of the Halifax Explosion. In 1930, the *Herald* noted that Mrs. Ella McCutcheon was a supervisor in the Detroit Receiving Hospital and Eva Martin was second anaesthetist at New York's Women's Hospital. Annie Lawrence, the first nurse to graduate, returned for a visit in 1934 and stayed with Dr. Wrinch. She commented on the changes in Hazelton since she had lived there. The only two things that had not changed, she said, were Rocher Déboulé and Dr. Wrinch.

Alice Wrinch died of cancer in early 1923. Her death caused much grief in the Hazelton community she had spent so many years serving.

Like her mother, Constance Hankin was fluent in half a dozen local languages. After her nursing days were over, she was for many years an interpreter in the Hazelton court. On one occasion when her services were required, she met E. Ruxton Cox, and in 1905 she married him, becoming Constance Cox.

Constance left Hazelton in December 1916. When her husband, who was manager of the telegraph office, was transferred to Prince Rupert, she went with him. When the Coxes were leaving, a delegation of employees from the telegraph office came to their house with a letter of warm wishes for their future and, more practically, a purse of gold. In 1934 they moved to North Vancouver. Throughout her life, Constance was a historian, translator, storyteller and advocate on behalf of the Indigenous Peoples of British Columbia.

When Dr. Wrinch was living in Vancouver in 1939 and suffering from the cancer that would kill him, Constance visited him and kept him informed about what was happening in Hazelton.[14] She died in May 1963.

18

James Maitland-Dougall and Policing in Hazelton

1909–1911

Chief Constable James St. Leger Maitland-Dougall was a blue-blooded Scottish aristocrat. It is unlikely, though, that the miscreants of Hazelton knew this, or would have cared, when, as police chief in Hazelton, he brought them before the local magistrate for trial. Born in 1867, he was the youngest son of Admiral Maitland-Dougall and the great-grandson of the sixth Earl of Lauderdale. Noble birth, however, did not guarantee wealth or ability. Young Jamie would have to make his own way in the world.

After a primary education at Fettes, one of Scotland's top private schools, he was pointed to a career in the army. Whether he objected or whether he was not made of the right stuff is not clear, but the army did not accept him. After that, still in his teen years, he was apprenticed to a large firm of brokers in Liverpool. After five years working there and playing golf at a local championship level, Jamie apparently had had enough. He and his brother Frederick came out to British Columbia together and bought land at Cowichan on Vancouver Island. James Maitland-Dougall spent his twentieth birthday in Victoria.

In 1890, after a brief visit to Scotland following the death of his father, James Maitland-Dougall returned to British Columbia and settled in the growing city of Vancouver. For a while he worked as a surveyor, and he is credited with laying out the town of Nelson. After that he was appointed assistant immigration officer in Vancouver, where he managed the office while his boss was away in England.

In June 1892, he joined the British Columbia Provincial Police. He wrote in his diary on July 16, "Sworn in as constable by H.O. [Harry Osborn] Wellburn." On July 18, he recorded that "Geo. Keir handed over keys and one pair hand-cuffs."[1] At this time there were only thirty-eight policemen in the British Columbia Provincial Police. Since many municipalities had their own police forces, policing was not as thinly spread as might appear. In 1895, the authorities recognized Maitland-Dougall's abilities and promoted him to chief constable in Cowichan. Additionally, in 1899 the government appointed him as a government agent. He earned a good reputation. Of the eight murder cases he worked on, he arrested the murderer in five. He was a competent, no-nonsense and decisive public servant. He left the police and set himself up as an insurance, estate and financial agent, but he appears to have tired of that because he soon sold that business. He also found

James Maitland-Dougall was the efficient and capable police chief who took over Hazelton's policing in 1909. Image 1987.05.5.2 courtesy of the Cowichan Valley Museum and Archives

time for romance, marrying Winifred McKinstry Watson in 1894.

When Superintendent of Police Frederick Hussey was looking for a new chief of police for the unruly town of Hazelton, he found in Maitland-Dougall a competent officer with practical experience. The town was growing fast and becoming a trouble spot. The one policeman there, John Deane, who had taken over from James Kirby, was clearly not up to the job. Hazelton needed a firm, experienced police chief, and more policemen. The tensions between the non-Indigenous and Indigenous populations were growing. New settlers and the new railway were occupying Indigenous land, and this was causing conflict. Rigid and unthinking enforcement of new fishery regulations added to the tension.

In August 1909, Maitland-Dougall packed his bags, collected the constables he was bringing with him and headed north. At Port Essington he boarded the river steamer *Hazelton* with his police party. Word of his approach and his reputation had already reached Hazelton. For the first time, the bartenders there started obeying the laws, closing on Sundays and even closing during the night.

Maitland-Dougall quickly established his control. As well as normal police work, he had inherited the task of trying to apprehend the two Gitxsan outlaws Simon Gunanoot and Peter Himadam. They had been accused of two murders in 1906 and were still on the run. Early that summer the government had hired two undercover Pinkerton's operatives, who went by their numbers, No. 28 and No. 6, to hunt for the two men. The name of No. 28, the leader, is now known to have been W.T. Bennett.

In Hazelton, Maitland-Dougall's main day-to-day problem was how to curb the pervasive abuse of liquor, though whether this was worse than anywhere else in the province is debatable. Nevertheless, it was a major challenge, and much of Maitland-Dougall's work was trying to stop the abuse. There were too many drunks in the streets. Furthermore, too many white residents were selling liquor to Indigenous people, which at the time was illegal.[2]

Maitland-Dougall kept a daily diary of his two and a half years in Hazelton. Diaries by their nature are episodic and fragmented. The extracts below provide an album of pictures of life in Hazelton at the time:[3]

August 1909

29th Arrived at Hazelton at 3:30 p.m. Met by Constable Deane.

30th At Hazelton. Called at Gov't office on Gov't Agent Allison. Making arrangements re quarters for constables. Took over charge of district. Inspected police quarters and lockup. Reported by letter arrival of party, also reported on condition of prisoner lock-up, and applied for immediate construction of new one. Made arrangements with Constable Deane that he should leave on steamer *Port Simpson* for Port Essington, leaving probably on 2nd September.

By appointment met operatives No. 28 and No. 6 after dark on road and discussed the Indian Simon Gun-an-noot and Peter's case. Agreed to meet next evening.

September 1909

7th Mrs. Pat Carey called and complained that her husband was drinking and asked me to try and stop it. Went to both hotels and requested them to stop supplying him. Two Indians called for information re killing of beaver.

29th Reported by Hudson Bay Coy that their liquor house had been broken into during the night. Could not say what had been taken. Went down and investigated. ...

Met Operative No. 28. Informed him that an order for medicine had been received by the doctor at the hospital, which was supposed to be for the Indian outlaw Simon, as it was the same kind that he used to get through Kispiox Indians. Out till 1 a.m.

October 1909

3rd Steamer *Port Simpson* arrived. Handed David W. Pratt his liquor license. Mr. Duncan Ross informed me that he thought he had made arrangements that the 40 or 50 tons of dynamite expected would be landed outside the village of Hazelton.

November 1909

17th Bought three suits of underwear, 6 pairs of socks, 3 shirts and 3 suits of overalls for prisoners at Hudson Bay store for use at gaol.

18th Made arrangements for prisoners cooking their meals in gaol. Prisoners' quarters being virtually finished. Secured seven more cords of wood, wood being scarce and hard to get at this season. Supervising gaol generally.

20th Assisted getting ballot boxes and papers ready for conveyance by dog team to outlying stations. Received wire from J.S. Campbell that specials were at Kitselas.

February 1910

23rd Called out at 1:30 a.m. Hazelton Hotel on fire. In close proximity to the gaol. Took prisoners out of cells and took precautionary measures to protect gaol. Hotel totally destroyed. No loss of life. Three men singed a little.

24th Up all night at fire. Went off duty at 7:30 a.m. to midday. On duty rest of day at gaol. Mail arrived.

28th McAfee called and made complaint that Charles G. Harvey had shot and killed a dog belonging to him and wanted to know what proceedings he could take. Informed him. Said he would come in next day.

Note: 16 prisoners during month. $277 in fines, fees and forfeitures.

March 1910

13th Received wire from Super't to send [Pinkerton's] operative to Victoria and pay off assistant. Failed to find operatives this day. Charles Sterritt, in course of conversation with him in the evening, informed me that Simon Gunanoot was a good friend of his and had called to see him at night at his house last October and had been in the vicinity some days. Simon told him that the Indians told him that the Government had given orders that he was to be shot on sight. Sterritt said that Simon was feeling very sorry about the murder and told him he had no recollection of doing it; he was drunk. Sterritt wanted to know if anything was being done about Simon. I told him no. Sterritt also said that Simon said that he would come back to see him the coming fall and wanted him to get a bottle of poison for him for foxes. After talking to Sterritt some time he promised to let me know if Simon came in and also would try to induce Simon to give himself up.

22nd Attending to office and gaol duties all day. In evening had another conversation with Charles Sterritt re Simon. Was informed that when Simon was in in the fall he got drunk and was looking for trouble, threatening to shoot the first white man he came across. Also that he came into Hazelton one night at midnight, and had a conversation with two white men whom he did not know, opposite the Hazelton hotel. Simon asked them if anything was being done about him (Simon). They replied they were new in the country and didn't know, but thought there was a warrant out for his arrest.

May 1910

15th Steamer *Operator* arrived with powder to discharge. Went on board and ordered Captain not to discharge at Hazelton. Steamer then proceeded upriver ½ mile and discharged. Usual duties.

20th Left Hazelton at 1:30 with Constable Bowdridge en route to Aldermere. Rode to 20 Mile house and stayed night.

23rd Looked over the Aldermere and Telkwa townsites re site for lock-up. Saw Mr. Eccleston, contractor and carpenter, re building of lock-up and gave him the proposed plan to estimate on.

24th Inspected Telkwa Hotel at Aldermere. Closed with Mr. Eccleston re building of lock-up for the sum of $1,356 this amount being $134 lower than the estimated cost given me by contractor Stevenson of Hazelton. Informed both at Telkwa and Aldermere that Mr. Eccleston was the best carpenter in the country.

25th Started on my return at 10:15 a.m. with two horses. Arrived Glacier Hotel 1:30 p.m. and had meal, fed horses and resumed journey. At thirty-two mile found Gramophone Creek bridge washed out, owing to flood, being unable to swim horses owing to current, assisted three other men to build bridge, finally getting horses over, had meal at Telegraph cabin at 31 Mile Point, arrived Twenty Mile House at 2 a.m.

June 1910

6th Made arrangements with William Dougherty to work as spotter in connection with blind pigs [illegal bars or speakeasies] at 2 Mile and Sealeyville at the rate of $5 per day.

7th Dougherty reported he and a friend, Arthur McCabe, had gone out to 2 Mile and bought liquor over the counter. Instructed him to proceed to Sealeyville and see what he could do there, as I had reason to believe a man named Hood was running a blind pig. In the evening Dougherty reported that Hood was running a blind pig alright but that he had been unable to buy liquor owing to the fact that Hood was out of stock having sold all he had. Laid information and had Nels Carlson arrested, charged with selling liquor by retail without a license at Two Mile.

16th Had Simon's [Gunanoot's] two children pointed out to me by Charles Barrett, could not get near enough to see them properly. Tried to locate Charles Sterritt. Found he was working on the telegraph line near Kitselas Canyon.

22nd Etienne, Indian of Babine, reported that a foreigner had stolen a 22 Winchester out of his camp and that he was in Hazelton. Sent Constable Harvey to bring him in. Mike Morris arrested for stealing rifle. Case dismissed. Indian Etienne having his rifle returned to him after order of court.

August 1910

9th Constable Rogers reported that prisoner Boddy refused to obey orders when ordered to carry water for gaol. Had prisoner brought before me. On his refusing to admit offence he was locked up, and to be placed on bread and water diet for one day and to again be brought before me at the expiration of that time. Prisoner paid fine.

11th Endeavouring to make arrangements to get spotter to act down at Sealey Landing. There being three blind pigs operating down there. Saw R. Palmer in connection with this.

12th On duty at gaol. Made inquiries re ten gallons rum shipped to Sealey Landing.

13th Saw Charles Sterritt who reported that Simon had been met by an Indian on the road between Glen Vowell and Kispiox at night of the 8th instant, had not yet been able to locate him.

23rd Charles Sterritt reported that Simon had called on him during the night, had a talk with him, advising him to give himself up. Simon stated he would like to, but was scared, was just starting out again, was going to consult his wife and would be back in about three weeks and would let Sterritt know what he intended doing. Sterritt tried to get him to stay at home, but Simon would not, stating that he was going right off that night.

24th John Lake, Finnlander, brought into station acting as if insane. Called in Dr. Wrinch to examine him. Dr. stated that he thought it was the effects of liquor & that he would be all right shortly. Complaint made at office by Andrew West that he had been short-changed by Ingenika barman on night shift.

25th Saw manager of Ingenika Hotel re West's complaint. Informed him that this was not the first complaint and that it was always on the same shift. Manager gave West $5, the amounts he claimed.

September 1910

5th Went out to hospital grounds for basketball match (Labour Day).

22nd Hans Carlson called me up at 6 a.m. and reported that 2 cases of liquor had been stolen out of his wagon during night, which had been loaded up with provisions for an early start this day to Aldermere, his load being for Broughton & McNeil. Was unable to tell me what kind of liquor had been taken. On getting up and going down found Carlson had gone off. Made inquiries afterwards at 8 a.m. from Messrs. Cunningham & Son, from whose warehouse load had been taken.

October 1910
22nd Made arrangements for raid on gambling houses at Sealey at midnight. Sent down Constables Bowdridge, Harvey and Special Constables Milne, Wilson and Palmer by boat.
23rd At 2 a.m. received word by phone from Constable Bowdridge that ten arrests had been made and asking that wagons be sent down for prisoners.

November 1910
7th Frank McLaine reported that he had been assaulted by C.F. Swanson of Sealeyville and that Swanson was running a gaming house and selling liquor and that he had done so on the 6th instant, and was doing so right along. Laid three different informations against Swanson, for keeping a common gaming house, selling liquor without a license and for assault. Obtained warrant. Arrested Swanson at 4:30 p.m. on his arrival with canoe at Hazelton.

December 1910
8th Charles Hall having served his term of imprisonment discharged from the gaol. Reported at 3 p.m. that the Ingenika liquor cellar opposite the Hudson's Bay store had been broken into and 2 5-gallon casks of rum and 2 cases of Burton's Beauty stolen. Went and investigated and found axe and a ring bolt, which had been used and left by person or persons.
14th Received wire that Joe Verschoyle had been buried by snow slide on 9 Mile Mountain. Also that a gang of men were trying to find him and dry him out. Supposed to have happened on Monday the 12th. ...

Indian feast begun, to last 3 days. Large numbers of Indians on reservation. Patrolled reserve, going off duty at 1 a.m.

January 1911
6th Prisoner Harman reported by Constable Harvey as insubordinate, refusing to wash and trying to prevent other prisoners from doing so on the 5th. Prisoner, on being brought before me, refused to go wash. So I

ordered him confined and put on bread and water for 3 days, this being second offence.

9th   Received mail. Made inquiries re Ernest Arthur Cole, having received letter of inquiry regarding him from his brother, A.M. Cole of London, England. Found he had gone out on last steamer, supposed to be on his way to England. Replied to letter.

11th   Prisoner Patrick Cassidy again reported by both Constables Harvey & Special Constable as insubordinate and refusing to obey. Had him before me, when he became violent and assaulted Special Milne. Handcuffed him and gave 2 days in cell with bread and water.

February 1911
24th   Received wire from W.J. Goepel offering me government agency job at Cowichan.

March 1911
9th   Busy in office all day. John Munro, late of Greenock Police, Scotland, called at office wished to get on Provincial Police Force. Had good discharge. Asked him to act as spotter. Consented to do so, to start operations tomorrow.

14th   Sent Constable Harvey with Government team to meet Constable Bowdridge at 20 Mile House, who was bringing an insane man (Charles Brown) from Aldermere.

15th   Placed O.A. Ragstad under section 76, Liquor Act. Trying to make arrangements for shipment of Charles Brown to coast. Made arrangements with mail contractors for conveyance of Brown to railway at Kitselas to start at 7:30 a.m.

In early 1911, Maitland-Dougall was offered the job of government agent at Duncan. Allegedly, he initially turned this down, but Premier Richard McBride persuaded him to accept it. Before he left, the citizens of Hazelton gave him a farewell "smoker," which was a term used for a rowdy male-only party. This was reported in the *Omineca Herald* on March 18, 1911:

Smoker a Success
The smoker given by the Omineca Aerie, F.O.E, at the town hall on Friday evening was a pronounced success in every way. A large crowd, estimated at well over 200, was present. The recently organized orchestra of five pieces was there and contributed much towards the entertainment of the audience. Cap Hood as chief police officer and assisted by Sanberg and Sweeney

thoroughly carried out the wishes of the presiding officer. Songs were rendered by Dorrien Mello, McCauley, Ogilvie, Gervais and several others. Dutch Kline [this was Sperry Cline] was accused of being a poet and proved it to the satisfaction of the audience.

A perfect gale of enthusiasm was aroused when Chief Maitland-Dougall was brought before the chairman. With one accord, comprising the bulk of the male population, rose to a standing position and began singing 'For He's a Jolly Good Fellow,' and followed this up with cheer after cheer. Mr. Maitland-Dougall briefly thanked his hearers for the kindly reception, following the announcement of his departure for the coast and was again cheered.[4]

Maitland-Dougall brought his diary to an end by recording his departure from Hazelton. He was taking witnesses south for a murder trial. Because the river was not yet open for steamers, he and his party went by canoe. On April 22, he wrote, "Left Hazelton by canoe, taking with me crown witnesses in Rex v Crosby. Started at 6 a.m. Reached Rankin's Camp 1½ miles before Kitwangah, at 10 p.m. Camped for night."[5]

He finished the trial in Vancouver and then went to his new job in Duncan. Here he spent the rest of his life. He and his wife, Winifred, had two sons, William and Hamish. Both were killed in the First World War. Hamish died at Vimy Ridge on April 9, 1917. William was the youngest captain of a submarine in the war (HMS *D3*) and the only one to be lost at sea. In March 1918, a French airplane sank his submarine after it failed to recognize the identification signals the submarine had displayed.[6] The wreckage was discovered in 2007.

Maitland-Dougall served as government agent in Duncan until he retired in 1932. Sperry Cline was among those at his retirement party. People remembered him as a fine sportsman and man of sterling probity. He was an excellent shot and missed few opportunities, it was said, to go out with his dog after pheasants or grouse. The billiard tables of Cowichan Country Club also knew his skill. He was one of the founders of this club and was for many years its president. He had an exemplary record on the bench. It was said that not one of his decisions was reversed on appeal. He died in 1940, after a long illness.

19

The People of Hazelton and Their Shocking Morals

1910

Mr. and Mrs. Ross Sutherland were shocked. Shocked! That their seventeen-year-old son, Victor, should be exposed to such flagrant vice was altogether too much to bear.

On July 30, 1910, the *Omineca Herald* reported that the Sutherlands were visiting the Hazelton district. With his family and a few friends, Sutherland had come upriver on the *Distributor*, one of the Grand Trunk Pacific steamers. He represented interests that were looking for investment opportunities in the district. This was the time of the Hazelton mining boom. A wise investor could make much money.

Ross Sutherland might have been impressed by the potential of the region for investment. He was not, however, impressed by the immorality he saw all around him. If his letter of complaint regarding the loose morals of the people of Hazelton is anything to go by, the police and clergy were fighting an uphill battle.

Sitting in his hotel room in Telkwa on August 12, 1910, he wrote to the top policeman in British Columbia, Superintendent Frederick Hussey:

My Dear Mr. Hussey:

You no doubt will be surprised to receive a letter from me but there is a matter which I feel impelled to advise you about which appears to me to be a very serious menace to the prosperity of the Province in this district and which lays your Department open to very severe criticism.

While you personally may not be aware of the situation and therefore not in a position to act in connection therewith, so in this spirit I write this letter to let you have the facts so far as they come under my observation.

I, accompanied by Mrs. Sutherland, Dr. and Mrs. Ewing of Prince Rupert and a lady friend from Vancouver took a trip up the Skeena River to Hazelton and remained there five days, the others returning from there and I am continuing my journey to Fort George, having my son Victor along with me.

At the only two hotels in Hazelton, the Ingenika and Omineca, we found things in a most filthy condition and the bar room open day and night and I saw more drunken men in one day at those places than I would see in two months time in Victoria or Vancouver and they are permitted to lie around on the sidewalk in front of the hotels, some asleep others rolling and staggering around and the foul language is beyond anything I ever heard. There is only one principal street in the place and people in order to use the sidewalk have to elbow their way through these drunken men or walk in the middle of the street to avoid them, and one morning we had to walk around a man drunk and asleep at 9:30 in the morning, he having fallen where there was a drop in the sidewalk at a lane beside some building.

Now I can safely say that the proprietors of these hotels pay little or no attention to the comfort of their guests but devote all their time night and day to the bar trade and there is neither any peace for a person day or night with the noise and clamor and shouting and swearing. These places are also frequented by bawdy women who are quite brazen and open in letting anyone know the class they belong to.

I made enquiry as to what police force there were and was surprised to learn that four or five men are on duty or supposed to be on duty. I also inquired why they did not enforce the law and was informed that they did not interfere unless there was a row or fight took place.

I have been in almost every new town in Manitoba, Saskatchewan and Alberta and I always found one mounted policeman able to suppress all this vice and drunkenness, in places four times the size of Hazelton.

The whole curse is in allowing men to run low saloons open night and day and presumably under the name of an hotel and if your police made it plain that every drunken person would be arrested and that the proprietor of these places was not allowed to furnish liquor to a man showing any signs of being intoxicated and bars open during the legal hours and also making it plain that no bawdy women were to be allowed in these hotels, a great deal of the evil would be quickly remedied and respectable people would not be annoyed by such degrading sights. We have to listen to foul language at every turn.

I know you have the reputation for suppressing all this when you were in the Interior and for God's sake, your own sake and the reputation of your department and the Government as a whole put a stop to this outrage upon all decency and make these small towns livable in for those who wish to see morality, law and order in the community.

I may say I find the same conditions exist in Telkwa and Aldermere but not on such an extensive scale. When I reached the Telkwa Hotel, I found an old harlot and a drunken brute sitting on the steps of the hotel, each drinking some sort of concoction and using language not fit to be repeated and my cheeks burned to think that my little son Victor had to be subjected to hearing such language and seeing such a sight.

Now, Mr. Hussey, I write this in a spirit of kindness and not fault-finding knowing well that personally you would not tolerate these conditions for a minute, and if you are not satisfied to act on my information write to Dr. Ewing or Wm. Fisher, Barrister of P. Rupert and I think they will corroborate me as to the actual conditions as they exist.

I trust I have not worried you with this long letter but prompt action ought to be taken and the matter put right before navigation closes and winter sets in.

With kindest regard and best wishes,

I am, yours sincerely,

R. Ross Sutherland.[1]

After reading this, and after perhaps giving a big sigh, Hussey wrote a letter to James Maitland-Dougall, in charge of the police in Hazelton. Hussey politely but firmly expressed the hope that the liquor laws were being enforced in Hazelton. The implicit message was clear: enforce the laws and report back. At the time, however, Maitland-Dougall was already striving to enforce the liquor laws and also to apprehend the accused murderer, Simon Gunanoot. He likely did not welcome interference from a meddler like Sutherland.

In his diary Maitland-Dougall recorded the efforts he was making to curb drunkenness, prostitution and the blind pigs (illegal bars) at Sealey's Landing and Two Mile. He was a busy man. On the day Sutherland composed his letter, Maitland-Dougall wrote that he was tracking two gallons of rum that had been shipped to Sealey's Landing. The previous day he had arrested a man named Jack Cail for being drunk in a canoe. Apparently, Cail had fallen in the river and had clambered into the canoe and refused to leave. Meanwhile, there was a litany of arrests, appearances in front of the magistrates and penalties of fines. For the miscreant who did not pay, there was time in the local jail. He was also trying to persuade Charles Sterritt to get Simon Gunanoot to give himself up. The last thing he needed was a high-minded busybody from out of town telling him how to do his job.

His diary does not show that his attempts to enforce the law ever led to significant reform in the morals of that particular slice of Hazelton life.

Victor Sutherland went on to study science at McGill University and in the First World War served as a lieutenant with the Canadian Field Artillery. He managed to survive both the trench warfare in France and his dangerous brush with vice in Old Hazelton.

20

The Soiled Doves of Two Mile

1911–1913

Every small town in the province seemed to have one. Respectable people knew about it but perhaps did not mention it above hushed, scandalized whispers. That house in the woods. That house, where illicit liquor, gambling, credit and women were readily available.

Forget Davy Crockett, Daniel Boone and the United States Cavalry; it was, it has been said, admittedly with a little hyperbole, the prostitutes who tamed the West, because they made their clients wash. The better class of brothels had carpets, lace curtains, piano playing, wallpaper with framed prints, cushions with "Forget-Me-Not" embroidered on them and a madam who enforced her rules more surely than the local sheriff enforced his.

Around Hazelton, there were two such places, although they were likely not refined enough to have pianos and lace curtains. The first was across the river at Sealey, which was convenient for the workers building the Grand Trunk Pacific Railway. Here was a notorious blind pig, as illegal drinking and gambling dens were known. The police were forever trying to sneak up on this place. Usually the bar owners and their spotters, who knew all the police, saw them coming and closed up.

In June 1911, James Maitland-Dougall, Hazelton's police chief, hired a man named William Dougherty and paid him five dollars a day to help catch them out. The bar owners were on to Dougherty at once, of course, and shut up shop as soon as they saw him coming. A new man, an ex-policeman, fresh from Scotland and therefore unknown, came into town one day and asked the police for a job. Maitland-Dougall hired him to find out when the blind pigs were open and selling alcohol. His first attempt failed because the bar had run out of liquor and was quiet. His second enabled the police to make a successful raid.

The second red-light district was at the hamlet of Two Mile. It was here that the accused murderer Simon Gunanoot had fought with Alex MacIntosh the night before the famous murders in 1906. Although Constable James Kirby had closed down that bar immediately, the hamlet remained and bars soon reopened. In 1911, this was where the prostitutes had their cribs. Trial records suggest that the women at Two Mile were not Indigenous.[1]

White men who took a bottle of whisky onto the Gitxsan reserve and used it to corrupt women were known as "squaw men." It is hard to assess how widespread this practice was, but it was seen as a social evil. The police tried to eliminate or at least reduce it. The tolerance of the prostitutes' cribs at Two Mile and probably those at Sealey may have been seen as a way of cutting down on white men corrupting Indigenous women and of reducing the racial unrest this caused. In the cribs at Two Mile there was, if only in theory, a willing buyer and seller.

The officers of the law no doubt did not approve of the activities of these women—"soiled doves," as the euphemism of the times had them—and of the men who sought their services, but they were realistic enough to accept them as an irrepressible evil. No doubt respectable citizens pestered the police to do more. Nevertheless, it is noticeable that the police took action against the women only when other offences had been committed. The few cases that appear in court records usually involved abuse of alcohol. Pimps were fair game, though. Maitland-Dougall recorded in his diary in June 1910 that he had ordered two pimps from Two Mile, men called Griffiths and Bert Jones, to leave town by the next steamer.

One case was that of Grace M. Grace had several encounters with the law. In 1911, she was charged with selling liquor without a licence. Convicted, she was fined one hundred dollars or—if she couldn't or wouldn't pay—one month's hard labour in the local lock-up. She paid the fine.

Then there was Rosie A., a known prostitute. In July, Jim M. was charged with being found unlawfully in her house at Two Mile between the hours of midnight and six in the morning. The court was told that he was a frequenter of this house of prostitution.

Acting on information received, Police Constable A.J. Harvey had gone to Two Mile to arrest Jim, whom he found in house number 10, Rosie's house. In order to catch him, Harvey stationed another man at the back door, knowing that if he went to the front, Jim would slip out of the back. Harvey knocked at the door several times and finally went in. Jim was inside on the bed with the doors locked. Harvey then arrested him. No one else was there. Rosie was found wandering about outside, very drunk and incoherent. Harvey told the court he had seen Rosie the previous night, at which time she had told him there was no reason why Jim should not go there if he wanted to. Harvey also told the court that Jim had been there several other times to his knowledge, adding he was sure he had hung around Rosie's place at night.

Jim pleaded not guilty. But it didn't help. The court convicted him and ordered him to leave the Hazelton police district within twenty-four hours. Rosie was not on trial herself, and there is no record of what happened to her.

That same month, August 1911, Grace was in court again. This time she was the offended party. Emilie G., another "soiled dove," was charged with biting her. Emilie pleaded not guilty. Grace testified:

I live at Two Mile. I know the accused. I saw her at Two Mile yesterday about noon. I was walking up to my own house when she called me up to the door and started fighting and I tried to hold her hands. She started fighting as soon as I got to her door. I was holding her hands and we fell down, she on top of me, and she bit me twice on the arm and on the face and eye. Her partner then took her into her house.[2]

Anna A., another witness, testified:

I reside at Sealeyville. I was at Two Mile yesterday. I saw the accused and I was with Grace. ... I was walking up the street with Grace ... and the two girls started to fight. The accused asked Gracie to come over to see her. She said, "I want you to come over here," and Gracie said, "I will." We were just passing the door when the accused asked. I don't know which one hit first. I think the accused hit first or rather she had grabbed hold of Gracie's hair. Grace caught hold of the accused's arms and accused bit her. I saw the marks. That is all I saw. Accused's partner then took her away.[3]

What did Emilie have to say in her defence? Presumably pleading justification, she argued, "Grace ... called me a French bastard on my step yesterday."[4] Despite this unusual defence of what she apparently thought was justified provocation, Emilie was convicted and fined ten dollars or, failing payment, seven days' hard labour.

In October 1913, Louisa S. was charged with keeping a disorderly house, though not one at Two Mile. Pleading not guilty, she defended herself vigorously. Constable S.M. Grant testified:

I am a provincial constable stationed at Hazelton. On the Sunday morning the 5th October about 1:30, I was in company with Constables [John] Russell and Caulkens, and proceeded to the house of the accused on the Hazelton Indian reserve. From information received, I had reason to suspect that this house was kept for immoral purposes. This house with two or three other houses on the Indian reserve have been under police surveillance for some time.

Constable Russell knocked at the door of the accused's house. There was no response. I knocked at the door, told it was the police and asked them to open the door. The accused opened the door to us and the three constables entered the house. The accused was undressed and a man named

Thomas ... was in bed undressed. The accused's youngest child was in the same bed. On the floor was a kind of a mattress the oldest boy was sleeping on. The house is a one room shack. Very untidy.

I spoke to [Thomas] and asked him what he was doing in the house. He said, "You know." I told him it was no place for him to be. I asked the accused if it was her house and she said, "Yes." I told the accused and [Thomas] to get dressed and come with me to the police station. Upon arrival at the station, I questioned [Thomas] if he had tendered to the accused any money. He said no, but had purchased some grub earlier in the day and took it to the house and gave it to the accused.[5]

Constable Russell testified:

I am a provincial constable stationed at Hazelton. I was on duty on Sunday morning. I visited the accused's house with two other constables. I confirm the conversation that took place between [Thomas] (the accused) and Constable Grant and given in court. I have been on night duty all summer up till last night. In the course of my patrols on the Indian reserve I have several times seen white men coming from accused's house after dark and I have turned back a few whom I have no doubt were going there in fact. Some of the boys around town have told me that they have visited there and that the house was a common whorehouse. I have never seen anyone go into the house, as any person who could not give a satisfactory account of himself always turned back. I have watched this place for some time. The woman has a bad character.[6]

Louisa, though, put up a spirited defence. She told the court:

Thomas ... wants to marry me. When Tommy left last spring, he left all his money with me and I lived on that all summer. When he left me, he told me to behave myself and not drink.

I have not been married to [Thomas] by white man's laws, but we were going to get married. I was in bed with him last Saturday night when the police came. I have been married before to a white man but he died four years ago. The oldest boy will be fifteen years in March. The youngest is nearly three years old. I was married to the white man nearly a year before the eldest boy was born. I earn my living at the canneries in the summer. I get $50 per month mending nets.[7]

The court did not believe her and convicted her, giving her a four-month suspended sentence.

Eva MacLean was the wife of the Presbyterian minister. She and her husband, Dan—Donald Redmond MacLean—had arrived in Hazelton in 1911. She wrote of the few years she spent there in her memoir, *The Far Land*. As the wife of the minister, she might be expected to have disapproved of the women and their occupation. She was, in fact, lively, broad-minded and compassionate. She became friendly with several of them. She wrote that the women of Two Mile came into town, shopped, ate in the cafés and were for the most part treated politely. One of her acquaintances, a former dancing-hall girl from the Klondike, was, MacLean wrote, saving up to give her children down south a chance at a good education.[8]

Before MacLean had left Ontario for British Columbia, respectable people had warned her she would be going to a godless place full of sin, wild men and wild women. After her arrival, she observed the more tolerant attitudes toward those who strayed from righteous paths. She noted wryly that, per capita, there were more churches and more missions in Hazelton than in her own hometown. She, a clergyman's wife, wrote:

> I was surprised to find in this new country that the women who were prostitutes were treated like human beings; while the town's women did not like them, they treated them civilly when they came in contact with them in the town. In my old home, prostitutes were looked upon as pariahs, and they were forced to always keep out of sight of the general public. For a respectable woman to be seen speaking to a known professional would have been considered scandalous. I found the professional prostitutes in the North preferable to the hypocritical amateurs I met during my years in the city.[9]

She recounted she once heard two such women from Two Mile complaining how bad times were becoming. "Migod! These are hard times, not like they used to be," one said. "Too many married women in this town."

To which the other replied, "Sure are. We can't compete with a free lunch counter."[10]

Whether the police prosecutions or the complaints of such morally upright citizens as Ross Sutherland (see "The People of Hazelton and Their Shocking Morals") and no doubt many others changed anything is doubtful. In July 1919, someone reported on the morals of the residents to the police. The *Omineca Herald* noted

that the town policeman—this would be Sperry Cline—said, "Practically every person in town is accused by the unknown informer of either frequenting immoral
houses, gambling or some other crime."[11] In all this, Hazelton was likely typical of
most of the small towns of the Canadian Old West.

21

Emily Carr and the Totem Poles of the Skeena

1912 and 1928

One day in the summer of 1912, a stout, determined lady left the boat and stepped onto the Hazelton riverbank.[1] She was carrying a bag, a bedroll, an easel and a box of painting supplies. Her name was Emily Carr. Trotting by her side was Billie, her crossbred Old English sheepdog and constant companion.

She had come to Hazelton to paint the totem poles and villages of the Gitxsan people. Her gaze would have swept along the riverbank to her left, past St. Peter's Church and up to the village of Gitanmaax on the low bench below the bluff, where approximately five or six totem poles stood. Seeing those totem poles, she would doubtless have been eager to pull out her brushes and tubes and start painting. That was what she had come for. She would have walked on to Government Street, the main street in town that ran parallel to the river, and taken in the bustle of settlers, the Gitxsan inhabitants and the large number of barking dogs.

Emily Carr came from a solid, middle-class, respectable home in Victoria. Born in 1871, she was the fifth child in a family of five girls. This dynamic conceivably powered her desire to be different. (A brother, born in 1875, had died young.) Her family was active in the Christian community and provided a welcome home away from home for missionaries travelling to or from their placements. When her religious sister died many years later, Carr found, in her words, "millions of tracts: prayer circle literature, missionary societies, little framed recipes for pious behaviour, pious poems, daily reminders ... and enough Bibles to supply the whole British and Foreign Bible Society."[2] This comment is significant. Consciously or not, Carr gives the impression of running away from her family upbringing all her life. Whatever there might have been in the family dynamics—a mother dying when Emily was young, a father with a faint question mark over his behaviour, and at least one domineering sister—she found a meaning for herself by being different from them. Art was the avenue of her escape. She found a way to what Gerta Moray, in her book *Unsettling Encounters: First Nations Imagery in the Art of Emily Carr*, called being "a missionary in reverse."[3]

Ever since 1898, when she had first seen totem poles at Ucluelet on the west coast of Vancouver Island, Carr had been fascinated by the cultures of Indigenous

Peoples. She deplored the damage being done to those cultures by the mission-aries and the colonial footprint. She challenged the social and religious ideologies predominant in British Columbia at the time. The missionaries and their sup-porters wanted to civilize those they saw as savages. Very well. She would honour them and celebrate their cultural richness. Some have criticized her for not being able to escape from the colonial attitudes of her class and race. However, she did try when not many others did—and that is important. She understood that the Indigenous Peoples of British Columbia had their own rich, valuable, separate identities and their own unique ways of artistic expression. She tried to under-stand and respect this.

Many missionaries mocked and laughed at totem poles. Like George Chismore fifty years before, they found them grotesque. With the missionary zeal Carr deplored, they diminished Indigenous cultures and tried to overlay—or even eradi-cate—them with Christian and colonial culture. In her 1913 *Lecture on Totems*, Carr wrote, "My object in going to these out of the way spots was a great love for the Indian and a determination to make as complete a collection of paintings and sketches of their villages, totem poles and houses as possible."[4] Moray writes, "With her documentary painting project, Carr sought to make a favourable record of a past that she saw many missionaries were misrepresenting and working to erase."[5]

In 1924 the anthropologist Marius Barbeau noted that twenty-six totem poles were still standing at Gitwangak, nineteen at Gitsegukla, eight at Gitanmaax, six at the Wet'suwet'en village of Hagwilget and twenty-three at Kispiox.[6] This dis-trict had—and arguably still has—one of the best arrays of totem poles in northern British Columbia, perhaps in the world. Emily Carr gives us rich pictures of these totem poles, both as paintings and as records of Indigenous culture.

"I shall come every summer among the villages of B.C.," she wrote, "and I shall do all the totem poles and villages I can before they are a thing of the past."[7] Following this resolve, she spent numerous summers in the North painting.

She visited Hazelton and the surrounding Gitxsan villages twice. The style and tone of her painting changed between her two visits. In 1912, she seemed to be trying to record Indigenous culture and make a statement about their value and richness. Her paintings, although freer in her use of paint than before she went to study in France, were, relative to her later work, still a little pedestrian. She recorded what she saw. In 1928, her focus appears to be more on the art. Her style was freer, more abstract and decidedly focused on forms, shapes and colours. She appears to have been less concerned with recording the culture than with expressing her feelings about it. Having moved from objective recording to sub-jective expression with confidence and skill, she would become British Columbia's best-known artist.

By 1912, Carr was already an accomplished painter. She had recently returned from eighteen months studying in France, where her art had been transformed by her observation of the works of the Impressionists, Post-Impressionists and Fauvists.[8] She was returning with new ideas about shapes and the use of colour, which would take her own work in a Fauvist direction. She was, the *Vancouver Daily Province* wrote in March 1912, "an enthusiastic disciple of the modern French school of art."[9] She settled in Vancouver and set up a studio at 1465 West Broadway.

A reporter from the *Province* visited her there and confessed to being startled by the vibrancy of the colours in the pictures lining the walls. "These modern painters," he quoted Carr as saying about what she had seen in France, "feel that almost anybody can be taught to sit down and make an exact copy of what they see before them if they only give enough time and effort to do it. Now a picture should be more than that. The trained eye of the artist should see more than meets the eye of the ordinary observer, who sees only what he has been in the habit of look-ing for. ... You will observe that I can get an effect of light that can only be obtained by a proper juxtaposition of colour."[10]

When she arrived in Hazelton in the summer of 1912, she had already spent some time in the North. Although her exact route is not entirely clear, it seems likely she had already been up to the Nass. She then came to Port Essington to stay with her niece Emily. This Emily was married to Marsh English, the manager of the BC Packers' Balmoral Cannery there.

Carr then travelled upriver to Hazelton on the sternwheeler *Skeena*. The Grand Trunk Pacific Railway was almost completed but had not yet reached Hazelton. Seeing the railway tracks for part of the way and the armies of railway workers, the blasting and disruption to Indigenous people along the route, she likely understood she was witnessing the end of the steamboat era on the Skeena. The last sternwheeler would leave Hazelton that September. "A mighty roaring river is Skeena," she later wrote, "treacherous—rapids, shallows, ledges, boulders—a violent river, tearing around curves, echoes shouting back her racket. Skeena used to be navigated by a fussy little sternwheeler, whose noisy going splashed and churned a moil of whiter whiteness than the river's own, foamier than Skeena's foaminess of hurried anger."[11]

In *The Heart of a Peacock*, Carr wrote that Hazelton was a tough little mining town with three hotels, as rough and turbulent as the rivers. She spent two weeks in the district. Despite her professed dislike of what missionaries were doing, she seems to have stayed some of the time at Kispiox with the Methodist missionary Rev. William Lee.[12] Here, approximately ten miles upriver from Hazelton, were

Kispiox, 1912, by Emily Carr. Image PDP00634
courtesy of the Royal BC Museum and Archives

some of the finest totem poles in the district. She made many drawings and paintings of them.

Staying in the village would have been convenient. She would have had ample opportunity to paint what was on her host's doorstep. She would also have somewhere dry to take refuge when it rained. By now she would have been familiar with one problem of painting totem poles. If she stood too close, she could paint only part of the pole and its details; too far away, and she could capture the majesty of its height but miss all the details. She did take some tall and narrow card panels with her. She also occasionally tried to solve the problem by joining two pieces of paper; nevertheless, this presented an artist trying to record the culture with a compositional problem.

One day Carr set up her easel on the riverbank near St. Peter's Church in Old Hazelton. While the Skeena flowed swiftly on her left, she painted the village of Gitanmaax. The now elderly Rev. John Field might have walked across the road from the manse to peer at what she was doing, engaging her in chatter when she wanted to be alone in her creative world. Ezra Evans, the old prospector from the gold-rush days, had a cabin next to the church. He too might have strolled across the street to peer at what she was doing. Carr painted four large Gitxsan houses with totem poles in front of each one. She did not paint these in detail as she did with other totem poles but laid them down as four dark pillars against the sky. Her focus, though, was on the poles and the houses. She painted the foreground and the hill and sky in the background in broad brush strokes of colour, reminiscent of the Cézanne paintings she had seen in Paris.

She wandered up the path on the hill behind Gitanmaax to the cemetery. Here the old-timers such as Joe Lyon and the murdered Charley Youmans and Alex MacIntosh were buried. Constructed over the Gitxsan graves were elaborate grave houses. This was the city of the dead, and full of spirits. She wrote:

Hazelton possesses a very quaint graveyard. It is on the bluff behind the town and the view from there is magnificent. The dead are buried in the

On the left, Carr's sketch of a grave house, likely to work up in a painting later. On the right, the cemetery. Images A-0656 and PDP00669 courtesy of the Royal BC Museum and Archives

ground, and perfect miniature little houses are built over them, having chimneys, windows, doors etc. You will see all the treasures of the dead: clothes, sewing machines, children's toys, women's hair, warrior's weapons, dishes, boots, hats and if possible a photo of the deceased (though this was only in the case of a young person as the old ones do not like pictures of themselves). This cemetery is divided into little streets. The little houses of the dead are gaily painted, no two are alike in colour and design.[13]

She painted approximately five watercolours in the graveyard. Since they are merely rough sketches, they were likely ideas for her to work up into paintings in her studio back in Vancouver.

She painted the river again and made three more sketches of Gitanmaax totem poles. On another day, she went four miles up the Bulkley River to paint the Wet'suwet'en village and totems of Hagwilget. At this time, the village was on a rise above the stony beach, out of reach of high water. The Indigenous bridge, still standing when Carr visited, was badly in need of repair. She did not include this bridge, nor indeed the high-level bridge being built almost above it, but concentrated her focus on Hagwilget, again laying in the foreground and background with broad sweeps of colour.

Leaving Hazelton, she boarded the sternwheeler *Inlander* and went downriver as far as Skeena Crossing. Here she disembarked and went to the adjacent village of Gitsegukla to do more sketching and painting. From here she was able to board a train for the rest of the journey. She was now able to use the free rail pass the Grand Trunk Pacific had given her to save money. En route, she stopped at Gitwangak. She wanted to visit Gitanyow but had been warned that

Gitanmaax, the Gitxsan village at Hazelton, inspired Emily Carr to a painting of this scene in 1912. Image A-06885 courtesy of the Royal BC Museum and Archives

this village was not safe. The Gitxsan community there, she was told, did not like non-Indigenous intruders. Reluctantly, she acquiesced, but made a mental note to return to the Skeena one day to paint the totems at Gitanyow. The train took her on to Prince Rupert, from where she took the steamer *Prince John* across to Haida Gwaii, then named the Queen Charlotte Islands, to paint more totem poles.

Carr returned to her studio in Vancouver after a journey of six weeks. She worked on the sketches she had made on the Skeena, producing many finished paintings. In October 1912, with other local artists, she exhibited at the Studio Club at 1126 Robson Street in Vancouver. The *Vancouver Sun*, in reviewing this exhibition, said, "Perhaps the most striking series in the hall came from the brush of Miss Emily Carr and are most weird and wonderful creations of Kispiox and Ktsikut villages where Miss Carr spent the summer."[14] The *Province* loftily commented that her vigorous descriptive painting of Indigenous villages and totem poles "might well find a place in a public gallery, where they would be a valuable memorial, though they scarcely come into the category of ordinary pictures."[15]

The public neither liked nor purchased her paintings. After a bigger and more important—but no more remunerative—exhibition in the Dominion Hall on Pender Street in Vancouver in April 1913, she gave up her studio and returned to Victoria. For fifteen years she did little painting. She took in lodgers and, because she had so little money, did all the work that this entailed. She cooked. She sold fruit from her garden. She bred rabbits. She also took up hooking rugs and sold these more easily than her paintings.[16] These were dark years for her.

––––––––––––

Carr's paintings, though, had become well known in artistic circles, earning both critical and positive attention. By 1927, her reputation had grown sufficiently for her to be drawn back into the artistic community. That year she had gone to Toronto, where she had been warmly welcomed by Lawren Harris and other members of the Group of Seven. They validated what she was doing and refreshed her confidence in her own painting. With a national reputation in the art world, she was now having more exhibitions and was increasingly being seen as British Columbia's most important painter. The National Gallery was buying her paintings and the Canadian Handicrafts Guild was buying her hooked rugs.

When Carr returned to Gitwangak in the summer of 1928, she was determined to see and paint the totem poles at Gitanyow. Again, she was warned the people there were unfriendly and she should stay away. The previous year some young men from Gitanyow had chased missionaries out and driven surveyors off their land, reportedly, but not reliably, with axes. Their subsequent imprisonment caused considerable resentment amongst the Gitxsan in Gitanyow and coolness toward her when she first arrived. Not that white people, she found, were any more friendly. They tended to mistrust or ignore her. The local newspapers made no mention of her presence in the district.

She described her visit to the Hazelton district to her friend Flora Burns and later lightly fictionalized it in her book *Klee Wyck*.[17] "Well, I had two weeks up the Skeena," she told Flora, "during which time it rained almost every day. I did quite a bit of work however, but it made it very difficult."[18]

At Gitwangak, she learned that a young man, Aleck Douse, the son of a Chief, was taking lumber to Gitanyow and would be returning in two days. Yes, he was prepared to have Carr accompany him there and back.

So here she was, sitting on a sack of oats in a four-wheeled wagon, "with nothing so jazzy as a spring," with her little griffon dog, Ginger Pop, on her lap.[19] She brought enough food and mosquito oil to last her two days, which she doubtless thought would be ample time to paint and gather sketches to work on in her studio

Isabella Douse, Emily Carr's host in Gitanyow, described by the police as the "chieftainess who supports the malevolent faction." Image PDP00629 courtesy of the Royal BC Museum and Archives.

later. The journey took seven hours and was a bumpy, dusty ride, even throwing some of the men travelling with them off the wagon a number of times. One sturdy old man walked behind the wagon for most of the way. When the cart arrived in Gitanyow, large dogs rushed out in a ferocious pack to greet them. The villagers came out to welcome one of the men enthusiastically, as though he were some sort of local hero.

Now what? There was no mission house in which to stay. Bears regularly came through the village at night. Camping outside no longer seemed such an attractive prospect. Aleck Douse told her that she could sleep on the veranda of his father's house. Here she spent the first night "with a fly over [her], but next morning an awful storm came on, hail, thunder and everything."[20] She now learned that Aleck's father, the Chief, was the man who had walked behind the wagon from Gitwangak. No one else paid her any attention.

The next morning, Mrs. Isabella Douse, the Chief's redoubtable wife, interrogated her. Why had she come to the village? "I want to make some pictures of the totem poles." Why? Mrs. Douse was neither friendly nor angry, Carr wrote. "Because they are beautiful," she answered. "The young people do not value the poles as the old ones did. ... I want to make pictures of them, so that your young people as well as the white people will see how fine your totem poles used to be."

Mrs. Douse said, "Go along, and I shall see."[21] Carr was not sure whether she would be turned out of the village or not.

As Carr was walking away from the house, toward the totem poles, she saw a menacing pack of large dogs coming out at her, snapping and barking. Whereupon, she wrote, Ginger Pop, all six pounds of him, put them all to flight. "Their tails were flat, their tongues lolled and they yelped." The Douses were highly amused by the sight, "and we all laughed together so hard that the strain, which before had been between us, broke."[22]

Carr went to see the totem poles. She sat in front of a totem mother and began to draw, not noticing the coming storm. When the rain came down in sheets, she took refuge in a grave house and then, aware of the spirits there, went to a broken-down and leaky community house and sat in the corner. Horses had also taken shelter there and they had, she discovered, taken all the dry spots and were not inclined to move. After two hours the rain ended, and, dripping wet, she returned to the Douses.

When she arrived back, she found that her hosts had moved her bed and things into the house, and they invited her to "live en family," she wrote. "They were extremely nice people and it was a most interesting insight into their life. It was a huge log house but only one room. The Chief, his son, a daughter and her husband (the jail man), three children

Gitanycw (Kitwancool). WikiArt

and a niece all lived in it. There were nine windows and all open and two doors. So it was airy and quite clean. The floor was scrubbed white. I was given a corner ... and a rocking chair. I hung my fly over the corner and put my bed behind that and was very comfortable."[23] She dried out. "When the Indians accepted me as one of themselves, I was very grateful," she wrote.[24]

In addition to Aleck and an orphan called Lizzie, two married daughters and their husbands and children lived in the Douse family home. Two babies swung in cradles suspended from the rafters. Everyone who passed gave the ropes a jerk so that the cradles kept swaying. "There was no rush, no scolding, no roughness in this household. When anyone was sleepy, he slept; when they were hungry, they ate; if they were sorry, they wept and if they were glad, they sang."[25] The families enjoyed Ginger Pop, his fiery temper, the tilt of his nose and particularly the way he kept the house free of Indigenous dogs. It was Ginger Pop, she wrote, who "bridged the gap" between their language and hers with laughter. "Ginger's snore was the only sound in that great room at night."[26]

For two days from dawn to dark, she drew and painted in the village of Gitanyow. In addition to her paintings, she filled notebooks with drawings to take back to her studio to work up into paintings there.

Every artist painting in the outdoors has to deal with the vagaries of weather and wildlife. Rain is the most common peril, but persistent mosquitoes can be more irritating. When the mists lifted, they attacked. Carr wrote to her friend Flora:

Emily Carr with Ginger Pop, her Brussels griffon dog that put the dogs of Gitanyow to flight on her visit there in 1928. Image F-01220 courtesy of the Royal BC Museum and Archives

But oh goodness! The mosquitoes. This whole country is blighted by them. They are beyond words an endurance. The Indians don't seem to get bitten. Much tho' they complain of them bitterly and they all sleep under nets. They attack my legs worst. ... They look like beef shanks. They swell and hang over my shoes. I only have low shoes with me and I've tried everything. Puttees [cloth wrapped around the ankle and calf] made out of table oil cloth of a loud design, but they slipped and the brutes got in between. Now I have a pair of canvas pant legs made loose and hanging right down over my boots like thin old pantalettes. I made a bag for my head of cheesecloth and a pair of glasses to see through fixed on with adhesive and wear two pairs of gloves, one kid and one long chamoisette and they bite through this tho' and my palms where they fasten are a mass of bites. Life's just torture every minute you are outdoors. It's terrible trying to concentrate on "significant form" or anything else with fiery states everywhere. They chew right through my khaki dress.[27]

On the day Aleck was to take her back to Gitwangak it started to rain, and it rained for three days and nights without stopping. Carr's problem now was that she had run out of food. All she had was hardtack and raisins. Because she could not bring herself to eat the Gitxsan food, she did not tell them how hungry she was. For four more days she lived on that hardtack and raisins.

As they were leaving, Mrs. Douse stopped the wagon and made Carr show them her sketchbooks and wet canvases again. Two of the best totem poles in the village belonged to the Douses. Carr offered several of her paintings of these poles to her. "Her head nodded violently and I saw her smile for the first time."[28]

When Carr arrived back at Gitwangak, the police told her that they would never have advised her to go to Gitanyow. In fact, they said, "One of the men who went in on the wagon with you was straight from jail, a fierce, troublesome customer."[29] Hence, she thought, the hero's welcome.

Either Carr did not know what had been happening in Gitanyow over the last year or she chose not to write about it. In her account of her visit, she makes no mention of the fact that she had stepped into the last chapter of a tense confrontation between the Gitxsan people and the Dominion government. In 2020, Professor Hamar Foster wrote about this incident in the *Manitoba Law Journal*.[30] The crisis, he notes, was significantly more serious than the mere chasing away of a surveyor. The previous year there had been a confrontation between the Gitxsan in Gitanyow, who claimed the valley was theirs, and the Dominion government, which claimed it was not. The Dominion government sent in surveyors, who asked for police protection. Both sides gave the other warnings. Plainclothes police investigated. The surveyors went in. In some magnitude of scuffle, the Gitxsan sent them away, taking one of their axes, smashing it and throwing it in the river. This was described as attacking the surveyors with axes. The police returned and arrested five of the ringleaders, who were tried, sentenced and sent to Oakalla Prison for a number of months. The police considered Isabella Douse one of the agitators, calling her a "chieftainess who supports the malevolent faction."[31] But they did not arrest her.

When Carr went to Gitanyow in the summer of 1928, several of the five jailed men were returning home after having served their sentences. The hostility to white people in the village would have been understandably high. It also explains the initial coolness Carr felt. She gives the impression of being blithely oblivious of the crisis, of being an innocent, tripping peacefully and unknowingly through dark woods. This has led some to criticize her for ignoring the crisis and not taking a stand with First Nations activism. Although she was not politically sophisticated, she did have a well of wisdom to draw from. It seems equally likely that, when *Klee Wyck* was published over a decade later, she realized she did not know enough of what had really happened and so thought it would be wise to avoid the topic. In her fictionalized account in *Klee Wyck*, she was choosing her words to describe her visit as carefully as she chose her colours to paint.

After her visit to Gitanyow, Carr went upriver to Kispiox, where she painted three large watercolours. In these she showed a markedly more artistic and confident handling of the totem poles with their large, powerful eyes. Necessarily she would have passed through Hazelton and Gitanmaax on her way to and from Kispiox. By now, her style had become more fully developed. Her work had an imaginative boldness, abstraction and power she had not yet found for her paintings in 1912. Her new paintings were full of unusual angles, strange near-Cubist shapes and swaths of colour.

Emily Carr preserved her understanding of the Gitxsan culture in and around Hazelton and in her own way honoured its separate and rich identity. She became the iconic painter of the forests and totem poles of British Columbia and one of Canada's most revered artists. Long unknown outside Canada, she has recently started to acquire an international reputation. An art critic for the London *Observer*, reporting on an exhibition of her work at the Dulwich Picture Gallery in London in 2014, wrote:

> Carr found a new way of painting that is unlike any other, in which the vision is radically joyful and modern, the paint as fine yet potent as the breezy air around her. Although she is often compared with her contemporary, Georgia O'Keeffe—two single-minded women out in all weathers, painting the great outdoors—at her best Carr has more in common with her fellow outsider Vincent van Gogh.[32]

22

Rene D'Egville and the Men from Hazelton Who Went to War

1913–1918

O ne evening in the winter of 1913, Sperry Cline pushed open the storm door, then stepped happily into the smoky, noisy, boozy bar in Old Hazelton. Outside, the temperature was twenty below; inside it was warm and convivial. He described the scene:

> All is hazy for a few moments. Kerosene lamps sway from the ceiling, well above reach and out of harm's way and as our vision clears we begin to get our bearings. The front of the sixty-foot bar is lined with customers and behind it are the usual six bar tenders. The professional bar tender of that era is a distinct specimen of humanity. His hair is smoothly plastered down by the liberal use of a perfumed pomade, sharply parted and brushed from his forehead into a perfect cowlick. A handle-bar moustache adorns his upper lip and is considered an absolute necessity. He usually works in his shirt sleeves and fancy white shirt, embroidered waist-coat which has a nugget watch chain crossed from pocket to pocket.[1]

Here men gathered, in Cline's words, "for companionship and a surcease of sorrow."[2] In the years before the First World War, the bar was the social centre of Hazelton. Townsmen, packers, telegraph operators, railway workers and prospectors in for a spree—but absolutely no women—from Hazelton congregated there each evening.

Cline paints a picture of the scene in the bar for us. The old packer known as Cataline is a regular, in his sombrero, frock coat, woollen trousers and long, curly hair, into which he rubs some rum from each glass he drinks. Beside him stands Get-Rich-Quick Davis, a dapper gentleman from "Virginny-uh," who modestly claims he is a nephew of the Confederate leader Jefferson Davis. Pete Enoch almost starts a fight, but someone orders another round of drinks and peace is preserved. Shell Robinson is trying to explain Darwin's theory of evolution, but Sanctimonious Bill interrupts him, quotes from Genesis and pronounces loudly that "beyond the peradventure of a doubt, Darwin and Huxley are bare-faced charlatans."[3] Johnny MacInnes is entertaining a number of French Canadians by reciting one of Dr. William Drummond's poems, except that Gustave Gervais,

Rene D'Egville was an artist. Here he illustrates the move of the *Omineca Herald* from Old Hazelton to New Hazelton. The sign says, "New Hazelton or Bust." Image P2564 courtesy of the Bulkley Valley Museum

eloquent with both hands, keeps interrupting with stories about his experiences as a voyageur on the river Nile in the attempt to rescue General Gordon. Over there leaning on the bar are James Turnbull and Tommy Brewer, both forest rangers, talking shop. A couple of Montenegrins are about to start a fight with some Serbs, their countries being at war with each other, but they are separated before it gets serious. Scotty Ogilvie, possessor of the best voice in the district, is then summoned from his desk in the lobby to restore conviviality by singing "Annie Laurie" and other Scottish ballads, which prompts Dave McPherson, heart swelling with Scottish pride, to start a speech about the antiquity of the Scottish race. Jack Bennett is somewhere in the milling crowd. Groundhog Jackson is still boring everyone by talking too much of the coalfields in the North. Whisky Jack orders yet another whisky and soda. He is a remittance man, a gentleman from England, and has never forgotten it, being smartly dressed and pretending to have a monocle. Big, kind-hearted Sourdough McKay—reared in Ontario on blueberries and catechism, it is said—comes in and buys a round of drinks.

Standing at the far end of the bar, quietly taking it all in, is a man in a Norfolk jacket. He takes out a pad of paper and starts drawing caricatures. His name is Rene D'Egville. He may be a remittance man. He applied for a homestead in Alberta in 1905 but the following year abandoned it as being unsuitable for cultivation. He now has a ranch near Telkwa but spends his summers in Hazelton as a fish guard. Born in 1881, he comes from a famous English theatrical family with a Huguenot heritage. He achieved some local renown in 1911 by shooting a bear that was demolishing his cabin. On at least one occasion he was a special constable helping in a raid on a blind pig, or illegal bar. A talented artist, he draws cartoons and humorous pictures of such topics as the *Omineca Herald's* move from Old Hazelton to New Hazelton. He has a reputation for eccentricity and is a familiar figure in Hazelton with his jacket, overalls, yellow-silver toque and Jack, his fox terrier. "We all considered that there was no future before Degg," the *Omineca Herald* would later note, "and some even looked upon him as a hopeless case."[4] No one thought he would come to much. He was known as "poor Degg" around town.

As with so many "before the cataclysm" scenes, this picture of Old Hazelton before the war that Cline described is both colourful and sad, poignant and a glimpse of a world of camaraderie that would soon be shattered. The old world was about to end. The coming war changed everything.

In August 1914, the major European nations stumbled into the First World War. With them, tied to the imperial government in London, went Canada. Like every community in the country, Hazelton endured the war as best it could, trying to keep a sense of normality amid ever-grimmer news. At the start, there was patriotism, jingoism and much distortion of what was really happening. In August, for example, the *Omineca Herald*, repeating the slanted news sent to it, announced that the Royal Navy had inflicted a crushing blow on the German Navy. "It is now almost universally looked for that Germany will be smashed in three weeks," the newspaper noted.[5] In September it announced in a headline as a known fact that the kaiser was "looking for peace."[6]

For the first three years of the war, the Canadian Army was composed of volunteers. Even after conscription was introduced, fewer than forty-eight thousand conscripts were sent overseas. Men from Hazelton stepped up to enlist, as did others from all over the country (see Appendix 2). Stanley Geary and Constable R. Ponder, both already in the naval reserves, were the first to be called to the colours. After a rousing send-off party at the Omineca Hotel, at which there were patriotic speeches and songs, the two men left town on August 4.

In the first days of the war, the government agent in Hazelton, Stephen Hoskins, received a telegram from an operator at one of the cabins on the telegraph line named John Reid Barker. His telegram read, "In case of need, please enrol my name among the volunteers for active service. Mounted or foot. Will take about ten days to reach town."[7] Barker, a man from Brierfield, Lancashire, had fought in the South African War and apparently did not want to miss this one. Wounded in the ankle at Ypres, he was later invalided out of the army with eczema. Bill Guiney

On To The War. — Hazelton Nov. 5th 1914

The first draft of men from Hazelton who volunteered to join the army in November 1914. In this group are Thomas Brewer, Spot Middleton, James Turnbull, Jack Frost, John Nesbitt, Lorne Fulton and Andrew Monour. Surprisingly, all survived the war. Andrew Monour, though wounded, resumed his career with the bank but died at the end of 1920. Image courtesy of the author

enlisted in October. Also a veteran of the South African War, Guiney was a good horseman and an expert marksman. His friends said they were confident he would give a good account of himself. Let the Germans beware!

On November 5, 1914, the Hazelton community gathered to wish good luck to the first group of volunteers leaving to join the Prince Rupert light infantry. George Reid Middleton (known for some reason as Spot) was a teller in the Union Bank, secretary of the athletics association and goalkeeper for the soccer team. Jack Frost was a rancher. James Turnbull and Thomas Brewer were forest rangers. John Nesbitt, a forest guard, was another veteran of the South African War, in which he had served with Lord Strathcona's Horse (Royal Canadians), a regiment raised and paid for by Lord Strathcona. Andrew Monour was a clerk with the Bank of Vancouver. Lorne Fulton, a druggist at the Up-to-Date Drugstore, joined up expecting to be in the medical corps.

In December 1914, Dr. Archibald MacAulay from the hospital staff left to join a regiment in Prince Rupert. Dr. Wrinch's nephew Hubert, who had been in Hazelton managing the drugstore, enlisted in May 1915. Other groups left later—six men in July and four men in August of 1915. Twenty-two more, after a rousing send-off in the Hazelton Hotel, left in September 1915. In June 1917, May Hogan, the lady superintendent and matron at the hospital, left to join the overseas

Another contingent about to leave for the war. But how many came back? Image courtesy of the author

nursing staff of the Canadian Forces. Her friends gave her a particularly good send-off at the Hazelton station.

The people of Hazelton, as in so many communities, supported their men and one woman in the war in Europe. They held a multitude of fundraising events. They formed a committee to raise $1,100 to buy a machine gun for the army. The ladies of the Red Cross knitted socks and sewed nightgowns for the wounded in hospitals. What the soldiers most craved, though, were newspapers and cigarettes. One soldier in France wrote that he had read and reread the *Omineca Miner* four or five times cover to cover so as not to overlook any news from home, even though by then the news would have been woefully out of date.

The *Omineca Miner* applauded the community:

Hazelton is cheerfully bearing its part in the war for world liberty. No call for men or money has gone unheeded, and our town has fairly earned an enviable reputation for contributions of soldiers and cash. Up to the present time we have sent more than fifty men with various corps, and the list of soldiers from Hazelton and vicinity is being constantly added to. Over ten per cent of our population and approximately half our men of military age are members of Canada's overseas forces.[8]

In the summer of 1916, Rene D'Egville was still doing his job around Hazelton as a fish guard and making detailed drawings of salmon and trout. Then he decided to go home and enlist in the British Army. He arrived in England on December 19, 1916.

Serving with the general staff "somewhere" in France, Lieutenant R. D'Egville wrote to Jack Frost at Soldiers' Aid in Hazelton:

> You've made me positively homesick, for the old brands of tobacco (in a Soldier's Aid parcel) looked so familiar, it only wanted a piece of smoked salmon to make the thing complete. ... I never expected to see much when I came out in a labour battalion but it was all I could do, the shape I was in, and I've seen quite enough in a short time to know that working under shell fire is not as funny as it looks in a Bairnsfather [a popular cartoonist in the English newspapers] drawing; nor can it be said that sleeping under canvas while the playful Hun empties machine guns from airplanes into the camp is conducive to steady nerves or restful slumber. ... I have seen the shells falling about sixty to the minute—not a bombardment, of course, merely an "artillery exchange"—and fellows playing football, with an occasional shell falling among the horse lines and the Canadian band playing O Canada in the offing. ... I have not been in the front line, no nearer than the twenty-five mile snipers, but a lot of our labour people are well "forrard" doing every conceivable job, pleasant or otherwise. And I know that "where-did-that-one-go" feeling, though I confess it does not interest me as much as the "where-in-h—-is-the-next-one-going-to-land" sensation. The man who says he doesn't mind being under fire is a — liar. When you have seen nothing you want to go up; when you've seen something, the back of the back looks mighty good. ... I am now confined to an office and do not get away until 11 or 12 at night, but I like it and manage to get some fresh air, though I sometimes feel I'd like to go out and split a little wood, and I found myself handling an axe lovingly some time ago. ... I miss the old trail and the campfire. It's going to be a hard job to stay this side. B.C.'s got me the same as the other fellow.[9]

James Turnbull was one of the volunteers in that first group of seven who, waving flags, had left Hazelton in November 1914. He was thirty-five years old. By March 1915, any glamour and excitement he may have felt when he enlisted was wearing off. "Amid the bleakness of a Belgian spring morning—colder than the rawest cold Canada can produce,"[10] he described graphically a life in the trenches that was "simply scientific murder."[11] The Germans, he said, were firing on stretcher-bearers as they were going about their humane duty. The Pats—Princess Patricia's Canadian Light Infantry—had just experienced another gas attack. Only about 150 men of the regiment remained on the front line. At the time of writing, he said, he had not had his clothes off for sixteen weeks.

In November 1915, Turnbull wrote home that he had been south of Armentières. "The boom and crash of high explosives goes on incessantly, day and night. Away down underneath the ground you can hear the tap tap of Germans who are mining with the amiable intention of blowing you up."[12]

In April of the following year, by now a lance corporal with the Pats in France, he wrote home:

We are living on the lid of hell these days and don't know the minute when she is going to blow up. ... We have been jumping around from place to place lately and there has been no time for anything. We've had frost and we've had snow, and we have fresh visitation of the white stuff this morning (March 4). Also where we are at present (of course I can't tell you where that is) is rather an important position, and the Germans shell the whole line and for the two miles behind the line most assiduously.

I am living in a shack composed of old poles, sacks and blankets and I expect to have the blessed thing caving in on my devoted head one of these days. The shells were landing 25 yards away last night. Fortunately they were high explosives, which either blow you to bits or miss altogether, so it's all right either way.

I saw Lorne Fulton two nights ago and Spot Middleton about three weeks ago. We are quite near each other, but it's hard to get away when things are so nervy as they are now. ... We have always very few casualties compared with fellow regiments in the same brigade, probably because we have ceased to be curious and don't expose ourselves unnecessarily. ...

(10 p.m.) I have just got back after having been up in the front trenches. They have got the wind up for fair up there tonight, expecting to get blown up by mines any minute, I think it's all tommyrot myself, but there is nothing like being prepared. I wanted to stick around and see the fun, but the major ordered me out of the trench and I'm back here again. It's a rotten sensation, though, waiting for the solid earth to heave you sky-high, though I would like to take part in the fight that follows.[13]

Soldiers may have been heroes, but they were not necessarily angels. Many got themselves into some kind of trouble, petty or otherwise. Turnbull was no exception. In June 1916, his superiors admonished him for neglect of duty while on active service. His offence? He had failed to hand over rations at a battalion dump when he was meant to. This story begs for an explanation, which now we shall never have.

On September 2, 1916, the *Omineca Miner* reported that James Turnbull of the Princess Pats had so far escaped injury, although only seven of the men who were on the roll with him when he joined remained in his company. Later that year he was in hospital with pneumonia. Later still, both he and Spot Middleton, another from that first November contingent, were both wounded, invalided out and discharged on service at Hastings.

Jack Bennett was Australian. He had been born in Lindenow in the state of Victoria in 1886 and arrived in British Columbia in 1910. How he came to be in Hazelton is not known. He may just have been knocking around the world before settling down. But there he was, a farmer, labourer—anything he could turn his hand to. He enlisted in Prince Rupert on November 6, 1914, and embarked for Europe in February of the following year.

Bennett went to war as a private with the Sixteenth Canadian Scottish. He reported to his friends in Hazelton that he was on a ten-day course where he was learning how to throw bombs.[14] This was at the Pioneer Camp at Seaford, in England, which was the base for the regiment. Then he returned to the front line in France. On June 13, 1916, he was wounded when he was hit by the fragments of a bomb near the Ypres Salient. In August, he was at the Canadian Convalescent Hospital in Epsom. "I am about fit for the firing line again," he wrote. "Tommy Brewer is here, also doing well. We were both hit in the same scrap."[15]

Then he was wounded again. He wrote:

I guess I can skip over our early experiences at Ypres, Festubert and Givenchy, as Jack will be able to tell you all about those places, the death trap at Festubert, where we were put against a regular hornets'-nest of machine-guns and our boys cut down like sheaves. I have seen much worse shellfire since then, but have not been in a warmer corner for machine-gun and rifle fire. All through want of shells too. It used to make us sore in those days to see our little light shells bursting almost harmlessly over the Hun trenches while they came back at us about five to one with heavy stuff that made us hunt our dugouts.

But all that slowly began to change. We got heavier shells and more of them, so that now we can beat the Hun himself at slinging the heavy stuff, with great shells that seem to rush up way from away to the rear, too far away to hear the gun that fires them. They pass overhead with a variety of sounds that seem to blend into one roar and hiss, and the sight of them going up in the air when they land is good for a man with a grudge against Fritz. A heavy bombardment nowadays is a terrible thing to see, and they are getting more concentrated and deadly as time goes on. If it lasts another year or two, I believe the opposing armies will hardly be able to approach each other for shell-fire.

You have heard of our scrap with the Germans on the —th. The Germans attacked the C.M.R.'s [Canadian Mounted Rifles] near Zillebeke, and after a fearful shelling, broke through on a front of 1,500 yards and penetrated 700 yards past the front line. Our brigade was about 12 miles to the rear, having a rest. We had to make a forced march to the scene of the action, arriving in the vicinity at 1:30 in the morning. The 14th, 15th and 7th Battalions made a counter-attack in broad daylight, but failed to drive the enemy out of his newly-won ground, and, of course, got badly cut up. So then it was our turn, but it was decided to get up some more heavy guns first and make a good job of it, as Fritz had done. We lay in a little disused ditch for six days while preparations were going on. Then it was decided to give us three days' rest before sending us over; so we marched out again, got a good bath (you know what that means, Jack) some good hot meals and some sleep. Then we marched up from business again.

We reached our old position about dawn on the —th and lay there all day and watched our big shells bursting along the German lines. Gee! it did our hearts good to see the great 9.2s and 12-inch howitzers sending up great columns of earth and smoke, sometimes black, sometimes yellow. They pounded them at intervals most of the day and again at 9 o'clock at night. Then we went silently up through our new front line and out into no-man's land. There we lay in a little, old trench while the artillery gave them the final intense bombardment. Our manoeuvre, though a bold one, was very successful and we were helped by the night being very dark and showery, with gusts of wind. Fritz might have made it hot for us had he discovered us out there, but he did not, thanks to the weather. We were just far enough forward to escape the terrible shellfire that he put up. It was an anxious hour we had there, with our own shells dropping ahead and the enemy's shells dropping so near behind us that we were sprinkled with falling earth, and could feel the hot smoke on our faces, while the ground shook and rocked under us.

Then our guns lifted at —a.m., and over we went amid crackling rifle fire and spattering machine gun fire. If ever a bunch of men got satisfaction it was us. There were three battalions of us attacking on a front of 500 yards each, the 13th, 16th and 3rd, and we sure gave them hell. I got within 20 yards of the second trench and lobbed a bomb into 7 or 8 of them who were potting away and throwing bombs, and then got knocked kicking by one of theirs, which burst alongside me. I was very lucky in getting off with only three small pieces in me, though I felt the shock for a week. Well, the boys took all the lost ground and held it all next day until relieved, in spite of a very heavy shell-fire, which lost us a lot of our boys, but, as I said before, the Huns lost more than we did. We did not stand on ceremony, and I guess very few Germans lived to go out of their own frontline trench. Tommy Brewer did fine work and accounted for more than one pair of Huns. He emptied his own revolver into them at close quarters and then I gave him mine, and he did the same with that.

I still have a piece of metal in my head and am recommended to take an operation to have it removed.[16]

Sergeant Jack Bennett—he had been promoted—was at the Battle of Vimy Ridge. There he was wounded again. This was his third wound, the first being at Hill 160 and the second at Zillebeke. He wrote from Seaford Hospital in Sussex to his friend Jack Frost about the battle:

That was some show on the 9th. It was the last thing in shell fire which our boys put up; some contrast to Festubert, I can tell you. Our guns had been giving it them at intervals for nearly a week, but the final three minutes before we went over was terrific; it nearly takes my breath away when I think of it.

We crept out into no man's land the night before and dug in our kicking-off trench. We were well dug in by daybreak, then we waited for the final moment to come. We did not have long to wait. At 5:27 the guns opened up as one. It was to be a three-minute preparation and then the barrage was to creep forward over his second and third lines and we were to climb over and follow. Three minutes don't seem long for a bombardment, but it did the work alright for there were not many Huns left in his front line or much of his front line left either.

The survivors were game though and did their best. I had the pleasure of lobbing a bomb between two of them who were still firing as we approached. It sure closed them up. I had a bit of good shooting with my rifle after we passed his front line. They could be seen getting away in bunches of from three to a dozen in the thick haze of smoke, but not many got away, for our barrage was dropping almost like a wall of smoke and fire ahead of them. We got to our first objective in a very short time and it was here I got pinked over. After the fury had passed on, I got a stick and with the aid of it hobbled back to the rear. It was a great start for the first day and I thought we were going to bust right through, but Fritz is a tough proposition to break up. I am now a grenade instructor here, just temporary of course, but I am going to hang on as long as I can and show the young bloods how to wield the grenade.[17]

In all this tangle of bombs, gas, rats, lice, blood, trench warfare and hospitals, Jack Bennett found one happy thread. On September 12, 1917, he married Alice Rogers—"the sweetest little girl in England."[18] But there were eleven more months of war. Seeming to attract German bullets, he had been wounded numerous times already. Would he survive to bring her home to Hazelton?

Cy North was a twenty-seven-year-old mining engineer from Nova Scotia. He was a valued player for the Hazelton soccer and hockey teams. His skill and experience had assisted Old Hazelton to thrash New Hazelton 10–0 in the opening game for the Duncan Ross Cup in January 1913.

He enlisted on September 13, 1914, as a private and sailed for Europe on October 3 with the First Field Company, Divisional Engineers. By June of the following year, he was a lieutenant with the 177th Royal Engineers. The next month, July, he wrote from a London hospital that he had been wounded by a bullet that had passed through his thigh bone. That meant he would be on the sick list for another six weeks. He praised the surgical work at the hospital and the fact that it took only sixteen hours to get a casualty from the front line to a hospital in London. He deplored the German practice of using the sulphur bullets that slowed recovery.[19]

By November 1916, he had risen to the rank of major and was the commanding officer of the First Canadian Tunnelling Company. "Cy," the *Omineca Miner* said proudly, "received his various promotions for acts of skill and daring which were to be expected of one with the pluck and brains which made him such a valuable member of our champion hockey and baseball teams. His latest distinction is the Military Cross, which he won by defeating a German attack on his trench. Coming out of his mine shaft, he found the infantry disorganized by a surprise attack, but rallied them, and with the assistance of his own men repulsed the Huns."[20] In January 1917, he was mentioned for distinguished conduct in Field Marshal Douglas Haig's dispatches, which led to his being personally invested with the Distinguished Service Order by the king at Buckingham Palace.

The toll on the men from Hazelton was heavy (see Appendix 3). The first reported fatality was that of Walter Smith, who was mortally wounded at Ypres. A New Hazelton boy, he had been one of the youngest men in the province to enlist. Andrew Monour had been wounded in the head. Invalided back home, he was recovering in the convalescent hospital in Esquimalt. Private Jack Frost was also invalided home and would have surgery to give him, it was hoped, full use of his injured foot. Private James Hevenor arrived home on leave "minus an arm but in good health and spirits."[21] He had gone away with the 102nd and had been wounded the previous September. In 1917 it seemed that almost every issue of the *Omineca Herald* or *Omineca Miner* carried tragic news. They announced the death of the Stoltze boy in February; Harold Findlay in March; H.P. Blake in April; Charles Helas and Frank Gray, killed at Arras, and H.L. Gibbs in May; and Major Tony McHugh in June. The death of Edward "Ned" Charleson, one of the best-known pioneers of the Hazelton district, was reported in December.

The war ended in November 1918. By the following summer, those of Hazelton's soldiers who were coming home were already back. Over 55,000 British Columbians, out of a population of fewer than 450,000, had served overseas. Of these, more than 6,000 had been killed and over 13,000 wounded.

In July 1919, Hazelton honoured its soldiers with a gala banquet. The assembly hall was decorated with flags and flowers. While Gray's Orchestra, all the way from Smithers, played in the background, the welcoming committee formally greeted guests at the doors. Practically everyone from Old Hazelton and New Hazelton was there, and many also came from Smithers and Terrace. There were songs and speeches. Harry Broadfoot delighted the crowd with his Harry Lauder renditions. Dr. Horace Wrinch, as chairman of the organizing committee, gave the main speech and presented the soldiers with certificates of honour and appreciation. Captain Thomas Brewer expressed the thanks of the returning soldiers to the people of the district, not only for the night's entertainment but also for the manner in which they had worked and supported them during the whole war. After the formalities, there was dancing until three in the morning. Present also, perhaps, were the ghosts of those who had not returned in person.

Remarkably, all seven men who had joined the Prince Rupert regiment in November 1914 in the first enlistment from Hazelton had survived. Four of them were present at that gala banquet: Captain Thomas Brewer, Captain J.F. Frost, Corporal James Turnbull and Sergeant Lorne Fulton. Spot Middleton was still in England with the Soldier Settlement Board. Andrew Monour was working at Molson Bank in Victoria, but he never really recovered from his wounds. He died in October 1920, aged twenty-nine.

Jack Bennett did survive the war and came from Europe on the ss *Metagama* in March 1919. After the war, he and Alice settled at Ganges, on Saltspring Island, where he died in 1984, aged ninety-seven. James Turnbull married Minnie Harbury in 1925 and became a timber cruiser and road foreman for the Department of Public Works. He died in 1950, aged sixty-nine.

Cy North also survived. He returned to his profession and became well known in British Columbia as a mining engineer and manager. During the Second World War, he went to Gibraltar and built an underground hospital in the rock. In 1958 he was the project manager for the destruction of Ripple Rock, the notorious navigational hazard in Seymour Narrows. The explosion was the world's largest non-nuclear peacetime explosion up to that time.

Whisky Jack, one of those present on that long-ago evening in the Hazelton bar, returned to England when the war broke out. His relatives managed to get him reinstated in the army. At the end of August 1914, he was killed at Mons. Scotty Ogilvie was also dead. Shell Robinson was wounded and went home to die in Ontario. "Many of the young and middle-aged," Cline wrote, "lie beneath the poppies of Flanders."[22] In remembering that convivial night, Cline mourned not only dead friends but also the death of the old way of life and the fragmentation of community and camaraderie.

After the war, the *Omineca Herald* noted with evident surprise that Rene D'Egville—poor Degg—had been mentioned in dispatches, had served as an efficient cipher officer with the General Headquarters Staff and had gone to the German headquarters at Spa with the Armistice Commission. It reported he had remained in England after the war and become a graphic artist.[23] The *Herald* may, however, have been misinformed on this. Rene D'Egville had a younger brother, Alan, who was also a noted cartoonist and who worked for the popular magazine the *Bystander*. Degg eventually settled in Exeter, Devon, and died in 1963.

The men from the Hazeltons who had gone to war with such enthusiasm, believing they would miss out on a great adventure if they did not hurry, believing all the wishful thinking about it being over by Christmas, understood all too soon that the reality was horribly different. The reticence of returning soldiers to talk about the war is well documented. They seldom spoke about it because they believed that those not there could never comprehend. The wounds were too deep. The losses too great. It was not until the mid-1920s that war memoirs and war poetry started appearing in bookstores. Only then did people begin to understand that the war had not been glorious, clean and heroic, that not all men had died quickly, bravely leading their comrades toward a fiendish foe.

23

May Hogan, the Woman from Hazelton Who Went to War

As the steamer chugged up the coast of British Columbia toward Port Simpson in that year of 1899, eighteen-year-old Eva May Hogan would have been excited to see her parents again. Her long journey from her native Ireland was almost over. She hadn't seen her parents for almost seven years. In those years, she had grown from a girl to a young woman.

She would have stood at the rails on the ship's deck, staring at the forested cliffs dropping down into the waters and at the multitude of fjords and islands. There, see, dorsal fins of orcas slicing through the waves. And there, in the trees, the white heads of eagles. Apart from the canoes and boats of the Indigenous people and the occasional village and the one or two mission settlements they stopped at, there were no people.

The journey across the Atlantic aboard the Allan Line ship *Parisian*, the train journey across Canada and then the steamer voyage up the coast would have seemed endless but intensely exciting. It was all new and the distances were vast.

In 1893 her missionary father, William Hogan, a large man famous for his big heart, and his Welsh wife, Margaret, had left Ireland for their Anglican mission post in northern British Columbia. Their daughter May had remained in Ireland to finish her education. Because she set down her occupation in the 1901 census of Canada as a schoolteacher, she may have acquired some teaching experience in Ireland. Now, here she was, on her way north to join her parents.

With an Irish lilt to her voice and a Dublin rose in her cheeks, May was now in the bloom of young adulthood, ready for life's adventures, ready for the new century, for love and fulfillment. And what did she get?

For the next few years, May lived in Port Simpson. She qualified as a nurse. It is possible that she went to Vancouver for her training at Vancouver General Hospital, one of the few nurse training schools in the province at that time. She spent a few years nursing at the small hospital at Swanson Bay, now a ghost town, on the northern coast. In 1912, she became lady superintendent at the twenty-two-bed Hazelton Hospital, reporting to Dr. Horace Wrinch. She had likely first met the Wrinches when they visited Port Simpson on their arrival on the northern coast in September 1900. At the hospital she was not only matron but also in charge of the nurse training school. Apart from her service during the war, May stayed at the Hazelton Hospital in various capacities for the next twenty-four years.

William and Margaret Hogan had moved to Masset on the Queen Charlotte Islands (now Haida Gwaii) in 1909. After William died in February 1914, Margaret went to Hazelton to be with her daughter. She worked as "a ray of Welsh sunshine"[1] in and around the hospital for many years, becoming a pillar of the local community. May, also community-minded, played the piano at events at the hospital and took part in amateur dramatics in Hazelton.

The Hazelton Red Cross was among the organizations that sprang up to support the soldiers at the front during the First World War. Mother and daughter worked on the Red Cross Committee with Dr. Wrinch. May Hogan remained on the committee until the spring of 1917.

May Hogan, photographed as a girl in Dublin. Image courtesy of the author

Then, after a good send-off from her friends at the station in New Hazelton, she went to Victoria and enlisted as a nursing sister with the Canadian Army Medical Corps. After receiving her basic medico-military training at the Ontario Military Hospital, she was sent to Europe.

She was one of the more than three thousand nursing sisters from Canada who served during the war. On account of their blue uniforms and white veils, the soldiers nicknamed them "bluebirds." Forty-five of them died, twenty-one from enemy action.

Hogan's nursing career as a bluebird during the war was probably typical of many. Her age and experience suggest, though, that she might have been seen as a square peg in a round hole. Thirty-six years old, she was considerably older than most of the other nurses, many of whom had joined up from their nursing schools or in groups from their training hospitals. One of the requirements of service was that the nurse had to be aged between twenty-one and thirty-eight. Although the age requirements were not always rigorously applied, Hogan was obviously among the older group. With her experience as a matron of a hospital and head of a nurse training school, she may have appeared intimidating to some of the younger nurses.

With the war in its third year, the organization of the Canadian Army Medical Corps was already well established. A bewildering array of medical establishments

Lieutenant May Hogan in her uniform as a nursing sister. Image courtesy of the author

in France, in England and in the eastern Mediterranean sprang up. There were general hospitals, stationary hospitals, casualty clearing stations, convalescent hospitals, hospital ships and more. Perhaps surprisingly, some of these were organized and sponsored by private organizations such as the medical faculties of various Canadian universities. Additionally, behind the hospitals and medical staff was the army of military clerks who maintained the all-important records and carefully noted on them wounds, convalescence, leaves, transfers and monthly pay. All too frequently, the records ended with a an abrupt line and a comment such as "killed in action" or "died of wounds."

Hogan was sent first to No. 16 Canadian General Hospital in Orpington, Kent. This huge, two-thousand-bed hospital had been sponsored and organized by the government of Ontario. The British colonial secretary, Andrew Bonar Law, a fellow Canadian, had opened the hospital in February 1916.[2] It contained twenty wards, arranged in pairs, but it expanded as the need for facilities grew. It had recreation rooms and even an excellent twenty-two-piece band to cheer everyone up. From here Hogan sent back a German helmet as a souvenir to her mother. (What happened to the head that was once inside it?)

Hogan volunteered to go to France and was posted to No. 10 Canadian Stationary Hospital, at that time stationed in Eastbourne, Sussex. She joined this hospital on November 4, 1917. When the hospital was moved to France in December, she and the other medical staff were temporarily posted elsewhere while the non-medical staff went to prepare the site. When it opened a month later, the authorities sent Hogan and the medical staff to the new location at Calais. She arrived on January 28 and started work at once. The day after she arrived, hostile aircraft raided Calais. At ten to eleven that night, a bomb fell in the hospital grounds and destroyed the men's cookhouse and mess room. Another bomb fell fifty yards north of the hospital. There were no casualties among the patients or personnel, but it was a taste of what was to come.

No. 10 Canadian Stationary Hospital was sponsored, organized and staffed by Western University of London, Ontario. The London Red Cross provided many of the supplies. The prime mover and commanding officer during its entire existence was Edwin Seaborn, professor of clinical surgery in the medical faculty, who was given the rank of lieutenant colonel.[3] An article in the *Canadian Journal of Surgery* describes this hospital:

> In December 1917, command of the No. 14 [Canadian General Hospital] was transferred to Lieutenant-Colonel Kenneth Douglas Panton, while Seaborn was tasked with taking a smaller group as the No. 10 Canadian Stationary Hospital to Calais, France. They were given a poor site by the Canal de Marck, which had been abandoned by a British hospital. They arrived to find the camp flooded, with no power. Although about 40 miles from the front at that time, they were subject to aerial bombardment because of the importance of the Calais port. The unit immediately set about rehabilitating the site by installing sewage, drainage, walkways and power, reinforcing patient areas and building bomb shelters. Soon they were receiving 250 new patients a day.
>
> The canal was used to transport the wounded. Seaborn soon noticed that the less injured arrived first. He developed a rapid admission system (canal to ward in less than one minute) so that he could keep treatment areas clear. A mobile surgical unit was created to treat patients injured by bombardment on site. Major General Carleton Jones complimented the unit, saying that they had achieved in one month what the Imperials could not do in six.
>
> The German offensive drive in March 1918 rendered the forward hospitals inoperative, dramatically increasing the number and severity of casualties. Most of the patients were British, as the Canadians were deployed far south of the hospital. ... The unit did not leave France until April 16, 1919. While in Calais, No. 10 had admitted 16,712 patients; only three other hospitals in France had taken so many.[4]

Being an embarkation port for troops and supplies coming from England, Calais was an important target for German bombers, which came over most nights. The nurses soon came to distinguish between friendly aircraft, which droned or hummed, and enemy aircraft, which throbbed with an ominous pulse. Many nurses preferred to be on duty during air raids, although the total darkness in the hospital while they were on duty made life difficult. They would stuff morphine, hypodermic needles and tourniquets into their apron pockets for their rounds. Another problem was the grumpiness of patients under skylights when they had to wake them to move them away from the risk of falling shrapnel and glass. Bombs landed on No. 10 Stationary Hospital twice, with little damage being done. The frequent German bombing raids were the closest times Hogan came to the enemy. That, she may have thought, was close enough.

What would it have been like, nursing at a stationary hospital in France? We get glimpses from what people wrote in diaries and articles.

Colonel Samuel Hanford McKee, who had commanded a stationary hospital, wrote in the *Canadian Medical Association Journal* in 1919:

> We used a large hospital marquee as the admission tent, and after the patient had been examined by the medical officer, three clerks took down the ... particulars. ... After the necessary forms were filled in, the patient was taken to an adjoining tent where he was stripped and given a bath. His clothes were quickly tied up, in an ordinary sack, and sent to the disinfector. ... The serious stretcher cases were, of course, taken straight to the wards. By means of a slate, with the hospital ward and bed arrangements upon it, the admitting officer was able to designate what bed he wished a patient sent to. ... Most of the convoys arrived at night with the men hungry, tired and sleepy. I have actually seen a man so tired that he was unable to stay awake while his arm was being set. No matter what time of night a convoy arrived, the men were always fed and given a smoke, and made comfortable for the night.[5]

Hogan stayed with No. 10 Stationary Hospital for most of the rest of the war. Together with the other staff, she had to deal with the huge number of casualties resulting from the German offensives that started on March 21, 1918. This huge push, powered in part by fifty-two divisions of soldiers brought from the eastern front after the collapse of Russia, punched a hole in the Allied lines and inflicted heavy casualties, many of whom were brought to No. 10. The Germans were banking on defeating the Allies before the American forces became too powerful. However, what the Germans hoped would be a decisive breakout failed when the Allies were able to bring in their reserves, including the newly arrived American troops. This contributed to the German collapse and ultimately to the armistice in November.

Extracts from the confidential war diaries of the hospital tell the day-by-day story and provide a vivid picture of hospital life:[6]

24/12/17 [day/month/year]   Arrived at Calais and proceeded to site of hospital (on eastern border of town). Hospital buildings consisted of eight large huts of rounded type and numerous huts of square construction. Estimated bed capacity of hospital huts—400. No patients in hospital at this time. Hospital previously occupied for a short time, during which period it was known as No. 38 General Hospital. Most of buildings unready for occupation in respect of Engineer Services, viz.—lighting, plumbing, sanitation, etc. Hospital grounds about 12 acres in extent. Land had been reclaimed and was of a loamy nature, with a tendency to become very muddy in wet weather. This defect was partially overcome by the laying down of slag footpaths in the grounds by a Belgian Labour Company. Unit personnel proceeded with work of organising, equipping and cleaning the hospital in preparation for receiving patients.

1/1/18   Personnel employed on following duties: protection of wards against action by hostile aircraft. Equipping of wards. Laying of footpaths, and improvement of grounds generally.

28/1/18   Nursing Sisters ... E.M. Hogan [and nineteen other sisters] reported from England.

31/1/18   Average number of patients during period 20-1-18 to 31-1-18: 100. Strength of unit at date: Officers, 12, Nursing Sisters, 28; Other Ranks, 114.

2/2/18   The wards are gradually opening and patients increasing.

5/2/18   A splendid concert was given by the personnel to the Officers and Sisters. The Matron and Sisters from the Isolation Hospital came over and all were very much pleased and thought the men did splendidly.

11/2/18   First evacuation of patients to England. (16 patients.)

12/2/18   A large Y.M.C.A. hut was put up this afternoon opposite the Administration Building, Captain Ridciford taking an active part in getting this desired recreation place for the patients.

14/2/18   The Sisters entertained the officers in their lounge. Dancing and cards were indulged in and a very pleasant evening was spent, this being the first social evening we have had since arriving.

15/2/18   There was an air raid. So far we haven't heard of any damage. It lasted a few minutes when "All Clear" was sounded. We are looking forward to the time when the moon does not appear.

18/2/18   Another air-raid this evening. No damage done, though it lasted two hours. We retired about 11:30 p.m. All tired out. The "All Clear" is a most welcome sound.

12/3/18   We held our first Tuesday "At Home" and entertained the Matrons, Officers and Sisters of No. 30 General Hospital and of the Isolation Hospital.

The day was lovely and everybody seemed to enjoy the afternoon. In the evening we were invited to the 222nd Anti-Aircraft Battery to attend a concert given by the A.T.C. Concert Party. When the concert was nearly over word was received of an impending air raid, which quickly dispersed the concert party, and we returned to camp. The alarm did not last very long, however, and soon the "All Clear" was sounded. No damage was done to the vicinity. It was reported that the enemy planes were on the way to England by way of Dunkirk.

18/3/18 The enemy planes were over Calais. Our guns put up a barrage but were of no avail. We heard the machine was brought down at Dunkirk.

20/3/18 One bomb fell 500 ft N.E. of Hospital grounds, another 500 S.E. of Hospital grounds.

The German offensive in March brought a rush of casualties. On the twenty-fifth, 84 cases, mostly gassed, arrived. Seventy patients arrived on the twenty-eighth, 150 on the twenty-ninth and 70 on the thirtieth. Another 170 patients arrived on April 10. The convoys of wounded men kept on coming. All available beds were being used and there were constant shipments of wounded soldiers to England to provide beds for new arrivals. For a time there was a fear that the front line, already broken, would be overwhelmed and the German offensive would succeed. Calais was bombed almost every night. The vulnerable hospital couldn't find labour to strengthen the wards against these bombs.

6/04/18 A confidential letter from Base Commandant, Calais, received, requesting that officers and other ranks infuse their utmost energy into their work during the present crisis in the military situation.

6/5/18 Convoy of 65 stretcher cases received. Air raid warning to 5:15 and 6:15 to 6:45.

9/5/18 An air-raid warning 12:45 to 3:30 a.m. Hostile aircraft over Calais. Many bombs were dropped but not in close vicinity to the hospital. ... Convoy of 97 cases admitted to hospital at 11 a.m. All available beds and tents being utilized for up-patients.

12/5/18 Another air raid warning was sounded last night at 10:40. Two hostile aircraft were plainly seen in the beam of the searchlights. Very heavy barrage was put up but was not successful in reaching the enemy.

15/5/18 We received a convoy of 62 patients during the afternoon from the barges. There was a great deal of activity in the air all afternoon. Three alarms were sounded. Hostile aircraft taking photographs. About 10:20 air raid alarm was sounded and immediately following the enemy planes were over us. Some eight bombs were dropped very close to the hospital. A French military office was destroyed. Twenty civilians, mostly women and children, were taken from the ruins by men from the unit and cared for in the hospital. Some of them were seriously wounded and one man died in the operating room. Five bombs were dropped on the Belgian hospital, which is in the next field to us, destroying five huts, killing seven and wounding quite a number. This is the worst raid we have experienced.

17/5/18 The 112th U.S.A. Infantry Band gave a concert during the afternoon and again in the evening, which was very much enjoyed by the patients. During this afternoon we admitted 250 cases from Beaumarais Camp suffering from ptomaine poisoning. They were all very ill. This made a busy afternoon. ... At present there are 24 of the personnel in hospital all suffering from what appears to be an epidemic of grippe. All available beds are taken and several patients were sent to the tents.

23/5/18 Received the word from No. 1 Canadian General Hospital of Sister K.M. MacDonald having been killed in the air raid of May 19, 1918, and also of Sister Lowe being dangerously wounded.

17/6/18 Convoy of 60 barge cases received.

19/6/18 Convoy of 88 patients, of which 50 were malaria cases. Two years ago today the Nursing Sisters of No. 10 Canadian Stationary Hospital left Canada. During the afternoon the personnel gave an open air concert to a large number of patients, including some of the officers and patients from the Belgian hospital, and in the evening the Sisters entertained a few of their friends in the Sisters' Mess. Dancing and cards.

1/7/18 Field Day Sports were held in the hospital grounds. The Y.M.C.A. Band played during the afternoon and in the evening an open air concert was given by local talent. Mr. Brownlee, U.S.A., sang several songs, which delighted the audience. ... A convoy of sixty patients was admitted in the morning.

22/7/18 Air raid warning sounded at 12:10. Almost immediately enemy planes were heard. Several bombs were dropped in the city, doing considerable damage. Some lives were lost. "All Clear" was sounded but the enemy returned shortly after and dropped three or four more bombs in close vicinity to the hospital, destroying a house and killing all the inmates.

11/8/18 Evacuation of 116 patients to England.

13/8/18 Convoy of 94 patients received. 69 patients evacuated to England. 10:25 p.m. to 1:10 a.m. air raid warning. Five bombs dropped in city proper.

23/8/18 Convoy of 56 barge patients received from the front. A very large percentage of these cases were Mustard Gas poisoning and many were severely burned.

31/8/18 [With two other nurses] E.M. Hogan proceeded to England on 14 days' leave.

16/9/18 [With other nurses] E.M. Hogan returned from 14 days' leave in the United Kingdom. Air raid alarm. Enemy machines raided the city intermittently.

11/10/18 A whist drive was given to the patients. A party of the Q.M.A.A.C. [Queen Mary's Army Auxiliary Corps] attended. A very enjoyable evening was spent with cards and dancing.

12/10/18 A convoy of 80 barge cases was received in hospital.

15/10/18 Today the sky is overcast and a fine rain is falling.

24/10/18 The number of influenza cases admitted is increasing rapidly. Wards 2 & 4 have been isolated for their accommodation.

26/10/18 A train convoy of 114 cases was admitted to hospital. 86 of these patients were suffering from Influenza. This sudden inrush of infectious cases necessitated the isolation of another ward. Mr. Chester of the British Y.M.C.A. gave one hour of character impersonations. Thoroughly enjoyed by patients.

The war diary becomes less about gassed and wounded soldiers and more about soldiers suffering from the influenza pandemic loose in the world. Finally, after all the suffering, came the armistice.

10/11/18 A wireless message from the Eiffel Tower was picked up by a Belgian Marconi station in Calais about ten o'clock this evening to the effect that the armistice had been signed. The French authorities are awaiting an official message.

11/11/18 There were 3 deaths today from broncho pneumonia following Influenza. The signing of the Armistice was celebrated by the blowing of whistles of boats in the harbour, ringing of bells and salvos from the anti-aircraft guns. The civilians and troops made great demonstrations in the city during the afternoon and evening.

12/11/18 A very enjoyable hour of music was given to the patients this evening by Miss Sarah Silvers of the Y.M.C.A.

19/11/18 Patients Day, set aside as a day of thanksgiving in commemoration of the cessation of hostilities, signing of the Armistice and to show in some humble way the great appreciation and regard which the Matron and Nursing Sisters held for the patients under their care who had so nobly fought and unflinchingly suffered to bring about such conditions. By kind permission to Lt-Col. Seaborn, November 19th was settled upon and the Matron and Nursing sisters set to work, sparing neither time nor expense to make the day a complete success. Tables were set up either side of the Red Cross Recreation Hut, a row up the center, two tables at the end near the stage and one long table on the stage itself. White tablecloths were laid and shaded electric lights. Flowers were profusely arranged on all tables and the whole appearance resembled a banqueting hall. Tables were arranged at the opposite end of the hut from the stage, for serving purposes.

Before commencing dinner, every person rose and headed by our padre, Captain Gibson, sang "Be present at our table Lord."

The following sumptuous repast, which was prepared under the supervision of Sgt. Duncan (Sgt. Cook), was served by the Matron and Nursing Sisters. Cream of tomato soup. Fresh roast (a donation by Lt.-Col. Seaborn, of an entire pig grown on our grounds) with apple sauce, boiled cabbage and mashed potatoes. Real Canadian pies—lemon and apple, fruited jellies and apples and apple cider and cigarettes. After dinner, the tables were cleared and set aside and Miss Sarah Silvers of the Y.M.C.A., and a very talented singer, entertained a delighted audience of blue boys and personnel, all of which joined in most heartily on choruses of songs which they knew. After Miss Silvers left, a short impromptu dance was enjoyed by all present and as a fitting finale of a very enjoyable and successful evening, the entire company formed a circle in the Red Cross Hut and sang "Auld Lang Syne."[7]

19/12/18 Request from P.C. Town Troop that everything possible should be done to provide entertainments, games etc. for the prevention of discontent among the troops.

May Hogan was at No. 10 Stationary Hospital in Calais when the war ended and would have been present at the grand banquet to thank the nursing sisters.

The soldiers put down their arms and started to dream of going home, which they did, though not as quickly as they wanted. The slowness of their return to Canada and of the demobilization led to a serious and almost forgotten mutiny in March 1919 at Kinmel Park, in North Wales. This resulted in five dead and twenty-three wounded Canadian soldiers. For many of the wounded soldiers and the people who looked after them, though, there was no going home, not yet anyway. Hogan's service in 1919 is a reminder that for the medical and nursing staff, the war had not ended. It merely meant no new arrivals. The hospitals were still full of men struggling to survive their terrible wounds.

May Hogan being welcomed home at New Hazelton station. Dr. and Mrs. Wrinch are in the closest automobile, May Hogan and her mother in the one behind. Image courtesy of the author

In January 1919, the authorities moved Hogan to No. 3 Canadian General Hospital. This was the hospital organized by McGill University shortly after the war broke out. The head of the medical faculty there, Colonel Birkett, had become the first medical director of the hospital. John McCrae, the writer of "In Flanders Fields," was the officer in charge of medicine at this hospital. But he had died of pneumonia in January 1918, long before Hogan was there.

Here Hogan could well have come across Dr. Archibald MacAulay from the Hazelton Hospital, who was also stationed there. Now a major, he had been mentioned in dispatches and decorated. It is pleasant to speculate that they found a little time amid their hectic schedules to reminisce about Hazelton and the long-ago days of peace by the Skeena River.

From there, Hogan went back to England to No. 2 Canadian Casualty Clearing Station at Shorncliffe. Then, after a spell at No. 16 Canadian General Hospital, she finally prepared to go home.

She returned to North America on the ss *Celtic*, reaching New York on September 4, 1919. Then there was the train journey across the continent to Vancouver and the steamer up the coast. This would doubtless have brought back memories of her journey twenty years before. How times had changed! Her mother, the Wrinches and the local citizenry gave her a warm reception at the New Hazelton station when she arrived. That evening there was a welcome-home banquet for her in Hazelton.

She was home. What should she do now? Her old job as matron at the hospital was held by someone else. She was too much a part of the Hazelton Hospital community not to have a contribution to make. With the administrative work of the hospital increasing, Dr. Wrinch now clearly needed assistance. Consequently, in the spring of 1920, Hogan became the secretary at the hospital.

Seven years later she took on another role. Dr. Wrinch's wife, Alice, had died of cancer in 1923. In September 1927, May Hogan and the widowed doctor married at a quiet wedding in Chown United Church in Vancouver. When Dr. Wrinch retired from the hospital in October 1936, he and May moved to Toronto, but they soon moved back to Vancouver, where, in October 1939, Wrinch died.

May Hogan became secretary of the Hazelton Hospital after her return from the war in 1919. Image courtesy of the author

May aged and fell ill. She died on April 5, 1945, in Hollywood Sanatorium in New Westminster. The short list of her possessions is poignant. They included two silver bangles, a black bead necklace, some family photographs, a glass scent spray, a rayon bedspread, a black evening dress, a biscuit jar and a few odd spoons.

24

The Hudson's Bay Company and the Anniversary Celebrations

1920

L ondon, 1666. The Great Plague is lately over, and the King and his cousin Prince Rupert are sitting in Whitehall. Médard Chouart des Groseilliers and his brother-in-law Pierre-Esprit Radisson, two French adventurers and fur traders, are looking for investors in London, the city of newly-restored-to-majesty King Charles II. Dutch privateers captured the ship on which they were returning from New France to Europe and dumped them on the coast of Spain. From there they worked their way back to France. This was not what they had in mind when they went searching for furs in the land beyond the French territories in North America. After their own government in France refused to support them in further ventures, they came to London for better luck.

Here they did persuade merchant adventurers to finance an expedition to explore the possibilities of the fur trade in the New World. The Duke of York (the King's brother) and Prince Rupert (the King's cousin) received them and, together with other aristocrats and leading merchants, each invested £300 in their venture. Prince Rupert became an important sponsor.

Their new ships, the *Nonsuch* and the *Eaglet*, sailed from Gravesend on June 3, 1668. One of their aspirations was to search for the elusive passage to the Indies around the top of North America. The other, more practical, was to find a fortune in the fur trade. The *Eaglet*, with Radisson on board, was dismasted in the Atlantic and had to turn back. Des Groseilliers, known by those who had trouble with his name as Mr. Gooseberry, carried on and spent the harsh winter at a fort he and his men built on the shore of Hudson Bay. He spent that time trading with the local Indigenous people and amassing beaver furs. Returning to England in October 1669, he had little difficulty persuading his investors to formalize the enterprise.

On May 2, 1670, King Charles awarded a monopoly of trading rights and effective governance to a vast area of land on the northern part of the American continent to the "Governor and Company of Adventurers of England, trading into Hudson's Bay," otherwise known as the Hudson's Bay Company. The fact that a large number of Indigenous people had lived on that land for millennia and considered it theirs was, in the context of the times, considered irrelevant, if considered at all. The King appointed his dearly beloved cousin Prince Rupert to be the Company's first governor. The land was consequently called Rupert's Land.

The two French venturers soon became disenchanted with their personal lack of fortune and returned to France. From there they went back to French Canada for further fur trading with other people in other places.

The Hudson's Bay Company prospered and established a formidable trading empire in a territory that was considerably enlarged by the merger with the North West Company in 1821. This extended the Company's trading rights to the Pacific coast. It governed this huge land—one-twelfth of the world's land mass—for approximately two hundred years. Its authority lasted until June 23, 1870, when the government of Queen Victoria approved the transfer of all the land under the Company's mercantile control to the new nation of Canada.

The Company's trading posts across the country formed the skeleton of non-Indigenous existence and expansion in Canada, and they prospered. The managers, or factors as they were called, were the key players in this trading empire. Between 1826 and 1830, young James Douglas was working for the Company at Fort St. James.[1] There he would have been aware of the Forks of the Skeena and also would have met William Brown, the trader who had tried so hard to get there. This was five years before the Company instructed Simon McGillivray to journey to the Forks. Douglas was then sent to Fort Vancouver, where he spent many years, rising in 1839 to be chief factor. Fort Vancouver (now Vancouver, Washington), though, was in American territory. The Oregon Treaty of 1846 had established a border between the Company's territory and the United States. This meant that the Company had to establish a new headquarters north of the border. In 1841 the Company directed Douglas to set up a fort at the southern tip of Vancouver Island, and he built Fort Victoria there not long after. In 1849, the British government established the Colony of Vancouver Island. After the first governor, Richard Blanshard, resigned, the British government appointed Douglas as the second governor. For a while, he held both positions: chief factor for the Hudson's Bay Company and governor of the Colony of Vancouver Island.[2]

Among the Company's posts in northern British Columbia were the ones at Fort Simpson, Fort Babine and Fort St. James. In 1866, the Company opened a store on the flat land at the Forks of the Skeena and appointed Thomas Hankin the first and only manager. On account of the poor furs, the Company closed this store in 1868. In 1880, taking over the premises of J. Walsh in Hazelton, it established a new store and appointed Alfred Sampare as its manager. After Sampare, the factors in Hazelton were William Sinclair, Charles Clifford, Joe Lyon, Richard Sargent, Alexander Murray and Alexander McNab, who took over in 1903. In the year 1920, the manager was William Anderson.

That year, 1920, the Hudson's Bay Company celebrated its 250th anniversary. Celebrations were held all over the country. How should it celebrate in Hazelton? As with so many celebrations in the small town, the Company organized a dinner, a dance and sports. It invited residents of the district to a banquet in the Hazelton assembly hall. Three long tables were set up, with the Gitxsan and Wet'suwet'en guests occupying two of them and the non-Indigenous guests the third. At the head table sat the host, William Anderson, and three long-time residents: Richard Loring (the Indian agent since 1889); Richard Sargent (the manager of the Company's store in Hazelton between 1896 and 1900); and Dr. Horace Wrinch (doctor and hospital superintendent since 1900).

The guests did ample justice to the sumptuous feast. Before dinner, a photographer took a now-lost flashlight photograph of the guests. Dr. Wrinch acted as chairman and proposed the toast to the King. Loring toasted the Company, and Anderson proposed a toast to the Indigenous people, to which Charles Martin replied. Bill Nye from Hagwilget then proposed a toast to the white population. In his toast, Anderson spoke of the Company's history and gave thanks to the Great Kind Giver of all things, who had been so lavish in his gifts to the country. The dance held in the assembly hall afterwards went on until two-thirty in the morning. When it ended, the dancers gave Mrs. Gibson hearty cheers for her excellent piano playing.

The following day, a non-Indigenous team from Hazelton played a celebration game of baseball with the Gitxsan team from Glen Vowell, a neighbouring community. The Glen Vowell players started well and were on their way to victory with three runs. In what may, uncomfortably, be seen as a metaphor for their relationship, the Hazelton team started to play the rule book and the Glen Vowell team "were called out, without knowing why or what for."[3] The Hazelton team started to score until they had won their thirteenth run in the bottom of the eighth inning and shut out the Glen Vowell team in the ninth. The score was 13–12. Understandably, players on the Glen Vowell team were not happy with this result. A match was also held between the Hazelton team and a team from the Grand Trunk Pacific Railway, but this was too one-sided to be enjoyable. When darkness ended the game, the Hazelton team was ahead 17–2.

The Hudson's Bay Company also held celebrations at its head office in Winnipeg. A group of Indigenous Chiefs from the Hazelton district travelled there to participate, taking with them a canoe that had been made at Fort St. James. This was to be used for a great paddle-down-the-river event.

The Chiefs who travelled to Winnipeg were Bill Nye from Hagwilget, Bill Williams from Kispiox, Charles Martin from Hazelton, John Williams from

Indigenous Chiefs in Winnipeg during the celebration of the 250th anniversary of the founding of the Hudson's Bay Company. With them are the manager and staff of the Union Bank. Image courtesy of the author

Babine, and Louis Billy and George Prince from Stuart Lake. They travelled first class, and for many of them this was their first time on a train. "Too much noise. Too much go fast," John Williams said.[4] Williams took marten and ermine skins to present to the governor of the Company, Sir Robert Kindersley. Sam Baptiste of Babine went with them, paying his own way. He impressed people there with his Royal Humane Society medal, which had been awarded to him for saving the lives of two prospectors in 1913. Baptiste had been caught in the wilderness with these two men, whom he had been able to get to safety, risking his own life in the process.

The manager of the Union Bank in Hazelton wrote to his colleague at the Union Bank in Winnipeg and asked him to show the visitors around. On May 6, the manager gave his guests a tour of the sights. They saw the stores, had a ride in automobiles and saw airplanes. The manager showed them around the Union Bank Building, where they inspected the gold and silver in the vaults. They then went up to the roof for photographs. In the elevator going up, one of the Chiefs counted the floors and said at the top, "Ten Houses."[5] To thank the bank for showing them around, the Chiefs performed on the roof the dance that honoured a new Chief on his elevation.

A hundred years later, on the 350th anniversary, the Hudson's Bay Company was still in business, though not in any form that Pierre-Esprit Radisson or

Médard des Groseilliers would recognize. Nor would King Charles or Prince Rupert have understood the department store business the Company—now universally known as the Bay—carries on, although they might recognize the reality of the plague that stalked the land in the early 2020s.

25

Captain Streett and the
Airplanes on Mission Point

August 1920

Bill Streett knocked apprehensively on the door of George Beirnes's house on Mission Point. Captain St. Clair "Bill" Streett of the United States Air Force was arguably the most historically significant foreigner ever to visit Hazelton. His objective in 1920 was to fly his Black Wolf Squadron from New York to Alaska and back. At this moment, though, his mission was at great risk of failing entirely. Streett knocked again.[1]

Beirnes was a Hazelton old-timer, having been a familiar person around the Upper Skeena for over twenty years. Like most Hazelton old-timers, he had worked at many jobs, including prospector, packer and carrier of mail to the coast. He had known the accused murderer Simon Gunanoot for much of that time and only the previous year had been instrumental in persuading Gunanoot to surrender to justice. Having been acquitted by a Vancouver jury, Gunanoot was now back on his traplines in the North. Beirnes knew all there was to know about dogsleds, pack trains and sternwheelers. Now he had a farm on Mission Point across the Bulkley River from Hazelton, and his crop of oats was ripening.

When Beirnes opened the door to Streett, he saw a young man in the uniform of the United States Air Force. Telling Beirnes he was the commander of the Black Wolf Squadron, Streett said he had a favour to ask. Could he land four airplanes on Beirnes's land on Mission Point? There was nowhere else suitable in the district. If Beirnes turned down his request, it might mean the end of his mission. This was his last chance.

Many important people visited Hazelton in these years, but, as yet, not one airplane. Premier John Oliver had visited earlier in 1920 and indeed would be coming again the week after the squadron's visit.[2] The Governor General, the Duke of Devonshire, and his retinue had visited Hazelton in 1919. Numerous foreigners visited over the years, but perhaps none had such a distinguished career as Bill Streett. But this was all in the future.

In less than ten years, modes of travel had moved from horseback, dogsled and sternwheelers to railway trains, automobiles and, if Streett was able to find a landing place, the first airplanes. In July the *Omineca Herald* announced that the first car to make the full journey from the southern part of the province to New Hazelton had arrived.[3] That claim was dented only slightly by the fact that for one stretch of a few miles near Burns Lake, the car had to be transported by train. The drivers, members of the Munger family from Kamloops, had navigated their Baby Grand Chevrolet through mud up to the top of the wheel in one bad patch, as well as through high water and over tree stumps. They also had to cut a new road through a stretch of forest at Quesnel. They might have wished for the ability to fly.

––––––––

Bill Streett had enlisted in the United States Army after high school. In 1916 he had joined the air force as a flying cadet. When his country joined the war the following year, he was commissioned as a second lieutenant and served in France.

After the war, the United States government wanted to strengthen its presence in Alaska and explore the possibility of regular flights there. It directed Streett to fly from Mitchel Field in New York to Nome, Alaska, with a squadron of four de Havilland DH-4B biplanes. This was officially known as the Alaska Flying Expedition. No aircraft had done this before. Powered by the 400-horsepower Liberty engines, these aircraft could fly as fast as 115 miles an hour. The squadron left Mitchel Field on July 15, 1920. Because reaching Alaska depended on being able to make repairs en route, each airplane carried a mechanic.

Called the Black Wolf Squadron on account of the wolves painted on the fuselage, the eight men—four pilots and four mechanics—flew 9,349 miles in a round trip of 112 flying hours.[4] One of the approximately eighteen planned stops was Hazelton. The stop before Hazelton would be Prince George. The stop after Hazelton was intended to be the Alaska community of Wrangell—if they got there.

This was by no means certain. By the time they reached Hazelton they had already overcome numerous challenges. The first day after he had left Mitchel Field, Streett had to land in a farmer's field to avoid a storm. This deeply rutted field broke the axle in his airplane. Send for another. It took three hours to install it. (Pennsylvania.) The refuelling truck became not only lost but stuck in deep mud. Find it. Dig it out. (Also Pennsylvania.) Rain fell so hard that they had to keep applying oil to prevent rusting. (Erie.) Lieutenant Crumrine's airplane dug deep into the mud on trying to take off from too soft a surface. Very well, bring some horses to pull it out and a truck roller to harden the surface. Then the horses became clogged in the mud. The roller also became stuck. No air pressure? Hand the controls over to the mechanic and use a hand pump. (Over Lake Michigan.) Too much hospitality? (Just about everywhere.) Broken wing skid and gas tank leaks. Stay a day and repair them. (Edmonton.) Streett mentioned that he thought the land around Edmonton looked as though it was full of oil, which was prescient of him. A fire in one of the motors? Hand the controls to Sergeant Henriques and find the fire extinguisher. (Over the Rocky Mountains.) Their journey was not uneventful.[5]

In early June 1920, Captain Howard Douglas of the American Air Service and Captain J. Achilles Learoyer of the Canadian Air Board had come to Hazelton to locate a suitable landing site. Richard Sargent showed them around. They decided that the lower field of the hospital would be an eminently suitable landing field. Stopping to chat at the offices of the *Herald*, they told the editor that the squadron would take about forty-five days for the round trip.[6] While in Hazelton, they also found time for a couple of enjoyable fishing trips.

People in the Hazeltons were excited. First, automobiles coming from Vancouver, and now, airplanes from New York! The modern world was arriving in a hurry. Fences on the proposed landing field in the hospital grounds were taken down. The crops on the field were cut early. July 20, the day scheduled for the landing, was declared Aviation Day, and a big town picnic was planned for the hospital grounds.

By July 16, everything was ready for the arrival of the squadron. People anxious to see the airplanes land were making plans to come from Prince Rupert and Burns Lake. The *Herald* excitedly told its readers that the picnic was set to start at ten in the morning—"not necessarily to eat then, but you had better be around by that time. ... Come on, boys, to the hospital on Tuesday. Make it a whole day. You can't work in this weather anyway."[7] Bring your food hampers, the *Herald* said. Be prepared to stay all day and help feed those from out of town who do not have food. The Red Cross planned to set up booths to dispense liquids and light refreshments.

Strong winds, storms and the need to make repairs delayed the aviators. This caused great disappointment in Hazelton, and the picnic had to be postponed. Not getting the message because the telegraph was down for a few days, some people came from Burns Lake and returned home disappointed. On July 30, it was announced that the squadron would be staying in Edmonton for two days for repairs. The aircraft needed some overhauling to enable them to climb over the mountains—what Streett called the fearful jump over the Great Divide.[8] Nor was the weather co-operating. By August 6, they had reached Prince George. Here Streett landed badly in heavy rain—landing blind, is how he described it—and ran into underbrush at the edge of the too-short runway. More repairs were needed. He enlisted a cabinetmaker to mend the spars. He also enlisted a local tailor to repair the torn linen fabric of the fuselage. One of the pilots concocted a special liquid from banana oil and gun cotton to shrink the repaired fabric to the framework.

While waiting for spare parts to come from San Francisco, Lieutenant Clifford C. Nutt, one of the pilots, came to Hazelton by train to inspect the proposed landing ground at the hospital. Nutt came to the conclusion that the hospital site would not do, being too short, too narrow and too soft. "Lieutenant Nutt returned," Streett wrote, "with the disquieting intelligence that he was sure no airplane could land safely at Hazelton."[9] Streett himself went to make a personal investigation and came to the same conclusion. But there was one field on Mission Point owned by a farmer named Beirnes that might just suffice. Indeed, it was the only place in the area that would do, but it was covered with a crop of oats. However, it was either land there or turn back.

The *Omineca Herald* reported the general disappointment at the delay. Not concealing his frustration, the editor reported that the arrangements had to be changed several times. It seemed strange, he wrote, that the officers who had chosen the original landing site could differ so badly on suitable places. And now Captain Streett had had an accident causing a delay of two weeks! "It should be a lesson to all governments to engage only the best men when undertaking something new."[10] Nevertheless, the people of Hazelton held a dance to honour the non-arrival of the squadron.

When Streett knocked on Beirnes's door, he had a lot riding on the answer to his request. Beirnes's farmland was covered with three-foot-high oats. What farmer would allow aircraft to land on his crops? "Accordingly," Streett wrote, "I called to see Mr. Beirnes and explained the situation to him. To my surprise and gratification, he immediately offered to cut a runway through the oats and furthermore declared he would roll the runway until it became firm enough to give us a smooth surface."[11]

Finally, on August 13, the biplanes left Prince George without further mishap. One party of people who wanted to see the landing drove furiously from Smithers but arrived too late. They had, though, seen the airplanes chugging past them in the air toward Hazelton.

Word was received in Hazelton at ten o'clock that the airplanes would land at eleven that morning. After all the anticipation, people were taken by surprise and scrambled to find ways of getting to Mission Point to see the landing. As it turned out, they had ample time to witness the arrival. One of the people watching may have been Cataline (Jean Caux), the old mule-train packer who had come into British Columbia at the time of the Fraser River Gold Rush in 1858. He had

The Black Wolf Squadron: (left to right) Capt. St. Clair Streett, 1st Lieut. Clifford C. Nutt, 2nd Lieut. Eric C. Nelson, 2nd Lieut. C.H. Crumrine and 2nd Lieut. Ross C. Kirkpatrick. Wikimedia Commons

lived on Mission Point for some years in a cottage Beirnes had put at his disposal for his old age.

"Aeroplanes Arrived This Morning Without Mishap," the *Omineca Herald* reported. "The 'planes left Prince George at five minutes past nine and the first machine landed at eleven minutes past twelve, thus the speed averaged about seventy miles an hour. ... No. 4 was the first of the planes to land and it took to the ground like a swan and was parked like an auto."[12]

One of the airplanes carried a letter—a billet-doux, perhaps?—from someone in Prince George to a woman named Inez Smith.

James Turnbull and other soldiers who had returned from the war organized a banquet in St. Andrew's Hall for the aviators that evening. This memorable affair was followed by a dance in the assembly hall. Tasty refreshments were served at midnight, and at one in the morning ice cream was served. "The revelry was kept until very late, or very early, being a tribute to the efforts of the returned soldiers to make the affair a success," the *Herald* reported.[13]

Streett decided that Beirnes's field was not firm enough for the takeoff. So a small army of residents, tourists and Gitxsan helpers marched up and down the field to make it firmer. "You ... smart man," a Gitxsan man, stamping down the field and perhaps doubting the wisdom of flying with a machine heavier than air, told Streett, "but a ... d— fool."[14]

Dr. Horace Wrinch (left) and Captain Streett (right), with Dr. Wrinch's daughter Ralphena in the mechanic's seat. Image courtesy of the author

Bill Streett in Hazelton. Image courtesy of the author

The four biplanes carried on their way to Alaska. They came back through the town in the second week of September. On landing, Lieutenant Nutt's plane plowed into the soft soil, forcing the plane to tip onto its nose. This slid the mechanic forward so that he too landed in the soft soil on his nose. Apart from that one scrape, neither pilot nor mechanic nor the dogs Lieutenant Nutt was bringing home with him were hurt. One propeller was broken, though, and supports had to be repaired.

On its return to Washington, the squadron was given a hero's welcome. Four squadrons comprising fifty-five airplanes and the country's biggest dirigible escorted Streett and his team to a landing. Thousands of spectators flocked to Bolling Field to watch them arrive. They

HAZELTON BC. NEW YORK TO NOME FLIGHT, AUGUST 13th 1920.

One of the Black Wolf Squadron over Mission Point. Image courtesy of the author

were now heroes. Generals John Pershing and William Mitchell as well as the secretaries for war and the navy were on hand to welcome them home. Doubtless to Streett's embarrassment, his mother "pushed through the crowd surrounding her boy, threw her arms about his neck and gave vent to her enthusiasm with a kiss.[15]

For this pioneering effort, which proved that Alaska could be linked by air to the United States, Streett was awarded the Distinguished Flying Cross and the Mackay Trophy, given to the most meritorious flight of the year by a US military airman. In an article in *National Geographic Magazine* in 1922, Streett presciently wrote, "Some day this trip may be made overnight—who knows?"[16]

No regular service seemed to come out of these exploratory flights, although by late 1922, the big monoplane *Hazelton* was planning to use Mission Point as an airfield to take parties to hunt big game in the mountains.

Bill Streett went on to have a brilliant career in the United States Air Force in peace and war. In 1928, he was the pilot in an experimental high-altitude flight that reached forty thousand feet, which was only a thousand feet less than the world record.[17] By March 1942, he had become a senior officer, being the chief of the Theatre Group of the Operations Division in the Office of the General Staff. The following year, he was the commanding officer of the Second Air Force in Colorado, where he was in charge of training bomber crews. In January 1944, he assumed command of the Thirteenth Air Force in the Pacific, where he served with General Douglas MacArthur.[18] He was in command of the air fleets that eventually brought Japan to unconditional surrender. Streett did not think highly of MacArthur. Prescient again, he had recommended against MacArthur's appointment to the supreme command in the Pacific, believing that he would not be able to co-operate with other commanders. Streett became known as a problem solver and troubleshooter for Henry "Hap" Arnold, who as general of the United States Air Force was one of the most senior officers in the armed forces. After the war, Streett organized and was deputy commander of the United States Strategic Air Command. Retiring in 1952 with the rank of major general, he died in 1970 and was buried in Arlington National Cemetery.

In landing and taking off on the land at Mission Point, Streett and his squadron would have flown over the stones at the Forks of the Skeena, where Simon McGillivray had stood less than ninety years before.

26

Premier Tolmie and His Famous Caravan Visit Hazelton

June 1930

The Hazeltons had never seen anything like it. Forewarned that the premier's caravan would arrive at five in the evening of June 20, 1930, eager residents of New Hazelton crowded down to the main road from Smithers to greet it. Indigenous and non-Indigenous people waited expectantly. They built an arch of evergreen boughs over the road as a welcome.

First came two red-coated mounted police on horseback. After them was Chilliwack bagpiper Bob Richardson. Then, on motorcycles, came three members of the provincial police in their khaki uniforms. Behind them and leading the motorcade was Perley Evans Sands, driving the same car he had brought to Hazelton in 1911. This was the feat for which he had been awarded a trophy for bringing the first car to reach Hazelton from the south, allegedly under its own power, though many, with good reason, doubted it.

The motorcade that followed had been dubbed "Premier Tolmie's caravan." It consisted of fifty automobiles containing the premier and his travelling companions. With Tolmie was Ernest Walker Sawyer, executive assistant to the United States secretary of the interior. The list of dignitaries accompanying Tolmie included William Alexander McKenzie, British Columbia's minister of mines, state senators and thirty to forty representatives of numerous boards of trade and motoring organizations from British Columbia, Alaska, Washington, Oregon and California. Later that day, the premier would meet Lieutenant-Governor Robert Randolph Bruce of British Columbia and Governor George Alexander Parks of Alaska, who, together with their own parties, would arrive by train from Prince Rupert.

Fifty-five members of the press came along to report on their progress. Among them was Bruce Hutchison, then a reporter for the *Vancouver Daily Province*. Later he became one of the best-known journalists in the province. A more private scribe was Jane Eva Denison, Tolmie's secretary. She kept a diary, which she entitled *Caravaning to the Land of the Golden Twilight*.[1] The melodious name—the Land of the Golden Twilight—was invented to publicize a proposed highway.

This was a high-level meeting of three separate governments. What had brought them all to Hazelton?

Grand ideas sometimes bring forth grand gestures. In June 1930, the grand idea was to build a road to Alaska. The governments of the United States and Alaska wanted to connect the territory of Alaska to the rest of the country by road. The British Columbia government wanted to open the northern part of the province for settlement, exploration and tourism. "The benefits to British Columbia," Denison wrote in her account, "would be simply immense. It would be necessary for visitors from south of the line to travel over a thousand miles on B.C. roads before reaching Hazelton, through a wonderfully attractive country to the tourist."[2] In describing the proposal, Sawyer said that "population and prosperity follow the motor-car."[3]

The grand gesture was for representatives of all three governments to meet in Hazelton to inaugurate the commencement of the building of the road. This road was to go from Hazelton up the Kispiox Valley, north to the Yukon and then west into Alaska. Agreeing with Denison, the people of Hazelton liked the project because it would bring more people into the area, thus promoting local farming, settlement and trade.

Premier Simon Fraser Tolmie had an impeccable Hudson's Bay Company heritage. Both his parents had deep roots in the Company's history. His father, William Fraser Tolmie, had come to British Columbia with the Company in 1833. A senior officer in Victoria, William was the chief factor who had removed Thomas Hankin from his post on Mission Point in 1868. He had also been a member of the colonial assembly before Confederation and a member of the legislative assembly after it.[4] The premier's mother, Jane, had Indigenous ancestry on her mother's side. Born in 1867, Simon Fraser Tolmie qualified as a veterinarian in 1891, farmed at Cloverdale and became the Dominion inspector of livestock. Entering politics as a Conservative in 1917, he served as federal minister of agriculture. His most lasting legacy to Canada in the end may be that he opened the British market to Canadian beef.

Although Tolmie had one foot firmly planted in federal politics, he had also been leader of the Conservative Party of British Columbia since 1926. A compromise candidate, he had not actually wanted to be the leader. Reportedly, when the persuasions and arguments made to him at the leadership convention held in Kamloops became heated, one Tory grandee and Tolmie, showing their Hudson's Bay Company heritage, continued their discussion in Chinook Jargon, which no one else present could understand. At the end of this conversation, Tolmie agreed to stand.[5] He was a farmer, a promoter of women's suffrage, a supporter of Indigenous heritage and a Tory. In 1928 he became the twenty-first premier of British Columbia. He was arguably one of the least successful of the province's premiers.

Lieutenant-Governor Bruce, Governor Parks and Ernest Walker Sawyer were all engineers. Bruce, a folksy man with a rolling Scottish accent, had been a prospector and made a fortune with the Paradise mine in the Kootenays. Generous in a quiet way, he had given his family home at Windermere to the community as a hospital. Parks, born in 1883, had impressed President Warren Harding and Herbert Hoover, then secretary of commerce, with his knowledge of Alaska when he had been their tour guide on a visit. They remembered him when they were looking for a territorial governor in 1925. He knew nothing about politics, but he did know Alaska. A quiet, modest man, he was overwhelmed when asked if he would serve.

In the United States, Secretary of the Interior Ray Lyman Wilbur had written to Tolmie enthusing that the international highway to Alaska gripped his imagination and spurred his pioneer spirit as nothing else had. He wrote he was sorry he could not join them, adding that President Hoover was all for the highway.[6] Wilbur did send Sawyer as his personal representative. Sawyer was an enthusiastic proponent of the highway and had already done much to bring it to the attention of the American public.

Premier Tolmie had decided that he, his wife and his party would drive to Hazelton in a convoy of automobiles. (His wife hated flying.) He invited his American guests to join him. Tolmie went to the border town of Blaine, Washington, to welcome his guests and bring them back to the Hotel Vancouver for a "get-to-know-you-banquet."[7] Bruce went to Prince Rupert to meet Governor Parks, who had come down from Alaska, and then accompanied him by train to Hazelton.

After gathering at eight o'clock for photographs at the courthouse the following morning, the contingent in Vancouver settled into their automobiles and set off. The caravan progressed north through the province: Chilliwack, where the piper joined them; Lytton, where they unveiled a monument to the Indigenous leader Spintlum; and Quesnel, where they made a detour to visit Barkerville.

In a marvellously ambiguous description, the *Province* reported that Barkerville gave the caravan "such a welcome that only Barkerville can give."[8] The whole population turned out to greet them. After dinner they all went to the ancient theatre for an old-time Cariboo dance. Six husky prospectors carried a piano up from Kelly's Hotel, and with the added delights of a concertina, the party danced the night away. Everyone was there: old-timers from Barkerville's glory days of the Cariboo Gold Rush and women who had not been out of town for fifty years. Every one of the sixty people in town was introduced to and shook hands with the premier. Some of the old-timers came and told the party their stories,

New Hazelton welcoming Premier Tolmie's caravan on its arrival. Image courtesy of the author

including Mrs. Houser, who had come to town as a child in 1868, and Dear Song, the cook at Kelly's Hotel, who had walked to Barkerville from New Westminster forty-three years before. As dawn arrived, the party ended with the playing of "God Save the King" on the accordion. Premier Tolmie was photographed panning for gold. It was, the *Province* said, a real adventure for the Americans.

The caravan moved on through Williams Lake to Burns Lake, where school-children waved to them as they passed. At Telkwa, one of the children, informed by her teacher that the premier was the biggest man of the province, excitedly told her parents that she had just seen one of the stoutest men of British Columbia, which, the *Province* observed, might well have been true.[9] Tolmie, it was said, weighed over three hundred pounds.

When it arrived in New Hazelton, the caravan stopped in front of the specially constructed stand. Here they were officially welcomed and invited to a dance that night, an invitation that was enthusiastically accepted. The caravan then drove across the high-level bridge and on into Old Hazelton, where the travellers settled in after the long journey. Dr. Horace Wrinch and Richard Sargent had volunteered to arrange for the accommodation of the visitors. Because the hotels in the Hazeltons could not accommodate such numbers, many visitors stayed as guests in homes of local residents. The Tolmies, Sawyer and Denison stayed at the home

Premier Simon Fraser Tolmie, standing third from the right, with some of his fellow travellers. Image courtesy of the author

of one of the leading families. They then went to greet Lieutenant-Governor Bruce, Governor Parks and the others in their party who had arrived from the coast.

That first evening over two hundred people attended the dance in the Omineca Hotel, which was, Denison wrote, only slightly marred by the fact that there were approximately twenty-five men to each lady.[10] The organizers brought in Gray's Orchestra from Smithers to provide the music. Since they got home at daylight, it may be assumed they all had a good time.

The next morning, Tolmie, Parks, Sawyer and others of their staffs went to the schoolhouse in Old Hazelton for a business meeting to plan the new road. After that, Tolmie met several local delegations that kept him busy until noon. The others were left to their own devices and spent the morning visiting the sights.

After lunch they went to a ceremony to turn the sod for the new hospital that was being built. Construction was about to start, and Dr. Wrinch was not going to miss the opportunity for his own grand event. At the designated time, Wrinch led the official party from the steps of the old hospital to the designated spot. First came the lieutenant-governor, who, as the king's representative, was to have the honour of turning the sod. After his introductory words, he handed his jacket to his niece, Miss Helen McKenzie, and grasped the long-handled spade. This was not a ceremonial turning over of previously dug soft soil, but hard work on unprepared turf. After some amusement, he finally dug into the soil and managed to turn it over. Tolmie, Parks, Sawyer, Sands and others each made a few appropriate remarks. Miss McKenzie was presented with a horn spoon made by Gitxsan

Lieutenant-Governor Robert Randolph Bruce turning the sod for the new hospital. Image courtesy of
the author

carvers as a souvenir. Little Leonora Wrinch, Dr. Wrinch's granddaughter, then
presented her with a bouquet. Chief Tom Campbell then stepped forward and
presented the lieutenant-governor with a stone axe, following which, to everyone's
delight, the lieutenant-governor gave him—"potlatched" was the word the *Omineca
Herald* used—his own walking stick.[11]

After the sod-turning ceremony, the sightseeing of the local beauty spots continued. Some went to the cemetery on the bluff. There the ghosts of the pioneers
would have been all around them: Charley Youmans, murdered in 1884; Cataline,
the packer; Alice Wrinch, the doctor's wife; and old prospectors such as Jim May
and Joe Lyon. Some of the visitors may have walked out on the stony point where
the Bulkley River merges into the Skeena, the point where Simon McGillivray had
stood less than a hundred years before. The Forks of the Skeena, they had called it
then. Others went to see the totem poles at Kispiox. The Gitxsan Chiefs there said
they were looking forward to driving their cars north on the new road. "To demon-
strate their interest in the scheme, they scattered eagles' down on the American
visitors, whom they called 'the Boston Men,' a name which has come down from fur
trading days."[12] Constance Cox, Thomas Hankin's daughter, was their interpreter.

The banquet that second evening was held in the Hudson's Bay Company
warehouse, tastefully decorated with flags, bunting and evergreen for the occasion.

From left to right, Lieutenant-Governor Robert Randolph Bruce, Governor George Alexander Parks of Alaska, Premier Simon Fraser Tolmie and Ernest Sawyer, special representative of the United States government, meeting outside the Hudson's Bay Company store in Hazelton. Image courtesy of the author

The ladies of the Hazelton social club had arranged the hall and the food. With Dr. Wrinch as chairman, the banquet was a great success, with many speeches and toasts to the king, the president and all three jurisdictions represented there.

"The weather during our stay at Hazelton was perfect," Denison wrote. "They call this the 'Land of the Golden Twilight.' The days we were there the sun shone nineteen hours and a half, then twilight until after 11:00 p.m.; dawn about 1:00; and daylight about 1:30. The climate there is most exhilarating. We felt we should not take time to sleep, and it was only when we felt we should get some rest that we turned in."[13]

Although surveyors were set to work almost at once, the road they planned to go up the Kispiox Valley was never built. The project of a road from the United States to Alaska rumbled through the bureaucracies of Washington, Ottawa and Victoria through the cash-strapped 1930s. Numerous routes were proposed. President Franklin Roosevelt was in favour of constructing the road, though, and kept the project alive. Then the Japanese attacked Pearl Harbor and invaded the Aleutian Islands in Alaska. This introduced an urgency to the project that had hitherto been lacking. Construction started in earnest in March 1942. The road was built farther to the east than originally planned in order to be farther away from the threat of Japanese bombers. Officially opened in October 1943, the Alaska Highway was not fully operational until the following year. Many years later a road was built up the Kitwancool valley to Stewart.

Tolmie had the bad luck to become premier of British Columbia a year before the Depression started. He applied his business skills to the human problems it caused, but these did not work. Arguably, they made the problems worse. Described as one of the kindest, gentlest and most honourable men to be premier of the province, by now he was finished. He paid the price at the election in 1933 and was thrown from office. "Fundamentally," it has been said, "Tolmie was completely out of his depth in the crisis that he had to face."[14] He returned to federal politics and was elected to his old seat in the 1936 election. He died of a heart attack in 1937.

Governor George Alexander Parks died in 1984, one hundred years old. His life neatly spans the years from the 1885 death of Thomas Hankin, who so many years before had settled on a piece of land at the Forks of the Skeena River.

The road up the Kispiox Valley to Alaska may not have been built, but the new Hazelton Hospital was completed by the end of the year. Dignitaries came from far and wide to join the two hundred people at the formal opening ceremony on a cold December day. Present were Dr. Horace Wrinch, of course, as well as the pioneers Richard Sargent and Constance Cox. The tearing down of the old wooden hospital after the new hospital became operational was the symbolic end of one era and the opening of another. Presiding majestically over the proceedings was snow-capped Rocher Déboulé (Stekyawden), with its stories of the many people who had made their mark on the town. Down in the valley, the Skeena River flowed as swiftly as always, carrying into the mists of time the old ways and memories of the people of the Upper Skeena.

Edgar Dewdney's Letter about the Founding of Hazelton

Forks of the Skeena River
May 20, 1871

Sir,

I have the honor to inform you that I returned to this place on the 17th ultimo [April] after inspecting the two routes from the Skeena River to Babine Lake, one starting from a creek about twelve miles below the Forks of the Skeena called Segucla and the other from the Forks.

I had been led to believe that the route by the Segucla was an improvement on the one usually travelled and as under any circumstances as it would have been necessary for me to go to Babine Lake and return before laying out the line for the trail, I thought it advisable to go by the one and return by the other.

The Segucla route has the advantage of the other only as regards elevation, being about 500 feet lower at the point where I crossed the summit, and the trail could be taken 500 feet lower than that. It would, however, take a great deal more work to make a trail and require a suspension bridge over the Agwilgate [Hagwilget, or Bulkley] River at the Canyon, and it also comes out too far up the Babine Lake to connect conveniently with the proposed second section of trail.

I have therefore come to the determination of adopting the present route. Its advantages over the other being directness of course and comparatively speaking making very little work.

The elevation of the respective summits—over Segucla pass, 4,580, old route, 5,140 feet above the sea level. The great elevation over which the trail must pass is the chief obstacle I see to what is known as the Skeena Route.

On my return I left Babine on the 15th May. About three miles from it, I met with snow which gradually deepened to the summit where it was five feet. The summit is from four to five miles in length. The snow trail was perfectly hard for that distance and I was enabled to travel on it without snowshoes. The total distance of snowshoe travelling was from 14 to 17 miles. On the day I crossed the summit, it snowed heavily, but on descending it turned to rain causing the snow to disappear rapidly. I feel confident, however, that pack animals will be unable to cross from here to Babine for a month at least, probably six weeks.

Since my arrival here I have selected a starting point for the trail and reserved for the Government all the land situated between the Agwilgate River and the lower line of a pre-emption taken up by Messrs. Mitchell and Farron. A portion of it I have reserved as a town site, the remainder as an Indian reserve for a tribe called the Ket-en-macks [Gitanmaax].

On the proposed town site I posted a notice (a copy of which I enclose). By it you will see that I have staked off a few lots, and should you think it advisable to lay out a small town site here before I return, I should be obliged if you would forward me the necessary instructions. The work would not take more than a week, as the ground is open and free from any underbrush. Three lots have been taken, one by Messrs. Cunningham and Hankin, one by a Mr. Reed and one by Wm. Moore. And buildings will be put up at once.

I trust that you will agree with me that it is fortunate I have been enabled to reserve a small tract for a town site as is invariably the case all the land that was thought to be open for pre-emption was taken up in the vicinity of the supposed starting point, and this would not have remained unoccupied had not the parties who had settled above the Reserve been of the opinion that an Indian Reservation existed from the mouth of the Agwilgate River two miles upstream.

I leave on Monday to blaze the trail as it is almost an open country. It will not take long. There are a few points on it that will require care in blazing but by far the greater part will follow the Indian track. I shall leave Mr. McNeil, who is working for me, to do most of the blazing on this section while I proceed to examine and blaze the second.

At Babine Lake on the 13th instant, I found the ice had not disappeared, and on the following day as I proceeded in a canoe from [Nesgat?] (an Indian ranch at the point where the trail from Seguckla comes out) I had to cut ice some hundred yards. On the following day it had entirely disappeared.

Almost all the men that had arrived at Babine from the Skeena (about two hundred) had crossed to Tacla by the Fry Pan Pass, Indians packing for them make that trip in four days, returning in two. As the snow disappears the travelling becomes more laborious on account of the fallen timber, which, I am informed, is in great quantities and in some places is six and eight feet deep.

I received a letter from Woodcock yesterday stating that owing to the non-delivery of an order for food which he had sent for to be used in the construction of the trail he was compelled to go to Victoria and could not be here for some weeks. This is more to be pitied as numbers of men here are willing to cut the trail through for the packing of their blankets and a little provisions.

W. Moore is here with his horses and a stock of goods for the Omineca market. He has made some such arrangement and started this afternoon with a number of men and his pack train—he will be able to go as far as the snow with very little work.

The distance from the Forks to Babine Lake will not exceed forty-five miles when the trail is completed. Indian men returning from packing travel it in a day and a half. There is an abundance of food for animals. From 450 to 500 men have come by this route and I have not heard a single man complain of it. The great drawback is the want of a trail on which pack animals can work, as the Indians are a most independent and dishonest lot, charging exorbitant rates for packing: 10 cents for hour to Babine, and their food and 20 cents from Babine to Tacla.

While at Babine an Indian returned from Tacla and informed me that the ice was out of the Lake, that boats had arrived at the landing and that flour was selling at $10.00 per sack.

The river has risen about twelve feet since I first arrived making boating from below much easier. It is the general opinion that a steamer can run with ease to the Kitselas Canyon and from the side of the Canyon to here.

There has been no disturbances in this part of the country, but I have been detained a couple of days longer than I should have been, inquiring into 2 or 3 cases of theft.

I shall write to you from Tacla Lake as soon as I arrive.

I have the honour to be, Sir, your most obedient servant,

Edgar Dewdney

(This letter is in the BC Archives, Colonial Correspondence, GR-1372.50.461(2), pp. 82–86.)

Those Who Served

The following were listed in the *Omineca Herald*, July 25, 1919, as men from Hazelton who "donned the colours" in the First World War. Note: This may not be the complete list. E. Charleson's name, for example, was omitted.

Affleck, B.C.
Anderson, J.
Ardagh, S.V.
Barker, J.R.
Bennett, J.E.
Berts, G.
Boe, G.
Brewer, B.
Brewer, T.W.
Burrington, G.
Campbell, W. McM.
Chappell, A.G.
Christianson, P.
Clothier, R.
Collins, F.H.
Cooling, S.
Cormier, J.
Corner, H.
D'Egville, R.
Dodimead, J.
Duncan, J.
Dunn, W.
Ellaby, C.E.
English, C.W.
Enoch, P.
Findlay, G.
Findlay, H.H.
Forster, K.B.
Fox, C.
Frost, J.K.
Frost, P.
Fuller, J.R.
Fulton, L.D.

Geary, S.
Gibbs, H.
Gore, G.R.M.
Gough, R.
Gray, F.
Guiney, W.
Hamblin, H.
Hankin, A.
Hankin, H.C.
Hadden, R.
Harrison, T.
Helas, C.
Hevenor, J.
Hicks-Beach, C.
Hill, B.T.
Hogan, E.M.; N.S.
James, H.
Jennings, F.W.S.
Johnson, A.
Johnson, J.
Kendall, M.C.
Kinghorn, H.C.
Larmer, W.
Leverett, W.
Lind, J.
Lind, O.
Loftquist, E
Loutit, J.C.
Mailan, J.
Macdonald, J.A.
MacKay, G.A.
MacKenzie, W.
Mathews, H.M.

Mathews, J.
Mathias, S.
Mathieson, R.
McBride, J.
McCormick, J.M.
McCubbin, J.
McDougall, A.
McDougall, P.A.
McGibbon, D.L.
McIntosh, A.
McIntosh, D.
McIntosh, K.C.
Middleton, G.R.
Millar, H.R.
Monour, A.
Morrison, J.W.
Munro, C.H.
Ogilvie, D.
Phillips, A.E.
Player, A.E.
Ponder, R.
Rex, G.
Rock, J.C.
Ruddy, A.M.
Schooling, A.
Sharpe, H.W.
Thompson, J.
Thorne, J.A.
Turnbull, J.
Walker, G.
White, J.
Williamson, G.
Wrinch, H.G.

First World War Casualties

These casualties were recorded in the *Omineca Miner* and *Omineca Herald* during the war. It may not be a definitive list. Some of the names on the list are of people who were merely known in the community, such as those who had worked on the building of the Grand Trunk Pacific Railway or who lived in the diaspora of settlers on the Upper Skeena. Mere statistics do not show how tragic the bloodshed was. It is noticeable, though, how the casualty rate dropped in 1918.

1915			
Name		*Date*	*Comment*
Walter Smith	Killed	June 11	Ypres
Andrew Monour	Wounded	June 19	
G.R. Middleton	Wounded	June 26	
B.T. Hill	Wounded		Captured
Stanley Geary	Wounded	July 17	Dardanelles
Cy North	Wounded		
D. Loughan	Wounded		
William J. Guiney	Wounded		
Al Chapple	Wounded		Festubert
J.R. Barker	Wounded		
E.N. Ford	Wounded		Prisoner of war
F.W.S. Jennings	Killed	August 21	From Kispiox
C.E. Ellaby	Wounded		

1916			
Name		*Date*	*Comment*
Jack Frost	Wounded	February 19	
T.W. Brewer	Wounded	July 1	
J.E. Bennett	Wounded	July 9	
Harold Price	Killed		Military Cross
George Walker	Killed	July 29	
Frank Jessup	Killed	August 12	
John Wadey	Killed	September 2	
W.F. Brewer	Killed	September 30	

1916			
Name		Date	Comment
Colin Munro	Wounded	October 14	
A.H. Wylie	Wounded	November 4	
Tom Brewer	Wounded		
George MacKay	Wounded		
Roy Clothier	Wounded		
J.W. Morrison	Wounded	November 11	
H.H. Findlay	Wounded	November 25	Missing; later found
Gilbert Burrington	Killed	December 9	Military medal for bravery
Alex McMillan	Killed		Formerly of Hazelton
E.E. Charleson	Killed	December 16	
Albert Schooling	Killed		

1917			
Name		Date	Comment
T.W. Brewer	Wounded	February 3	
A.W. Stultze	Killed	February 24	
Alex Gray	Wounded	March 3	From Smithers
J. Preece	Wounded		
W.F. Brewer	Wounded	April 7	
H.P. Blake	Killed		
James Hevenor	Wounded	April 14	
H.L. Gibbs	Killed	May 5	
K.B. Forster	Wounded		
Jack Bennett	Wounded		Third time
Charles Helas	Killed	May 19	Arras
Frank Gray	Killed		Arras
A.L. McHugh	Killed	June 2	
Harry James	Missing	December 1	

1918			

None

Endnotes

Preface

1 Neil Sterritt, *Mapping My Way Home: A Gitxsan History* (Smithers, BC: Creekstone Press, 2016), p. 328.

2 *Daily British Colonist*, January 30, 1870, p. 3.

3 L.P. Hartley, *The Go-Between* (London: Readers Union, 1954), p. 1.

1: William Brown, Simon McGillivray and Their Early Explorations

1 Simon McGillivray, D.4/126, Hudson's Bay Company Archives (HBCA). Simon McGillivray (1791–1840) wrote two accounts of his journey. His account in the Fort Simpson post journals is the most detailed account, being the daily journal he kept on his journey. This "Journal of a Voyage to Simpson's River by Land, Summer 1833" is set out in the Fort St. James post journal, 1833, B.188/a/18, HBCA. The second account is the letter he wrote to Hudson's Bay Company governor George Simpson, which is a little more formal but contains the map, in Governor George Simpson, Inward Correspondence Book, D.4/126. The two accounts do not differ, but the post journal includes more details.

McGillivray did write that he and his men were astonished by their first sight of the confluence of the Skeena and Bulkley Rivers. He was likely standing close to where the 'Ksan Historical Village and Museum is today. The point across the Bulkley River to the south, later known as Mission Point or Mission Flats, is now called Anderson Flats Provincial Park.

These are some of the earliest days in the history of British Columbia. Alexander Mackenzie of the North West Company had made his epic journey to the coast in 1793. Simon Fraser established Fort St. James in 1806 at the southern end of Stuart Lake, named after John Stuart, his lieutenant. It was not until 1841 that the Hudson's Bay Company asked James Douglas to set up a trading post at the southern end of Vancouver Island, which became Victoria. Fort Langley on the mainland was initially established in 1827 but moved to its present location in 1839. Vancouver itself was not founded until 1885.

Neil Sterritt describes McGillivray's visit to the Forks in his book *Mapping My Way Home: A Gitxsan History* (Smithers, BC: Creekstone Press, 2016). This book is the most informative history of pre-1900 Hazelton. See also the biography of William McGillivray, Simon's father, *McGillivray, Lord of the Northwest*, by Marjorie Wilkins Campbell (Toronto: Clarke, Irwin, 1962).

2 McGillivray, B.188/a/18, HBCA.

3 Daniel William Harmon, *A Journal of Voyages and Travels in the Interior of North America* (Andover, MA: Flagg and Gould, 1820), p. 203 reprinted as *Sixteen Years in the Indian Country: The Journal of Daniel William Harmon, 1800–1816*, ed. William Kaye Lamb (Toronto: Macmillan, 1957); reissued as *Harmon's Journal, 1800–1819* by TouchWood Editions in 2006, with a foreword by Jennifer S.H. Brown. This quotation is from the 2006 edition, p. 125. Daniel Harmon, a North West Company employee, was likely the first white man to enter the Skeena River watershed. It was reportedly Harmon who first came into contact with the Gitxsan (Atnah) people and started trading with them. He would have learned of the merger of the two rivers at the Forks.

Father Adrien-Gabriel Morice wrote about the history of the area. Without any explanation or evidence, he dismissed Harmon's report of white traders having visited the Forks as being wrong. They were, he said, simply "Indians from the coast" (A.G. Morice, *The History of the Northern Interior of British Columbia* [Toronto: William Briggs, 1904], p. 88). I am inclined to believe that American traders, seemingly mostly from Boston, on account of which they were called "Boston men," who, we know, had been on the coast since 1787, may have seized the opportunity of going up the Skeena to the major trading site at the Forks. But it could easily have been Russian or English traders.

4   George Simpson to William Brown, September 16, 1820, B.39/a/16, HBCA.

5   William Brown, October 23, 1820, B.39/a/16, HBCA. Brown (1790–1827) wrote numerous reports and post journals. These reports are in the HBCA. In addition to the post journals for Fort Kilmaurs, he wrote two reports: *Report of the Establishment of Fort Kilmaurs, Babine Country, New Caledonia*, 1823, B.11/e/1, and *Report of the Babine Country, and Countries to the Westward*, 1826, B.11/e/2. The Babine Correspondence Book, 1825–1826, B.11/b/1, contains a number of his letters.

6   Fort Chipewyan post journal, December 4, 1820, B.39/a/16, HBCA; Peter C. Newman, *Caesars of the Wilderness* (Markham, ON: Penguin Books, 1987), pp. 264–65.

7   Brown, *Report of the Establishment of Fort Kilmaurs*.

8   Brown, *Report of the Establishment of Fort Kilmaurs*.

9   George Simpson to William Brown, April 4, 1825, B.11/b/1, HBCA.

10   Fort Kilmaurs post journal, July 21, 1825, B.11/a/3, HBCA.

11   William Brown, April 13, 1826, journal kept at Fort Kilmaurs, March 1–June 18, 1826, R7759-0-0-E, MG19-D8, Library and Archives Canada (LAC), p. 20.

12   Brown described his journey in R7759-0-0-E, MG19-D8, LAC, p. 20. See also Nancy Marguerite Anderson, *The York Factory Express: Fort Vancouver to Hudson Bay, 1826–1849* (Vancouver: Ronsdale Press, 2021), p. 17. William Brown attended the meeting of the Hudson's Bay Company Northern Council on July 6, 1826. For reasons that are not entirely clear, the council severely censured him for mismanagement of his post at Fort Kilmaurs in 1825.

13   The name of Fort Simpson was changed to Port Simpson in approximately 1880 because incoming mail was often sent to Fort Simpson in the North-West Territories, and vice versa. It is now known as Lax Kw'alaams.

14   Simon McGillivray to George Simpson, April 30, 1833, B.188/b/9, HBCA.

15   McGillivray, B.188/a/18, HBCA.

16   McGillivray, B.188/a/18, HBCA.

17   McGillivray, B.188/a/18, HBCA.

18   McGillivray, B.188/a/18, HBCA.

19   McGillivray, D.4/126, HBCA.

20   McGillivray, D.4/126, HBCA.

21   McGillivray, B.188/a/18, HBCA.

22   McGillivray, B.188/a/18, HBCA.

23   McGillivray, D.4/126, HBCA.

24   McGillivray, B.188/a/18, HBCA.

25   McGillivray, B.188/a/18, HBCA.

26   McGillivray, July 15, 1833, D.4/126, HBCA.

27   McGillivray, B.188/a/18, HBCA.

28   McGillivray, B.188/a/18, HBCA.

29   Peter Ogden, February 23, 1833, quoted in McGillivray, B.188/a/18, HBCA.

30   McGillivray, B.188/a/18, HBCA.

31 McGillivray, D.4/126, HBCA.

32 Fort Liard post journal, 1840–41, B.116/a/18, HBCA.

2: George Chismore and the Western Union Russian-American Telegraph

George Chismore wrote three accounts of his visits to the Forks of the Skeena and the Upper Skeena: "From Nass to the Skeena," *Overland Monthly* 6, no. 35 (November 1885), pp. 449–58; "Log-Book of a Trip among the Siwash of British Columbia," BANC MSS-P-K 219, George Chismore Papers, Bancroft Library, University of California, Berkeley; and "Record of Travel from Skeena Mouth to the Peace River Mines," BANC MSS 81/84, George Chismore Papers, 1871–1900, Bancroft Library, University of California, Berkeley.

1 Chismore, "Log-Book," p. 12.

2 Chismore, "Log-Book," p. 11.

3 Chismore, "Log-Book," p. 9.

4 Chismore, "Log-Book," p. 9.

5 Chismore, "Log-Book," p. 12.

6 Chismore, "Log-Book," p. 15.

7 Chismore, "Log-Book," p. 15.

8 Chismore, "Log-Book," p. 16–17.

9 Chismore, "Log-Book," p. 17.

10 P.J. Leech, "The Pioneer Telegraph Survey of British Columbia," *British Columbia Mining Record* 5, no. 1 (January 1899), pp. 17–26. This contains the description of the work on the telegraph line.

11 *Daily British Colonist*, July 31, 1866, p. 3.

12 Fort Simpson post journal, B.201/a/9, Hudson's Bay Company Archives.

13 Charles Morison, MS-0001, box 18, file 8, BC Archives (BCA).

14 Emil Teichmann, *A Journey to Alaska in the Year 1868* (Kensington: Cayne Press, 1925), pp. 123–25.

15 Letters of Sophia Cracroft, MS-0245, BCA.

16 Chismore, "From Nass to the Skeena," pp. 454–55.

17 *Pacific Rural Press*, August 24, 1872, p. 121.

18 Chismore, "From Nass to the Skeena," p. 456.

19 Chismore, "From Nass to the Skeena," p. 458.

20 Chismore, "Record of Travel," p. 1.

21 Chismore, "Record of Travel," p. 6.

22 Chismore, "Record of Travel," p. 7.

23 Chismore, "Record of Travel," pp. 13–14.

24 *Washington Standard*, August 5, 1871, p. 3.

25 Chismore, "Record of Travel," p. 16.

26 Chismore, "Record of Travel," p. 16.

27 Chismore, "Record of Travel," p. 31.

28 "Pavy's Expedition to the North Pole," *Overland Monthly* 8, no. 6 (June 1872), p. 551.

29 *San Francisco Examiner*, November 6, 1873, p. 3.

30 Douglass W. Montgomery, "George Chismore," *California State Journal of Medicine* 12, no. 5 (May 1914), p. 169.

31 Douglass W. Montgomery, "George Chismore: A Sketch of a True Physician," *California and Western Medicine* 26, no. 5 (May 1927), p. 646.

32   *San Francisco Examiner*, January 12, 1906, p. 11.

3: Thomas Hankin and the Founding of Hazelton

1   Fort Simpson post journal, B.201/a/9, Hudson's Bay Company Archives (HBCA).
2   Roderick Finlayson to Robert Cunningham, April 17, 1868, B.226/b/36, HBCA.
3   E/B/H19, Old Manuscript Collection, BC Archives (BCA).
4   Louis LeBourdais, "Billy Barker of Barkerville," *British Columbia Historical Quarterly* 1, no. 3 (July 1937), p. 165; reprinted in *British Columbia History* 45, no. 1 (Spring 2012), p. 11. See also *Daily British Colonist*, February 27, 1863, p. 3; *London Times*, May 6, 1863, p. 26; and *Victoria Daily Chronicle*, October 28, 1864, p. 2.
5   *British Columbian*, September 12, 1861.
6   J.T. Scott, letter to the editor, *British Columbian*, October 31, 1861.
7   Fort Simpson post journal, B.201/a/9.
8   Roderick Finlayson to William Manson, August 23, 1866, B.226/b/35, HBCA.
9   William Tolmie to William Manson, August 2, 1867, B.226/b/33, HBCA, pp. 116–17.
10   Roderick Finlayson to Thomas Hankin, April 17, 1868, B.226/b/36, HBCA.
11   James Bissett to James Grahame, October 12, 1870, B.226/b/44/a, HBCA, p. 673.
12   *Vancouver Daily Province*, May 10, 1947, p. 55.
13   Bissett to Grahame, October 12, 1870.
14   James Grahame to Robert Cunningham, November 11, 1870, B.226/b/44/a, HBCA, p. 865.
15   R.G. Large, *The Skeena: River of Destiny* (Vancouver: Mitchell Press, 1957), pp. 29–30.
16   *Daily British Colonist*, January 7, 1870, p. 3.
17   *Daily British Colonist*, January 9, 1870, p. 3.
18   *Daily British Colonist*, July 15, 1870, p. 3.
19   *Cariboo Sentinel*, June 3, 1871, p. 3.
20   *Daily British Colonist*, December 28, 1870, p. 2.
21   *Daily British Colonist*, December 11, 1870, p. 3.
22   Thomas Hankin to the commissioner of land and works, December 12, 1870, Colonial Correspondence, GR-1372.68.708, BCA.
23   Thomas Hankin and Robert Cunningham to the chief commissioner, land and works, January 28, 1871, Colonial Correspondence, GR-1372.68.708, BCA.
24   *Daily British Colonist*, January 20, 1871, p. 2.
25   *Daily British Colonist*, February 21, 1871, p. 3.
26   Neil J. Sterritt, *Mapping My Way Home: A Gitxsan History* (Smithers, BC: Creekstone Press, 2016), pp. 131–32.
27   *Daily British Colonist*, March 17, 1871, p. 3.
28   *Daily British Colonist*, August 3, 1871, p. 2.
29   Large, *The Skeena*, pp. 44–45.
30   Sterritt, *Mapping My Way Home*, p. 131.

4: Edgar Dewdney, Charles Horetzky and Other Passersby

1   At this time Gitanmaax had not yet moved from its location close to the confluence of the two rivers to the low bench below the bluff to which it moved after a fire in 1876.
2   Edgar Dewdney, Colonial Correspondence, GR-1372.50.461(2), BC Archives (BCA), p. 88. One chain is twenty-two feet. It is subdivided into one hundred links or four rods. There are eighty chains to a mile.

3. E. Brian Titley, "Dewdney, Edgar," in *Dictionary of Canadian Biography*, vol. 14, University of Toronto/Université Laval, 2003–, http://www.biographi.ca/en/bio/dewdney_edgar_14E.html.

4. This is the generally known version. There is another. In "The Artful Dewdney," *British Columbia History* 42, no. 2 (2009), pp. 11–17, C.J. Cooney argues that Edgar Dewdney was living a bluff all his life. Rather than having grown up a gentleman in a respectable middle-class family in England and having received a good education there, he was in reality the son of a boatman who worked on the river canals. He had a poor education and used a "bread and butter" letter of recommendation as a formal reference from high authorities in England to high authorities in British Columbia. The money a well-educated Englishman would be expected to have brought with him, he said, he had lost on unidentified sins in New York on his way over. All his life he concealed his origins and obfuscated the records. This theory appears to depend almost entirely on the discovery of a possible set of 'other parents.' Genealogical research in the early Victorian era is always murky and fraught with the possibility of error. I have not investigated this intriguing theory and so retain an open mind.

5. Edgar Dewdney to Benjamin W. Pearse, May 20, 1871, Colonial Correspondence, GR-1372.50.461(2), BCA, pp. 82–86.

6. Benjamin W. Pearse, report on Edgar Dewdney's letter of May 20, 1871, Colonial Correspondence, GR-1372.50.461(2), BCA, p. 89.

7. Colonial Correspondence, GR-1372.50.461(2), BCA, p. 89.

8. Letter to the editor, June 5, 1871, *Daily British Colonist*, June 14, 1871, p. 3.

9. *Daily British Colonist*, July 19, 1871, p. 2.

10. *Daily British Colonist*, July 9, 1871, p. 3.

11. Peter O'Reilly to the colonial secretary, July 16, 1871, Omineca Gold Commissioner Records, GR-0233, BCA.

12. George Chismore, "Record of Travel from Skeena Mouth to the Peace River Mines," BANC MSS 81/84, George Chismore Papers, 1871–1900, Bancroft Library, University of California, Berkeley, p. 27.

13. Dancing Bill deserves an explanation. He was a Rhode Islander called Bill Latham who ran pack trains on the Hazelton-Omineca route. In 1874, he moved to Cassiar to open up a dance hall with "an organ and four klootchmen" (*Daily British Colonist*, May 14, 1874, p. 3), but he soon went back to packing and mining. He died in 1880, exhausted by the hard work of mining.

14. Charles Horetzky, *Canada on the Pacific: Being an Account of a Journey from Edmonton to the Pacific by the Peace River Valley* (Montreal: Dawson Brothers, 1874), pp. 100–105. See also Jane Stevenson, "Horetzky's Hike across Northern BC," in *A Trail of Two Telegraphs: And Other Historic Tales of the Bulkley Valley and Beyond* (Halfmoon Bay, BC: Caitlin Press, 2013), pp. 26–32.

5: Jim May and the Miners of the Omineca Gold Rush

Sperry Cline, who was a Hazelton resident and a friend of Jim May, wrote about him in "Jim May," Sperry Cline Reminiscences, MS-409A, BC Archives (BCA). See also the transcript E/E/C61, BCA. His article about Jim May was published in the *Northern Sentinel*, April 21, 1960, p. 10. Sperry Cline's recollections occur frequently in this book.

1. Jim May, quoted in Eva MacLean, *The Far Land* (Prince George, BC: Caitlin Press, 1993), p. 120.

2. Daniel Marshall, *Claiming the Land: British Columbia and the Making of a New El Dorado* (Vancouver: Ronsdale Press, 2018). This excellent book on the Fraser River Gold Rush points out the early discoveries of gold made by Indigenous people.

3   W.H. McNeill, letter to the board of management of the Hudson's Bay Company, Fort Victoria, August 26, 1852, letter book, November 20, 1851–November 2, 1855, Fort Simpson (Columbia Department) Fonds, PR-1678, BCA.

4   William Downie to Governor James Douglas, October 10, 1859; this letter is an attachment to a letter that Governor James Douglas sent to Henry Pelham-Clinton, November 1, 1859, CO 60:5, no. 880, Colonial Despatches, University of Victoria.

5   *Daily British Colonist*, October 3, 1860, p. 2.

6   *Daily British Colonist*, November 17, 1863, p. 3.

7   Nathan Simpson (Sebastopol) to Governor Frederick Seymour, July 17, 1865, Colonial Correspondence, GR-1372.125.1599, BCA.

8   *Daily British Colonist*, August 13, 1864, p. 3.

9   Allan Stanley Trueman, "Placer Gold Mining in Northern British Columbia, 1860–1880" (master's thesis, University of British Columbia, August 1935), pp. 46–47.

10   MacLean, *The Far Land*, p. 118.

11   *British Colonist*, August 1, 1859, p. 3.

12   Cline, "Jim May," Sperry Cline Reminiscences, p. 4.

13   *British Columbia Tribune*, April 10, 1866, p. 3.

14   Omineca mines record book, Omineca Gold Commissioner Records, GR-0225, vol. 4, box GR0255-002, BCA.

15   James May to John McLean, June 8, 1870, *Cariboo Sentinel*, June 25, 1870.

16   *Daily British Colonist*, December 11, 1870, p. 3.

17   *Daily British Colonist*, August 15, 1875, p. 3.

18   *Daily Telegram* (Nanaimo, BC), December 7, 1893, p. 6.

19   Cline, "Jim May," Sperry Cline Reminiscences, p. 5.

20   Cline, "Jim May," Sperry Cline Reminiscences, p. 5.

21   Hudson's Bay Company Archives, diary, Hazelton, 1894–1897, quoted in Neil J. Sterritt, *Mapping My Way Home: A Gitxsan History* (Smithers, BC: Creekstone Press, 2016), p. 153.

22   *Skeena District News*, February 6, 1904, p. 1.

23   *Omineca Herald*, October 17, 1908, p. 1.

24   *Omenica Miner*, January 6, 1912, p. 1.

25   Constance Cox, *Vancouver Daily Province*, May 10, 1947, p. 55.

26   Richard Sargent, Edward Stephenson and Rev. John Field, letter to the government agent in town, Frederick Valleau, Omineca Gold Commissioner Records, 1899–1904, GR-0255, vol. 1, BCA.

27   Wiggs O'Neill, *Northern Sentinel*, November 29, 1962, p. 11.

28   Cline, "Jim May," Sperry Cline Reminiscences, p. 6.

29   *Omineca Miner*, December 29, 1917, p. 1.

30   *Omineca Miner*, April 20, 1918, p. 1.

6: Jack Gillis and His Helpful Grave

1   Sperry Cline, "Gillis's Grave," Sperry Cline Reminiscences, MS-409A, BC Archives (BCA). This account was also published as an article in the Kitimat *Northern Sentinel*, April 30, 1959, birthday supplement, p. 85.

2   William Gordon, statement, August 18, 1897, William Adam Gordon Fonds, 1897–1898, PR-1406, BCA.

3   Cecil Clark, "Gillis' Grave," *Daily Colonist*, April 4, 1971, p. 68.

4   *Cariboo Sentinel*, August 12, 1871, p. 3.

5   The facts in this chapter mostly come from the inquest on Hugh Gillis, August 21, 1872, Coroner's Inquiries/Inquests, GR-0431, box 1, file 3, BCA.

6   George Mitchell, testimony at inquest on Hugh Gillis.

7   Adam McNeily, quoting George Mitchell, testimony at inquest on Hugh Gillis.

8   Mitchell, testimony at inquest on Hugh Gillis.

9   Mitchell, quoting Jack Gillis, testimony at inquest on Hugh Gillis.

10   McNeily, testimony at inquest on Hugh Gillis.

11   Charles Camsell, *Son of the North* (Toronto: Ryerson Press, 1954), p. 235.

7: Thomas Riley, Barney Devine and Their Dead Ends

1   *Cariboo Sentinel*, July 6, 1872, p. 3.

2   *Cariboo Sentinel*, July 6, 1872, p. 2.

3   George Chismore, "Record of Travel from Skeena Mouth to the Peace River Mines," BANC, MSS 81/84, George Chismore Papers, 1871–1900, Bancroft Library, University of California, Berkeley, pp. 21–24.

4   W.B. Robinson, quoting Thomas Riley, testimony at inquest on Thomas Riley, 1872, Coroner's Inquiries/Inquests, GR-0431, box 1, file 11, item 11, BC Archives (BCA).

5   Robinson, quoting Riley, testimony at inquest on Thomas Riley.

6   Archibald McConnell, quoting Thomas Riley, testimony at inquest on Thomas Riley.

7   George Bent, testimony at inquest on Thomas Riley.

8   Arthur W. Vowell to the provincial secretary, October 2, 1873, letter book of correspondence inward, Omineca Gold Commissioner Records, GR-0233, box 1, BCA.

9   For the comments of his friends on his death, see *Daily Independent* (Helena, MT), March 24, 1874, p. 3. For his death, see *San Francisco Examiner*, October 23, 1873, p. 3.

8: Bishop William Ridley, Jane Ridley and the *Hazelton Queek*

1   Eugene Stock, *Metlakahtla and the North Pacific Mission of the Church Missionary Society* (London: Church Missionary House, 1881), p. 125.

2   *Church Missionary Intelligencer*, n.s., vol. 2 (1866), p. 267.

3   Eugene Stock, *The History of the Church Missionary Society, Its Environment, Its Men and Its Work* (London: Church Missionary Society, 1899), p. 565.

4   The college was probably Edwardes High School, which had been founded by the Church Missionary Society in 1855 and was the only institution providing Western-style education on the northwest frontier. It is now named Edwardes College, Peshawar.

5   Stock, *History*, p. 566.

6   William Ridley, *Church Missionary Gleaner*, vol. 19 (1869), p. 140.

7   Ridley, *Church Missionary Gleaner*, vol. 19, p. 141.

8   Stock, *History*, p. 566.

9   *Huddersfield Chronicle and Yorkshire Advertiser*, July 18, 1874, p. 6. An article describes the turmoil in the two Yorkshire parishes.

10   Stock, *Metlakahtla*, p. 126; *Daily British Colonist*, April 16, 1879, p. 3; *Church Missionary Gleaner*, vol. 1 (1874–1887), p. 48.

11   *John Bull*, July 26, 1879.

12   *Daily British Colonist*, October 15, 1879, p. 3.

13   *Church Missionary Intelligencer and Record*, new series (n.s.), vol. 5 (February 1880), p. 128.

14   *Church Missionary Intelligencer and Record*, n.s., vol. 5, p. 126.

15   Constance Cox, *Vancouver Daily Province*, May 10, 1947, p. 5.

16   *Church Missionary Gleaner*, vol. 8 (1881), pp. 78–79.

17   William Ridley, letter, October 29, 1881, *Church Missionary Gleaner*, vol. 9 (1882), pp. 119–20.

18   *Victoria Daily Times*, November 9, 1903, p. 2.

19   One copy of an original edition of the *Hazelton Queek* is in the BC Archives, NWs 971.1Haz H429. Some of the text is illegible. The records in the BCA include Helen Kate Woods's explanatory note.

20   The 1881 census shows that there were more miners in Hazelton that winter than the *Queek* recorded, including James May, Charles McKinnon and Ezra Evans. It also shows that the mix was a very international one. In addition to Chinese miners, there were also miners from France (Peter Gaston, Rene August, Felix Bau), miners from Germany (Henry Bode, Luke Bachte and Gill Brabeau), one from the Netherlands (Henry Froats) and those from Ireland (George Kenney and Pat Smith), Wales (Samuel Griffiths and William Williams), Scotland (James Brown and James Buchanan) and, of course, the United States (John Robinson and Nathaniel Heffward). Nor is this the complete list. Since the 1881 census document is in some places faded, almost illegible and the victim of Victorian penmanship, some of these names may be spelled wrong. Froats, for example, could just as easily be Groats or Franks. Strangely, neither Charley Youmans nor Thomas Hankin and his family are listed in the census, which suggests that some pages may be missing.

21   William Ridley, letter, October 29, 1881, *Church Missionary Gleaner*, vol. 9 (1882), p. 120.

22   *Daily British Colonist*, June 20, 1882, p. 3.

23   William Ridley and William John Macdonald, *Senator Macdonald's Misleading Account of His Visit to Metlakatla Exposed by the Bishop of Caledonia* (s.n., 1882), p. 1.

24   *Church Missionary Intelligencer and Record*, n.s., vol. 7 (February 1882), p. 2, and p. 507 (August 1882); *British Columbian*, October 24, 1883, p. 3.

25   *Church Missionary Gleaner*, vol. 9 (1882), p. 120.

26   *Nanaimo Daily News*, November 2, 1887, p. 3.

27   Charles Henry Mockridge, *The Bishops of the Church of England in Canada and Newfoundland* (Toronto: F.N.W. Brown, 1896), p. 320; *Guardian*, March 29, 1911, p. 9.

28   William Ridley, *Among the Indians in the Far West* (London: Church Missionary Society, 1905), p. 27; William Ridley, letter, December 11, 1896, in *Snapshots from the North Pacific*, ed. Alice J. Janvrin (London: Church Missionary Society, 1904), chap. 11.

29   *Sydney Morning Herald*, February 24, 1904, and August 26, 1904, p. 5.

30   *Daily Mail*, November 27, 1905, p. 4.

9: Richard Loring and the Mystery of the Swedish Balloon

Richard Loring provided facts about his life in his letter of September 5, 1896, to the librarian to the legislative assembly, Victoria, R-7479-0-5-E, Library and Archives Canada (LAC).

1   Richard Loring to A.W. Vowell, July 31, 1896, letter book, Department of Indian Affairs: Babine Agency, microfilm C-14856, image 131, LAC.

2   This was during the 1888 Skeena River crisis, when Loring's colleague Constable Daniel Green shot Kamalmuk (Kitwancool Jim) dead.

3   Loring, R-7479-0-5-E, LAC; Constance Cox, in "Notes of a Talk with Mrs. E.R. Cox," March 29, 1940, box 2147, Prince Rupert Presbytery–Hazelton, Archives Reference Collection, United Church of Canada Archives (Vancouver).

4   Loring to Vowell, July 31, 1896.

5   *Daily Colonist*, August 12, 1896, p. 8.

10: Father Morice and His Trembling Knees

1   Adrien-Gabriel Morice, *Fifty Years in Western Canada: Being the Abridged Memoirs of Rev. A.G. Morice, O.M.I.* (Toronto: Ryerson Press, 1930), p. 142.

2   Morice, *Fifty Years*, p. 111.

3   Morice, *Fifty Years*, p. 6.

4   David Mulhall, "Morice, Adrien-Gabriel (Marie-Gabriel-Adrien-Arsène)," in *Dictionary of Canadian Biography*, vol. 16, University of Toronto/Université Laval, 2003–, http://www .biographi.ca/en/bio/morice_adrien_gabriel_16E.html. This provides a full but less than laudatory account of the life of Father Morice. This article is largely based on David Mulhall, *Will to Power: The Missionary Career of Father Morice* (Vancouver: UBC Press, 1986).

5   Mulhall, "Morice, Adrien-Gabriel."

6   Morice, *Fifty Years*, p. 87.

7   Morice, *Fifty Years*, p. 140.

8   Morice, *Fifty Years*, p. 186.

9   Morice, *Fifty Years*, p. 112.

10   *Omineca Herald*, October 3, 1913, p. 8.

11   *Omineca Herald*, August 24, 1917, p. 1.

12   Mulhall, "Morice, Adrien-Gabriel."

13   Mulhall, "Morice, Adrien-Gabriel."

14   Mulhall, "Morice, Adrien-Gabriel."

11: James Kirby and Mexican Tom, the Hazelton Bully

1   Much of the information in this chapter comes from James Kirby's memoirs, MS-1572, PR-0062, BC Archives; and "A Short Sketch of the Life of James Kirby," PF1, box 1, Bulkley Valley Museum. See also *The Shoulder Strap*, July 1940, Northern BC Archives & Special Collections, University of Northern British Columbia Archives, p. 44.

2   Kirby, "A Short Sketch," p. 2.

3   Kirby, memoirs, p. 1.

4   Kirby, memoirs, p. 4.

5   Kirby, memoirs, p. 8.

6   Kirby, memoirs, p. 15.

7   Kirby, memoirs, p. 25.

8   Kirby, memoirs, p. 30.

9   Kirby, memoirs, p. 30.

10   Kirby, diary entry, June 1, 1904, PF1, box 1, Bulkley Valley Museum.

11   *Northern Sentinel*, February 25, 1965, p. 1.

12   Winnie Robinson, in *Bulkley Valley Stories* (Smithers, BC: Heritage Club, 1973), p. 172.

13   *Interior News*, February 24, 1965, p. 1.

12: Horace and Alice Wrinch and Their Arrival in Kispiox

1   William Henry Pierce, *From Potlatch to Pulpit: Being the Autobiography of the Rev. William Henry Pierce, Native Missionary to the Indian Tribes of the Northwest Coast of British Columbia* (Vancouver: Vancouver Bindery, 1933), p. 57.

2   For a biography of Horace Wrinch, see Geoff Mynett, *Service on the Skeena: Horace Wrinch, Frontier Physician* (Vancouver: Ronsdale Press, 2019).

3   Rev. Robert Whittington, *Western Methodist Recorder* 2, no. 4 (October 1900), p. 10.

4   Rev. Robert Whittington, *Western Methodist Recorder* 6, no. 4 (November 1904), p. 1.

5   Constance Cox, in "Notes of a Talk with Mrs. E.R. Cox," March 29, 1940, box 2147, Prince-Rupert Presbytery—Hazelton, Archives Reference Collection, United Church of Canada Archives (Vancouver).

6   Dr. Horace Wrinch, letter to the young people of Albert College, Belleville and the Picton District, *Canadian Epworth Era* 3, no. 4 (April 1901), p. 117.

7   Horace Wrinch to Rev. Egerton Doxsee, September 27, 1900, *Albert College Times* 13, no. 1, pp. 8–9.

8   Wrinch to Doxsee, September 27, 1900.

9   *Western Methodist Recorder* 2, no. 9 (March 1901), p. 12.

10   *Vancouver Sun,* October 20, 1939, p. 21.

13: Sperry Cline and the Suspended Corpse

1   Field Marshal Frederick Roberts, VC, first Earl Roberts, in his official report dated November 8, 1900, *Nottinghamshire Guardian*, November 17, 1900, p. 10.

2   Sperry Cline, "The Prospector," Sperry Cline Reminiscences, MS-409A, BC Archives, p. 6.

3   Details from the story of the frozen corpse and inquest come from Sperry Cline, "Six Good Men and True," Sperry Cline Reminiscences, MS-409A, BC Archives.

4   Cline, "Six Good Men and True," Sperry Cline Reminiscences, p. 5.

5   Cecil Clark, "Sperry Cline: Frontier Policeman," in *Pioneer Days in British Columbia*, vol. 4, ed. Art Downs (Surrey, BC: Heritage House, 1979), p. 43.

14: Mr. Sargent, Mr. Loring and Their Bitter Feud

1   J.D. McLean, "Memorandum for the Information of the Deputy Minister Relative to the Complaint by Mr. Sargent and Others against Mr. Agent Loring," July 22, 1902, Office of the Deputy Superintendent of Indian Affairs, microfilm C-9003, image 823, Library and Archives Canada (LAC).

2   "Sargent, Richard S.," biographical sheet, Hudson's Bay Company Archives (HBCA).

3   E.C. Stephenson to the attorney general, July 31, 1902, Attorney General Correspondence, inward, GR-0429, box 9, file 2, BC Archives (BCA).

4   R.E. Loring to the deputy commissioner of lands and works, BC, April 18, 1901, microfilm C-14856, image 897, LAC.

5   Richard E. Loring to Robert Tomlinson, October 19, 1899, letter book, Department of Indian Affairs: Babine Agency, microfilm C-14855, image 853, LAC.

6   Richard E. Loring to Arthur Vowell, October 23, 1899, Attorney General Correspondence, GR-0429, box 5, file 4, BCA.

7   Petition signed by some citizens of Hazelton, sent to Joseph Martin, attorney general, dated January 9, 1900, Attorney General Correspondence, inward, 1900, GR-0429, box 5, file 4, BCA.

8   *Daily Colonist*, February 28, 1900, p. 4, and March 1, 1900, p. 4.

9   Richard S. Sargent to Joseph Martin, attorney general, January 27, 1900, Attorney General Correspondence, inward, GR-0429, box 5, file 4, BCA.

10   Richard E. Loring to Arthur Vowell, January 30, 1900, letter book, Department of Indian Affairs: Babine Agency, microfilm C-14855, image 816, LAC.

11 Richard Sargent to Albert McPhillips, attorney general, May 14, 1900, Attorney General Correspondence, inward, GR-0429, box 5, file 5, BCA.

12 Richard E. Loring to Arthur Vowell, January 5, 1900, letter book, Department of Indian Affairs: Babine Agency, microfilm C-14855, image 827, LAC.

13 Richard E. Loring to Church Missionary Society, London, January 20, 1900, letter book, Department of Indian Affairs: Babine Agency, microfilm C-14856, image 661, LAC.

14 J.D. McLean to G.N. Maxwell, July 25, 1900, letter book, Department of Indian Affairs: Babine Agency, microfilm C-8451, image 1139, LAC, p. 514.

15 John Lewis, government agent, to the attorney general, April 16, 1902, Attorney General Correspondence, GR-0429, box 8, file 5, BCA. He recommended that the resignation of R.S. Sargent as a magistrate be requested.

16 McLean, "Memorandum for the Information of the Deputy Minister."

17 A.C. Murray to Jas. Thomson, HBC Victoria. September 15, 1902, Port Simpson Project File, Letters x-y, B.226/b/53, file 1/H, HBCA.

18 *Omineca Miner*, August 24, 1918, p. 1.

19 Pinkerton's report to Philip Ahern, August 2, 1909, Attorney General Correspondence, GR-0429, box 17, files 1–4, BCA.

15: Sperry Cline and the Winter Mail

1 *Omineca Herald*, September 12, 1908, p. 4.

2 Sperry Cline's comments on his mail run experiences in this chapter come from "Skeena River Mail," Sperry Cline Reminiscences, MS-409A, BC Archives.

3 Dr. Horace Wrinch, letter to the young people of Albert College, Belleville and the Picton District, *Canadian Epworth Era* 3, no. 4 (April 1901), p. 117.

4 Cline, "Skeena River Mail," Sperry Cline Reminiscences, p. 11.

5 Cline, "Skeena River Mail," Sperry Cline Reminiscences, p. 15. See also Art Downs, *Pioneer Days in British Columbia* (Surrey, BC: Heritage House, 1975), vol. 4, pp. 42–43.

6 Cline, "Skeena River Mail," Sperry Cline Reminiscences, p. 10.

16: George McKenzie, the Missing Medicine Chest and Runaway Dogs

1 *Vancouver Daily Province*, July 27, 1903, p. 2.

2 This story is told in May 1906 editions of the *Vancouver Daily Province* and the *Boundary Creek Times*.

3 *Vancouver Daily Province*, May 8, 1906, p. 5.

4 *Boundary Creek Times*, May 4, 1906, p. 2.

5 *Boundary Creek Times*, May 4, 1906, p. 2.

17: Constance Cox and the Nurses of Hazelton Hospital

1 *Vancouver Daily Province*, May 10, 1947, p. 125.

2 Constance Cox, quoted in Arthur Barner, *Surgeon of the Skeena, a Brief Resumé of the Life and Work of Rev. Horace Wrinch, M.D., D.D., Hazelton B.C.* (Committee on Missionary Education, Women's Missionary Society and the United Church of Canada, n.d.), p. 22.

3   Constance Cox, in "Notes of a Talk with Mrs. E.R. Cox," March 29, 1940, box 2147, Prince-Rupert Presbytery—Hazelton, Archives Reference Collection, United Church of Canada Archives (Vancouver).
4   Richard E. Loring to Dr. N. Aikins, October 26, 1901, letter book, Department of Indian Affairs: Babine Agency, microfilm C-14857, image 29, Library and Archives Canada.
5   Cox, in "Notes of a Talk."
6   Constance Cox, oral history, interviews, Imbert Orchard Fonds, T0313:0001–0008, BC Archives.
7   *Canadian Nurse*, vol. 3 (March 1907), p. 122.
8   Dr. Horace C. Wrinch, *Rules and Regulations of Hazelton Hospital*, received May 1, 1909, Toronto, fonds 14, series 2, subseries 2, correspondence of Alexander Sutherland, 78.081C, box 1, file 4, United Church of Canada Archives (Toronto).
9   *Hazelton Hospital Annual Report 1908*, United Church of Canada Archives (Toronto).
10   *Hazelton Hospital Training Record*, United Church of Canada Archives (Vancouver).
11   *Hazelton Hospital Training Record*, United Church of Canada Archives (Vancouver).
12   *Omineca Herald*, November 14, 1924, p. 1.
13   *Omineca Herald*, March 26, 1926, p. 1.
14   Horace Wrinch to his son Harold Wrinch, August 18, 1939, and to his daughter Ralphena, May 6, 1939, in the author's possession.

18: James Maitland-Dougall and Policing in Hazelton

1   James Maitland-Dougall, diary entry, August 25, 1909, Maitland-Dougall, James St. Leger, MS-2177, BC Archives (BCA).
2   Amendments to the Indian Act in 1884 maintained the prohibition of selling alcohol to First Nations individuals and made it a felony for a First Nations person to buy or drink alcohol on or off the reserve.
3   James Maitland-Dougall kept detailed diaries up until 1911, which can be found in MS-2177, BCA. Since his daily diary entries that relate to Hazelton cover over seventy pages, the entries here are necessarily selective.
4   *Omineca Herald*, March 18, 1911, p. 3.
5   Maitland-Dougall, diary entry, April 22, 1910.
6   *Daily Colonist*, March 22, 1918, p. 7. See also the war service records for Hamish Maitland-Dougall with Library and Archives Canada.

19: The People of Hazelton and Their Shocking Morals

1   R. Ross Sutherland to Frederick S. Hussey, August 12, 1910, Attorney General Correspondence, GR-0429.3091, box 18, reel B09324, file 2, BC Archives.

20: The Soiled Doves of Two Mile

1   Hazelton and Smithers Magistrate's Record Books, vol. 1, GR-3122, BC Archives.
2   Magistrate's Record Books, p. 25.
3   Magistrate's Record Books, p. 26.
4   Magistrate's Record Books, p. 27.
5   Magistrate's Record Books, pp. 235–36.
6   Magistrate's Record Books, p. 236.
7   Magistrate's Record Books, p. 237.

8   Eva MacLean, *The Far Land* (Prince George. BC: Caitlin Press, 1993), p. 79.

9   MacLean, *The Far Land*, p. 70.

10 MacLean, *The Far Land*, p. 43.

11 *Omineca Herald*, July 18, 1919, p. 2.

21: Emily Carr and the Totem Poles of the Skeena

1   In her account of her arrival at Hazelton in "Eagles of Skeena River," in *The Heart of a Peacock* (Toronto: Oxford University Press, 1953), p. 60, Emily Carr says she left the steamboat at the end of steamer navigation at Skeena Crossing, close to Gitsegukla, and went on to Hazelton by canoe. This is puzzling because the steamers had been reaching Hazelton since 1891. Moreover, Wiggs O'Neill had started a launch service in 1908. Either Carr's memory played tricks on her when she wrote this many years later, or for some reason she had disembarked at Skeena Crossing, perhaps to see the totem poles in Gitsegukla, and neither ferry nor launch was available to take her on to Hazelton.

2   Emily Carr, August 14, 1936, *Hundreds and Thousands: The Journals of Emily Carr* (Toronto: Clarke, Irwin, 1966), p. 255.

3   Gerta Moray, *Unsettling Encounters: First Nations Imagery in the Art of Emily Carr* (Vancouver: UBC Press, 2006), p. 34.

4   Emily Carr, *Lecture on Totems*, in *Opposite Contraries: The Unknown Journals of Emily Carr and Other Writings*, ed. Susan Crean (Vancouver: Douglas & McIntyre, 2003), quoted in Moray, *Unsettling Encounters*, p. 35.

5   Moray, *Unsettling Encounters*, p. 49.

6   Moray, *Unsettling Encounters*, p. 100.

7   Emily Carr, quoted in Laurie Carter, *Emily Carr's B.C.: Northern B.C. & Haida Gwaii* (West Kelowna, BC: Little White Publishing, 2016), p. 11.

8   *Vancouver Daily Province*, March 25, 1912, p. 8.

9   *Vancouver Daily Province*, March 27, 1912, p. 13.

10 *Vancouver Daily Province*, March 27, 1912, p. 13.

11 Carr, "Eagles of Skeena River," in *The Heart of a Peacock*, p. 59.

12 Maria Tippett, *Emily Carr: A Biography* (Toronto: Oxford University Press, 1979), p. 107.

13 Carr, *Lecture on Totems*, in *Opposite Contraries*, p. 199.

14 *Vancouver Sun*, October 10, 1912, p. 3.

15 *Vancouver Daily Province*, October 12, 1912, p. 42.

16 Paula Blanchard, *The Life of Emily Carr* (Vancouver: Douglas & McIntyre, 1987), p. 140.

17 Emily Carr to Flora Burns, July 11, 1928, Flora Alfreda Hamilton Burns Papers, MS-2786, box 1, file 4, BC Archives; Emily Carr, "Kitwancool," chap. 19 in *Klee Wyck* (Toronto: Penguin Canada, 2006), p. 385.

18 Carr to Burns, July 11, 1928.

19 Carr to Burns, July 11, 1928.

20 Carr to Burns, July 11, 1928.

21 Carr, *Klee Wyck*, p. 101.

22 Carr, *Klee Wyck*, p. 102.

23 Carr to Burns, July 11, 1928.

24 Carr, *Klee Wyck*, p. 104.

25 Carr, *Klee Wyck*, p. 104.

26 Carr, *Klee Wyck*, p. 105.

27 Carr to Burns, July 11, 1928.

28   Carr, *Klee Wyck*, p. 107.

29   Carr, *Klee Wyck*, p. 107.

30   Hamar Foster, "Two 'White' Perspectives on Indigenous Resistance: Emily Carr's *Klee Wyck*, the
      RCMP, and Title to the Kitwancool Valley in 1927," in "Essays in Legal History in Honour of
      DeLloyd J. Guth," special issue, *Manitoba Law Journal* 43, no. 1 (2020), p. 1.

31   Constable T.E.E. Greenfields in a report to his commanding officer, quoted in Foster, "Two
      'White' Perspectives," p. 40.

32   Laura Cumming, reporting on the exhibition *From the Forest to the Sea: Emily Carr in
      British Columbia* at the Dulwich Picture Gallery, November 2014–March 2015, *Observer*,
      November 2, 2014.

22: Rene D' Egville and the Men from Hazelton Who Went to War

Many of the details in this chapter are taken from the war records of the participants and the hospitals held by Library and Archives Canada.

1   Sperry Cline, "One Night in a Bar Room," Sperry Cline Reminiscences, MS-409A, BC Archives,
      p. 3. Cline's description of the scene in the bar on that night may have been a composite picture
      drawn from his notes and recollections.

2   Cline, "One Night in a Bar Room," Sperry Cline Reminiscences, p. 2.

3   Cline, "One Night in a Bar Room," Sperry Cline Reminiscences, p. 3.

4   *Omineca Herald*, March 14, 1919, p. 1.

5   *Omineca Herald*, August 14, 1914, p. 3.

6   *Omineca Herald*, September 18, 1914, p. 1.

7   *Omineca Herald*, August 14, 1914, p. 1.

8   *Omineca Miner*, January 22, 1916, p. 1.

9   Rene d'Egville to Jack Frost and W.J. Carr, *Omineca Miner*, July 28, 1917, p. 2.

10   James Turnbull to Forester Allan, March 23, 1915, *Omineca Miner*, April 24, 1915, p. 3.

11   James Turnbull to H.C. Kinghorn, May 28, 1915, *Omineca Miner*, June 26, 1915, p. 2.

12   James Turnbull to Forester Allan, *Omineca Miner*, November 13, 1915, p. 1.

13   James Turnbull to Forester Allan, *Omineca Miner*, April 8, 1916, p. 2.

14   *Omineca Miner*, July 17, 1915.

15   Jack E. Bennett to W.J. Carr and Jack Frost, *Omineca Miner*, August 26, 1916, p. 1.

16   Jack E. Bennett to Jack Frost, *Omineca Miner*, November 4, 1916, p. 2.

17   Jack E. Bennett, letter written from Seaford Hospital, *Omineca Miner*, August 18, 1917, p. 2.

18   *Omineca Miner*, December 8, 1917, p. 1.

19   *Omineca Miner*, July 17, 1915.

20   *Omineca Miner*, November 25, 1916, p. 1.

21   *Omineca Miner*, April 14, 1917.

22   Cline, "One Night in a Bar Room," Sperry Cline Reminiscences, p. 11.

23   *Omineca Herald*, March 14, 1919.

23: May Hogan, the Woman from Hazelton Who Went to War

1   *Omineca Herald*, March 19, 1930, p. 1.

2   Record of service, No. 16 Canadian General Hospital (narrative), Government of Canada, https://
      www.canada.ca/content/dam/themes/defence/caf/militaryhistory/dhh/ledgers/medical/narrative
      -gen16.jpg.

3   Alexandra C. Istl and Vivian C. McAlister, "Western University (No. 10 Canadian Stationary Hospital and No. 14 Canadian General Hospital): A Study of Medical Volunteerism in the First World War," *Canadian Journal of Surgery* 59, no. 6 (December 1, 2016), pp. 371–73.
4   Istl and McAlister, "Western University."
5   Samuel Hanford McKee, "The Work of a Stationary Hospital in the Field, 1919," *Canadian Medical Association Journal* 145, no. 9 (November 1, 1991), pp. 1123–24.
6   Unless otherwise indicated, all extracts come from the war diaries of No. 10 Canadian Stationary Hospital in RG9-III-D-3, vol. 5034, microfilm reel number T-10923–T-10924, file 850, Library and Archives Canada (LAC).
7   The extract from November 19, 1918, is in RG9-III-B-2, vol. 3747, file part 24, LAC.

24: The Hudson's Bay Company and the Anniversary Celebrations

1   John McLoughlin, *Letters of Dr. John McLoughlin Written at Fort Vancouver, 1829–1832*, ed. Burt Brown Barker (Portland, OR: Binfords & Mort, for the Oregon Historical Society, 1948), pp. 304–05.
2   Peter C. Newman, *Caesars of the Wilderness* (Markham, ON: Penguin Books, 1987), pp. 399–408; Margaret Ormsby, *British Columbia: A History* (Vancouver: Macmillan, 1958), pp. 162–63.
3   *Omineca Herald*, May 28, 1920, p. 1.
4   *Omineca Herald*, April 30, 1920, p. 1.
5   *Omineca Herald*, April 30, 1920, p. 1.

25: Captain Streett and the Airplanes on Mission Point

1   St. Clair Streett, "The First Alaskan Air Expedition," *National Geographic Magazine* 41, no. 5 (May 1922), pp. 499–552. See also Stan Cohen, *The Alaska Flying Expedition: The U.S. Army's 1920 New York to Nome Flight* (Missoula, MT: Pictorial Histories, 1998), pp. 56–60.
2   *Omineca Herald*, September 3, 1920, p. 1.
3   *Omineca Herald*, July 23, 1920, p. 1.
4   Members of the squadron were: No. 1, Captain St. Clair Streett and Sergeant Edmund Henriques, mechanic; No. 2, Lieutenant Clifford C. Nutt and Lieutenant Erik H. Nelson, navigating and engineering officer; No. 3, Lieutenant C.E. Crumrine and Sergeant James D. Long, mechanic; No. 4: Lieutenant Ross C. Kirkpatrick and Master Sergeant Joseph E. English, mechanic.
5   Streett, "First Alaskan Air Expedition."
6   *Omineca Herald*, June 11, 1920, p. 1.
7   *Omineca Herald*, July 16, 1920, p. 1.
8   Streett, "First Alaskan Air Expedition," p. 499.
9   Streett, "First Alaskan Air Expedition," p. 539.
10 *Omineca Herald*, August 6, 1920, p. 2.
11 Streett, "First Alaskan Air Expedition," p. 541.
12 *Omineca Herald*, August 13, 1920, p. 1.
13 *Omineca Herald*, August 13, 1920, p. 1.
14 Streett, "First Alaskan Air Expedition," p. 543.
15 *Washington Herald*, October 22, 1920, p. 3.
16 Streett, "First Alaskan Air Expedition," p. 552.
17 *Honolulu Advertiser*, December 23, 1928, p. 25.

18   Kent G. Budge, "Streett, St. Clair (1893–1970)," in Pacific War Online Encyclopedia, http://pwencycl.kgbudge.com/S/t/Streett_St_Clair.htm.

26: Premier Tolmie and His Famous Caravan Visit Hazelton

The *Vancouver Daily Province* and the *Omineca Herald* both reported on the premier's visit to Hazelton.

1   Jane Eva Denison, *Caravaning to the Land of the Golden Twilight*, RBSC-ARC-1165, J.E. Denison Fonds, University of British Columbia Library Digitization Centre Special Projects.

2   Denison, *Caravaning*, p. 13.

3   *Vancouver Sun*, September 18, 1930, p. 21.

4   W. Kaye Lamb, "Tolmie, William Fraser," in *Dictionary of Canadian Biography*, vol. 11, University of Toronto/Université Laval, 2003–, http://www.biographi.ca/en/bio/tolmie_william_fraser_11E.html.

5   S.W. Jackman, *Portraits of the Premiers: An Informal History of British Columbia* (Sidney, BC: Gray's Publishing, 1969), p. 211.

6   Ray Lyman Wilbur to Simon Fraser Tolmie, May 23, 1930, box 9 (files 37–40), Simon Fraser Tolmie Fonds, RBSC-ARC-1555, Rare Books and Special Collections, University of British Columbia Library.

7   Denison, June 13, 1930, in *Caravaning*.

8   *Vancouver Daily Province*, June 19, 1930, p. 1.

9   *Vancouver Daily Province*, June 20, 1930, p. 1.

10   Denison, June 20, 1930, in *Caravaning*.

11   *Omineca Herald*, June 25, 1930, p. 1.

12   *Vancouver Daily Province*, June 23, 1930, pp. 1–2.

13   Denison, June 21, 1930, in *Caravaning*.

14   Jackman, *Portraits of the Premiers*, p. 213.

Acknowledgements

I acknowledge the unrivalled support and skill of my wife, Alice, who carefully read this book with a fine pencil and made many valuable suggestions, and Stephen Mynett, Annika Reinhardt and Peter Mynett for their unstinting support and encouragement. Peter Newbery of Hazelton has been an enthusiastic supporter of my books about Hazelton history and I thank him for his ideas for the title of this book. I also want to thank Vici Johnstone and her team at Caitlin Press for their continued support and for publishing my books. Again I thank Meg Yamamoto for sharp and incomparable editing and Morgan Hite of Hesperus Arts in Smithers for his illustrative maps. Apart from what I could find online, most of the research for this book was done before the COVID-19 pandemic struck in March 2020. I want to thank the staff at BC Archives for their assistance and Jhoanne Villegas of the Hudson's Bay Company Archives in Winnipeg for her patience with my inquiries. Thanks also are due to Axgoodim Ts'etsaut, Victor Robinson, Wing Chief of Wilp Nikate'en for reviewing the photographs in the chapter on Emily Carr.

About the Author

Geoff Mynett was born in Shropshire, England. After qualifying as a barrister in England, he came to British Columbia in 1973 and requalified as a barrister and solicitor. Geoff practised law in Vancouver until his retirement. A believer in the importance of knowing our histories, he is also an amateur artist. He and his wife, Alice, live in Vancouver.

In 2019, Ronsdale Press published his biography of a pioneer doctor in Hazelton in northern British Columbia from 1900 to 1936: *Service on the Skeena: Horace Wrinch, Frontier Physician*. In 2021 it won the Jeanne Clarke Local History Award and the George Ryga Award for Social Awareness in Literature. He has also written *Pinkerton's and the Hunt for Simon Gunanoot*, published by Caitlin

Photo by Stephen Mynett

Press in 2021. His third book, also published by Caitlin Press in 2021, was *Murders on the Skeena: True Crime in the Old Canadian West, 1884–1914*.